YOUR PASSAGE TO EVERYTHING THAT MATTERS IN THE GREAT LAKES

The *Herbert C. Jackson* upbound, entering the MacArthur Lock, Sault Ste. Marie, MI

Contents

Marine Publishing Co. Inc.
317 S. Division St. #8
Ann Arbor, MI 48104
1-855-KYS-SHIP (855-597-7447)

roger@knowyourships.com
www.KnowYourShips.com

Editor/Publisher: Roger LeLievre
Crew: Nancy Kuharevicz,
Audrey LeLievre, Matt Miner,
Kathryn O'Gould-Lau,
Neil Schultheiss, William Soleau,
Wade P. Streeter, John Vournakis
and George Wharton

Founder: Tom Manse (1915-1994)

ISBN: 978-1-891849-22-0 © 2017

FRONT COVER: Saginaw on the St. Clair River. BACK COVER: Lee A. Tregurtha on Lake Huron. THIS PAGE: Baie Comeau on lower Lake Huron. *(All images, Marc Dease)*

4

Passages

A look at the shipping scene since our last edition

Algosoo unloading at Point Edward, Ont., on June 27, 1992. She was scrapped in 2016. (Marc Dease)

JUST A FEW NEW FACES

As has been the case for the last several years, Great Lakes and St. Lawrence Seaway fleets lost more ships to scrap than they gained in new construction. Even though eight new vessels are being built for Canada's Algoma Central Corp., they have yet to arrive from their overseas shipyards, although *Algoma Innovator* is due in late 2017. Even so, the Montreal-based Fednav fleet saw the debut of several new vessels, with more on the way. Canada's McKeil Marine continues to expand with the addition of the former saltwater vessel *Arklow Willow*, which was renamed *Florence Spirit* last summer. The fleet has also modernized its stack monogram and houseflag. Another former saltie, *Ardita*, has also joined the fleet. Quebec City-based Groupe Desgagnés is also welcoming two new eco-friendly additions, *Mia Desgagnés* and *Damia Desgagnés*, built in Turkey, this year.

Florence Spirit on the Seaway near Montreal, Que. (René Beauchamp)

New Federal Caribou. (René Beauchamp)

FLORENCE SPIRIT

A number of vessels that usually only trade on the upper lakes made unusual trips down the Seaway with ore in 2016, including Joseph L. Block, Herbert C. Jackson, Michipicoten, Saginaw and several American Steamship Co. vessels. (Jeff Cameron)

Herbert C. Jackson was back in action in 2016 after her steam turbines were replaced by diesels at Fraser Shipyards. She's shown loading at Monroe, Mich. (Paul C. LaMarre III)

The former Italian vessel Ardita is now part of the McKeil Marine fleet. (Ted Wilush)

The former East Coast tugs Katie G. McAllister and Colleen McAllister arrived on the Great Lakes late in 2016. (Jeff Cameron)

HEDDLE MARINE SERVICE

TRANSITIONS

The Canadian tanker *Thalassa Desgagnés*, her usefulness to the Groupe Desganés fleet at an end thanks to newer vessels being built, has been sold for overseas use. The fleet has also sold Thalassa Desgagnés to foreign owners. ... *John G. Munson* returns to service in 2017 with new diesel engines under the hood. ... VanEnkevort Tug & Barge of Escanaba, Mich., has picked up the lease on the tug/barge combo *Ken Boothe Sr./Lakes Contender* from the American Steamship Co. The tug will be renamed *Clyde S. VanEnkevort,* after the company's founder, and the barge will be renamed *Erie Trader,* a nod to the city in which it was built.

Thalassa Desgagnés at Port Weller, Ont. (Alain Gindroz)

John G. Munson spent 2016 being converted from steam to diesel. She was ready to return to service in 2017. American Courage sat out 2016 due to a lack of demand. (Roger LeLievre)

Erie Trader is the new name for the barge Lakes Contender. (VanEnkevort Tug & Barge)

COURAGE

LAY-UPS

Arthur M. Anderson may sit 2017 out at Duluth, Minn. *American Victory* and *Edward L. Ryerson* will most likely sit out another season at Superior, Wis. *Manistee, American Valor* and *Sarah Spencer* will stay in mothballs at Toledo, Ohio. *McKee Sons* will likely stay sidelined at Muskegon, Mich. *Adam E. Cornelius* may sit out another season at Huron, Ohio. *CSL Tadoussac* will probably notch her third season of inactivity at Thunder Bay, Ont.

Of course, these and other vessels may fit out if demand improves, while others may not run if business conditions decline.

Gone But Not Forgotten

The march to the cutting torch, led by a parade of Canadian-flagged vessels, continued in 2016. Algoma Central Corp. purged its fleet of four vessels. *Algoma Navigator* left Montreal for Turkey May 27, 2016, with the saltwater tug *Boulder*. *Algomarine* and *Peter R. Cresswell* left for Turkey under tow last May as well. The tanker *Algosar* was scrapped at Port Colborne, Ont. *Algosoo,* the last vessel built on the lakes with its pilothouse up front, sailed proudly under her own power up the Welland Canal Oct. 2, also to the breaker's yard at Port Colborne. Canada Steamship Lines disposed of one vessel, the 1984-built *Atlantic Erie*, temporarily renamed *Spirit of Shpongle* for the tow.

Canadian registry was closed on July 21, 2016, for Transport Desgagnés' cargo vessel *Melissa Desgagnés*. The vessel was launched as *Ontadoc* for N.M. Paterson & Sons Ltd., Thunder Bay, Ont., in 1975. Renamed *Ethan*, she now flies the flag of Tanzania.

Melissa Desgagnés
(Roger LeLievre)

The 1963-built crane-equipped *Yankcanuck* was towed away for scrapping in December at her home port of Sault Ste. Marie, Ont. The vessel – often one of the earliest out in the spring and the last one to lay up in January – was owned by Purvis Marine Ltd.

Two vintage U.S.-flagged sandsuckers bit the dust in 2016. *F.M. Osborne* of 1910 and *Emmet J. Carey* of 1948 were hauled ashore and scrapped at Fairport, Ohio.

Algomarine was towed from Montreal by the tug Diavlos Pride on May 18, 2016. Their final stop was Aliaga, Turkey. (René Beauchamp)

Atlantic Erie arriving at Duluth / Superior. She was towed out of Montreal Nov. 4, 2016, headed for Turkey and scrapping. (Diane Hilden)

The sandsucker F.M. Osborne and her Osborne Materials fleetmate Emmet J. Carey have been dismantled at Fairport, Ohio. (Jim Hoffman)

Algosoo sailed up the Welland Canal under her own power last fall and was quickly torched at the Marine Recycling Corp. yard. (Main photo, Jeff Cameron; inset, Ted Wilush)

Yankcanuck, which often hauled steel coils from Sault Ste. Marie, Ont., to the lower Great Lakes, has been scrapped after several years of inactivity. (Viktor Kaczkowski)

Shipwatcher's Favorite for Over 20 Years !

DIAMOND JACK'S
RIVER TOURS

2 Hour Narrated Detroit River Tours
Detroit and Wyandotte

www.diamondjack.com

Vessel Index

Joseph L. Block at the ArcelorMittal steel mill in Indiana Harbor, Ind. (Peter Groh)

INNOVATION

Interlake Steamship's reputation is built on its proud history of growth and innovation. Interlake keeps on top of customers' requirements and ahead of regulatory changes by investing in its fleet. Capital improvements emphasize technology, safety, and efficiency. Re-powering and the installation of exhaust gas scrubbing systems allow Interlake to meet all North American EPA air emission standards. Improvements like these assure Interlake's customers of flexible service and reliable cargo delivery. Interlake's nine-vessel self-unloading fleet, with capacities ranging from 24,800 to 68,000 gross tons, permits targeted solutions for customers' needs.

Great Lakes transportation is our business, our only business. Let us deliver for you.

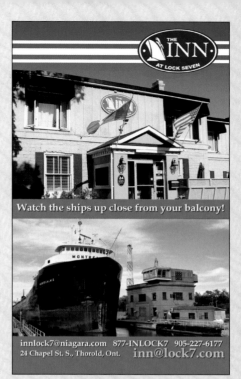

Georgian | Centre for Marine Training and Research

CENTRE FOR MARINE TRAINING AND RESEARCH

Steer toward superior training and certification.

As one of the most advanced marine simulation training centres in North America, we are leaders in innovation, customized training, research and development.

MarineTraining.ca

Fleet Listings

Lower Lakes Towing's tug Defiance laid up for the winter of 2016-'17 at Sarnia, Ont. Saginaw is astern. (Roger LeLievre)

LAKES / SEAWAY FLEETS

Listed after each vessel in order are: Type of Vessel, Year Built, Type of Engine, Maximum Cargo Capacity (at midsummer draft in long tons) or Gross Tonnage*, Overall Length, Breadth and Depth (from the top of the keel to the top of the upper deck beam) or Draft*. Only vessels over 30 feet long are included. The figures given are as accurate as possible and are given for informational purposes only. Vessels and owners are listed alphabetically as per American Bureau of Shipping and Lloyd's Register of Shipping format. Builder yard and location, as well as other pertinent information, are listed for major vessels; former names of vessels and years of operation under the former names appear in parentheses. A number in brackets following a vessel's name indicates how many vessels, including the one listed, have carried that name.

KEY TO TYPE OF VESSEL

2B ....Brigantine	**DS**.................................Spud Barge	**PF** ....Passenger Ferry
2S ....2-Masted Schooner	**DV** ....Drilling Vessel	**PK**.........................Package Freighter
3S ....3-Masted Schooner	**DW** ....Scow	**PV** ....Patrol Vessel
4S ....4-Masted Schooner	**ES** .... Excursion Ship	**RR**.............................Roll On/Roll Off
AC..............................Auto Carrier	**EV** ....Environmental Response	**RT** ....Refueling Tanker
AT ....Articulated Tug	**FB** ....Fireboat	**RV**...........................Research Vessel
ATB ....Articulated Tug/Barge	**FD**.......................Floating Dry Dock	**SB**................................Supply Boat
BC.............................Bulk Carrier	**GC** .... General Cargo	**SC** .... Sand Carrier
BK...........Bulk Carrier/Tanker	**GL**................................Gate Lifter	**SR** .... Search & Rescue
BT ....Buoy Tender	**GU** ....Grain Self-Unloader	**SU** ....Self-Unloader
CA ....Catamaran	**HL**...................Heavy Lift Vessel	**SV** ....Survey Vessel
CC .... Cement Carrier	**IB** ....Ice Breaker	**TB**....................................Tugboat
CF......................................Car Ferry	**IT** .... Integrated Tug	**TF** ....Train Ferry
CO...................Container Vessel	**ITB**...............Integrated Tug/Barge	**TK** ....Tanker
CS...............................Crane Ship	**MB** ....Mailboat	**TS**....................................Tall Ship
DB ....Deck Barge	**MU** ....Museum Vessel	**TT** ....Tractor Tugboat
DH...........................Hopper Barge	**PA** ....Passenger Vessel	**TV**........................ Training Vessel
DR ....Dredge	**PB** .... Pilot Boat	**TW** ....Towboat

KEY TO PROPULSION

B...Barge	**R**...................Steam – Triple Exp. Compound Engine
D...Diesel	**S** .... Steam – Skinner "Uniflow" Engine
DE.............................. Diesel Electric	**T** ....Steam – Turbine Engine
Q...................Steam – Quad Exp. Compound Engine	**W** ....Sailing Vessel (Wind)

Fleet Name Vessel Name	Vessel IMO #	Vessel Type	Year Built	Engine Type	Cargo Cap. or Gross*	Overall Length	Vessel Breadth	Vessel Depth

A

ABACO MARINE TOWING LLC, CLAYTON, NY

Bowditch		TB	1954	D	76*	65' 00"	22' 00"	8' 04"
Built: Missouri Valley Steel Inc., Leavenworth, KS (Oriskany, Hot Dog)								
Carina		TB	1954	D	64*	61' 05"	17' 09"	8' 03"
Built: Higgins Inc., New Orleans, LA (Charles R. Higgins, Augusta Withington)								

ALGOMA CENTRAL CORP., ST. CATHARINES, ON *(algonet.com)*

Algolake	7423093	SU	1977	D	32,807	730' 00"	75' 00"	46' 06"
Built: Collingwood Shipyards, Collingwood, ON								
Algoma Discovery	8505848	BC	1987	D	34,380	729' 00"	75' 09"	48' 05"
Built: 3 Maj Brodogradiliste d.d., Rijeka, Croatia (Malinska '87-'97, Daviken '97-'08)								
Algoma Enterprise	7726677	SU	1979	D	33,854	730' 00"	75' 11"	46' 07"
Built: Port Weller Dry Docks, Port Weller, ON (Canadian Enterprise '79-'11)								
Algoma Equinox	9613927	BC	2013	D	39,400	740' 00"	78' 00"	48' 03
Built: Nantong Mingde Heavy Industry Co. Ltd., Nantong City, China								
Algoma Guardian	8505850	BC	1987	D	34,380	729' 00"	75' 09"	48' 05"
Built: 3 Maj Brodogradiliste d.d., Rijeka, Croatia (Omisalj '87-'97, Goviken '97-'08)								
Algoma Harvester	9613939	BC	2014	D	39,400	740' 00"	78' 00"	48' 03"
Built: Nantong Mingde Heavy Industry Co. Ltd., Nantong City, China								
Algoma Innovator	TBA	SU	2017	D	24,900	650' 08"	78' 00"	xx' 00"
Built: 3 Maj Brodogradiliste d.d., Rijeka, Croatia								
Algoma Integrity	9405162	SU	2009	D	33,047	646' 07"	105' 06"	xx' 00"
Built: Estaleiro Ilha S.A., Rio de Janeiro, Brazil (Gypsum Integrity '09-'15)								

Fleet Name Vessel Name	Vessel IMO #	Vessel Type	Year Built	Engine Type	Cargo Cap. or Gross*	Overall Length	Vessel Breadth	Vessel Depth
Algoma Mariner	9587893	SU	2011	D	37,399	740' 00"	77' 11"	49' 03"

Built: Chengxi Shipyard Co. Ltd., Jiangyin City, China (Laid down as Canadian Mariner {2})

Algoma Niagara	N/A	SU	2017	D		740' 00"	78' 00"	xx' 00"

Built:Yangzijiang Shipbuilding Group Limited, Jingjiang City, Jiangsu Province, China

Algoma Olympic	7432783	SU	1976	D	33,859	730' 00"	75' 00"	46' 06"

Built: Port Weller Dry Docks, Port Weller, ON (Canadian Olympic '76-'11)

Algoma Spirit	8504882	BC	1986	D	34,380	729' 00"	75' 09"	48' 05"

Built: 3 Maj Brodogradiliste d.d., Rijeka, Croatia (Petka '86-'00, Sandviken '00-'08)

Algoma Transport	7711737	SU	1979	D	32,678	730' 00"	75' 11"	46' 07"

Built: Port Weller Dry Docks, Port Weller, ON (Canadian Transport '79-'11)

Algomarine	6816607	SU	1968	D	26,755	730' 00"	75' 00"	39' 08"

Built: Davie Shipbuilding Co., Lauzon, QC; converted to a self-unloader by Port Weller Dry Docks, St. Catharines, ON, in '89; entered probable long-term lay-up at Goderich, ON, January 2016 (Lake Manitoba '68-'87)

Algorail {2}	6805531	SU	1968	D	23,810	640' 05"	72' 00"	40' 00"

Built: Collingwood Shipyards, Collingwood, ON

Algosteel {2}	6613299	SU	1966	D	26,949	730' 00"	75' 00"	39' 08"

Built: Davie Shipbuilding Co., Lauzon, QC; converted to a self-unloader by Port Weller Dry Docks, St. Catharines, ON, in '89 (A. S. Glossbrenner '66-'87, Algogulf {1} '87-'90)

Algoway {2}	7221251	SU	1972	D	23,812	646' 06"	72' 00"	40' 00"

Built: Collingwood Shipyards, Collingwood, ON

Algowood	7910216	SU	1981	D	32,253	740' 00"	75' 11"	46' 06"

Built: Collingwood Shipyards, Collingwood, ON; lengthened 10' in '00 at Port Weller Dry Docks, St. Catharines, ON

Capt. Henry Jackman	8006323	SU	1981	D	30,590	730' 00"	75' 11"	42' 00"

Built: Collingwood Shipyards, Collingwood, ON; converted to a self-unloader by Port Weller Dry Docks, St. Catharines, ON, in '96 (Lake Wabush '81-'87)

John B. Aird	8002432	SU	1983	D	31,000	730' 00"	75' 10"	46' 06"

Built: Collingwood Shipyards, Collingwood, ON

John D. Leitch	6714586	SU	1967	D	34,127	730' 00"	77' 11"	45' 00"

Built: Port Weller Dry Docks, Port Weller, ON; rebuilt with new mid-body, widened 3' in '02 (Canadian Century '67-'02)

Radcliffe R. Latimer	7711725	SU	1978	D	36,668	740' 00"	77' 11"	49' 03"

Built: Collingwood Shipyards, Collingwood, ON; rebuilt with a new forebody at Chengxi Shipyard Co. Ltd., Jiangyin City, China, in '09 (Algobay '78-'94, Atlantic Trader '94-'97, Algobay '97-'12)

Tim S. Dool	6800919	BC	1967	D	31,054	730' 00"	77' 11"	39' 08"

Built: Saint John Shipbuilding & Drydock Co., Saint John, NB; widened by 3' at Port Weller Dry Docks, St. Catharines, ON, in '96 (Senneville '67-'94, Algoville '94-'08)

ALGOMA TANKERS LTD., ST. CATHARINES, ON – DIVISION OF ALGOMA CENTRAL CORP.

Algocanada	9378591	TK	2008	D	11,453	426' 01"	65' 00"	32' 08"

Built: Eregli Shipyard, Zonguldak, Turkey

Algoma Dartmouth	9327516	RT	2007	D	3,512	296' 11"	47' 11"	24' 11"

Built: Turkter Shipyard, Tuzla, Turkey; vessel is engaged in bunkering operations at Halifax, NS (Clipper Bardolino '07-'08, Samistal Due '08-'09)

Algoma Harvester at Port Colborne, Ont. (John C. Knecht)

Fleet Name Vessel Name	Vessel IMO #	Vessel Type	Year Built	Engine Type	Cargo Cap. or Gross*	Overall Length	Vessel Breadth	Vessel Depth
Algoma Hansa	9127186	TK	1998	D	16,775	472' 07"	75' 06"	40' 08"
Built: Alabama Shipyard Inc., Mobile, AL (Amalienborg '98-'98)								
Algonova {2}	9378589	TK	2008	D	11,453	426' 01"	65' 00"	32' 08"
Built: Eregli Shipyard, Zonguldak, Turkey (Eregli 04 '07-'08)								
Algoscotia	9273222	TK	2004	D	19,160	488' 03"	78' 00"	42' 00"
Built: Jiangnan Shipyard (Group) Co. Ltd., Shangahi, China								
Algosea {2}	9127198	TK	1998	D	17,258	472' 07"	75' 04"	40'08"
Built: Alabama Shipyard Inc., Mobile, AL (Aggersborg '98-'05)								

OPERATED BY ALGOMA CENTRAL CORP. FOR G3 CANADA LTD. (g3.ca)

G3 Marquis	9613941	BC	2014	D	39,400	740' 00"	78' 00"	48' 03
Built: Nantong Mingde Heavy Industry Co. Ltd., Nantong City, China (CWB Marquis '14-'16)								
G3 Strongfield	9613953	BC	2015	D	39,400	740' 00"	78' 00"	48' 03
Built: Nantong Mingde Heavy Industry Co., Ltd., Nantong City, China (CWB Strongfield -'15-'17)								

Editor's note: Algoma Central Corp. has five 740 by 78 foot vessels and one 650 by 78-foot vessel being built at shipyards in China and Croatia for late 2017 delivery.

ALPENA SHIPWRECK TOURS, ALPENA, MI *(alpenashipwrecktours.com)*

Lady Michigan		ES	2010	D	90*	65' 00"	19' 00"	11' 00"

AMERICAN STEAMSHIP CO., WILLIAMSVILLE, NY *(americansteamship.com)*

Adam E. Cornelius {4}	7326245	SU	1973	D	29,200	680' 00"	78' 00"	42' 00"
Built: American Shipbuilding Co., Toledo, OH; spent '15-'16 in lay-up at Huron, OH (Roger M. Kyes '73-'89)								
American Century	7923196	SU	1981	D	80,900	1,000' 00"	105' 00"	56' 00"
Built: Bay Shipbuilding Co., Sturgeon Bay, WI (Columbia Star '81-'06)								
American Courage	7634226	SU	1979	D	24,300	636' 00"	68' 00"	40' 00"
Built: Bay Shipbuilding Co., Sturgeon Bay, WI; spent '16 in lay-up at Sturgeon Bay, WI (Fred R. White Jr. '79-'06)								
American Integrity	7514696	SU	1978	D	80,900	1,000' 00"	105' 00"	56' 00"
Built: Bay Shipbuilding Co., Sturgeon Bay, WI (Lewis Wilson Foy '78-'91, Oglebay Norton '91-'06)								
American Mariner	7812567	SU	1980	D	37,300	730' 00"	78' 00"	42' 00"
Built: Bay Shipbuilding Co., Sturgeon Bay, WI (Laid down as Chicago {3})								
American Spirit	7423392	SU	1978	D	62,400	1,004' 00"	105' 00"	50' 00"
Built: American Shipbuilding Co., Lorain, OH (George A. Stinson '78-'04)								
American Valor	5024738	SU	1953	T	26,200	767' 00"	70' 00"	36' 00"
Built: American Shipbuilding Co., Lorain, OH; lengthened 120' by Fraser Shipyard, Superior, WI, in '74; converted to a self-unloader in '82; entered long-term lay-up Nov. 13, 2008, at Toledo, OH (Armco '53-'06)								
American Victory	5234395	SU	1942	T	26,700	730' 00"	75' 00"	39' 03"
Built: Bethlehem Shipbuilding and Drydock Co., Sparrows Point, MD; converted from saltwater tanker to a Great Lakes bulk carrier by Maryland Shipbuilding in '61; converted to a self-unloader by Bay Shipbuilding Co., Sturgeon Bay, WI, in '82; entered long-term lay-up Nov. 12, 2008, at Superior, WI (Laid down as Marquette, USS Neshanic [AO-71] '42-'47, Gulfoil '47-'61, Pioneer Challenger '61-'62, Middletown '62-'06)								

Ice coats American Integrity on Dec. 16, 2016. (Shaun Vary)

Fleet Name Vessel Name	Vessel IMO #	Vessel Type	Year Built	Engine Type	Cargo Cap. or Gross*	Overall Length	Vessel Breadth	Vessel Depth
Buffalo {3}	7620653	SU	1978	D	24,300	634' 10"	68' 00"	40' 00"
Built: Bay Shipbuilding Co., Sturgeon Bay, WI								
Burns Harbor {2}	7514713	SU	1980	D	80,900	1,000' 00"	105' 00"	56' 00"
Built: Bay Shipbuilding Co., Sturgeon Bay, WI								
H. Lee White {2}	7366362	SU	1974	D	35,400	704' 00"	78' 00"	45' 00"
Built: Bay Shipbuilding Co., Sturgeon Bay, WI								
Indiana Harbor	7514701	SU	1979	D	80,900	1,000' 00"	105' 00"	56' 00"
Built: Bay Shipbuilding Co., Sturgeon Bay, WI								
John J. Boland {4}	7318901	SU	1973	D	34,000	680' 00"	78' 00"	45' 00"
Built: Bay Shipbuilding Co., Sturgeon Bay, WI; spent 2015 in lay-up at Huron, Ohio (Charles E. Wilson '73-'00)								
Sam Laud	7390210	SU	1975	D	24,300	634' 10"	68' 00"	40' 00"
Built: Bay Shipbuilding Co., Sturgeon Bay, WI								
St. Clair {3}	7403990	SU	1976	D	44,800	770' 00"	92' 00"	52' 00"
Built: Bay Shipbuilding Co., Sturgeon Bay, WI; spent '16 in lay-up at Sturgeon Bay, WI								
Walter J. McCarthy Jr.	7514684	SU	1977	D	80,500	1,000' 00"	105' 00"	56' 00"
Built: Bay Shipbuilding Co., Sturgeon Bay, WI (Belle River '77-'90)								

AMHERSTBURG FERRY CO. INC, AMHERSTBURG, ON

The Columbia V		PA/CF	1946	D	46*	65' 00"	28' 10"	8' 06"
Built: Champion Auto Ferries, Algonac, MI (Crystal O, St. Clair Flats)								
The Ste. Claire V		PA/CF	1997	D	82*	86' 06"	32' 00"	6' 00"
Built: Les Ateliers Maurice Bourbonnais Ltée, Gatineau, QC (Courtney O., M. Bourbonnais)								

ANDRIE INC., MUSKEGON, MI (andrietg.com)

A-390		TK	1982	B	2,346*	310' 00"	60' 00"	17' 00"
Built: St. Louis Shipbuilding & Steel Co., St. Louis, MO (Canonie 40 '82-'92)								
A-397		TK	1962	B	2,928*	270' 00"	60' 01"	22' 05"
Built: Dravo Corp., Pittsburgh, PA (Auntie Mame '62-'91, Iron Mike '91-'93)								
A-410		TK	1955	B	3,793*	335' 00"	54' 00"	17' 00"
Built: Ingalls Shipbuilding Corp., Birmingham, AL (Methane '55-'63, B-6400 '63-'71, Kelly '71-'86, Canonie 50 '86-'93)								
Barbara Andrie	5097187	TB	1940	D	298*	122'00"	29' 07"	16' 00"
Built: Pennsylvania Shipyards Inc., Beaumont, TX (Edmond J. Moran '40-'76)								
Endeavour		TK	2009	B	7,232*	360' 00"	60' 00"	24' 00"
Built: Jeffboat LLC, Jeffersonville, IN								
Karen Andrie {2}	6520454	TB	1965	D	516*	120' 00"	31' 06"	16' 00"
Built: Gulfport Shipbuilding, Port Arthur, TX (Sarah Hays '65-'93)								
Rebecca Lynn	6511374	TB	1964	D	433*	112' 07"	31' 06"	16' 00"
Built: Gulfport Shipbuilding, Port Arthur, TX (Kathrine Clewis '64-'96)								
Sarah Andrie	7114032	TB	1970	D	190*	99' 05"	32' 04"	6' 07"
Built: Main Iron Works, Houma, LA (Seminole Sun '70-'97, Declaration '97-'99, Caribe Service '99-'15)								

Paul R. Tregurtha on a perfect St. Marys River day. (Jarrett Dodge)

OPERATED BY ANDRIE INC. FOR OCCIDENTAL CHEMICAL CORP., MUSKEGON, MI

Spartan	7047461	AT	1969	D	190*	121' 01"	32' 01"	10' 09"

    Built: Burton Shipyard, Port Arthur, TX; paired with barge Spartan II
    (Lead Horse '69-'73, Gulf Challenger '73-'80, Challenger {2} '80-'93, Mark Hannah '93-'10)

Spartan II		TK	1980	B	8,050	407' 01"	60' 00"	21' 00"

    Built: Sturgeon Bay Shipbuilding Co., Sturgeon Bay, WI (Hannah 6301 '80-'10)

ANDRIE SPECIALIZED, NORTON SHORES, MI *(andriejackup.com)*

Meredith Ashton	8951487	TB	1981	D	127*	68' 08"	26' 01"	9' 04"

    Built: Service Marine Group Inc., Amelia, LA (The Rock, Specialist, Alpha)

Robert W. Purcell		TB	1943	D	29*	45' 02"	12' 10"	7' 08"

    Built: Sturgeon Bay Shipbuilding, Sturgeon Bay, WI

APOSTLE ISLANDS CRUISES INC., BAYFIELD, WI *(apostleisland.com)*

Ashland Bayfield Express		PA	1995	D	13*	49' 00"	18' 05"	5' 00"
Island Princess {2}		ES	1973	D	63*	65' 07"	20' 05"	7' 03"

ARCELORMITTAL MINES CANADA INC., PORT CARTIER, QC *(arcelormittal.com)*

Brochu	7305899	TT	1973	D	390*	98' 11"	36' 00"	12' 04"

    Built: Star Shipyards Ltd., New Westminster, BC

Vachon	7305904	TT	1973	D	390*	98' 11"	36' 00"	12' 04"

    Built: Star Shipyards Ltd., New Westminster, BC

ARNOLD FREIGHT COMPANY, ST. IGNACE, MI

Corsair		CF	1955	D	98*	94' 06"	33' 01"	8' 01"

    Built: Blount Marine Corp., Warren, RI

ASHTON MARINE CO., NORTH MUSKEGON, MI *(ashtontugs.com)*

Candace Elise	8016380	TB	1981	D	199*	100' 00"	32' 00"	14' 08"

    Built: Modern Marine Power Inc., Houma LA (Perseverance '81-'83, Mr. Bill G '83-'90, El Rhino Grande '90-'97, Stephan Dann '97-'15)

ASI GROUP LTD., ST. CATHARINES, ON *(asi-group.com)*

ASI Clipper		SV	1939	D	64*	70' 00"	23' 00"	6' 06"

    Built: Port Colborne Iron Works, Port Colborne, ON (Stanley Clipper '39-'94, Nadro Clipper '94-'08)

ATLAS MARINE SERVICES LLC, FISH CREEK, WI

Atlas		PA	1992	D	12*	30' 04"	11' 05"	5' 04"
Northern Lighter		GC	1973	D	5*	36' 00"	9' 09"	1' 06"

AZCON METALS, DULUTH, MN *(azcon.net)*

J.B. Ford		CC	1904	R	8,000	440' 00"	50' 00"	28' 00

    Built: American Shipbuilding Co., Lorain, OH; converted to a self-unloading cement carrier in '59; last operated Nov. 15, 1985; most recently used as a cement storage and transfer vessel at Superior, WI, and now awaiting scrapping at Duluth, MN (Edwin F. Holmes '04-'16, E. C. Collins '16-'59)

B

B & L TUG SERVICE, THESSALON, ON

C. West Pete		TB	1958	D	29*	65' 00"	17' 05"	6' 00"

    Built: Erieau Shipbuilding & Drydock Co. Ltd., Erieau, ON

BASIC MARINE INC., ESCANABA, MI *(basicmarine.com)*

BMI-192		DB	2009	B	1219*	220' 02"	55' 00"	12' 00"
BMI-FDD-1		FD	1981		301*	160' 02"	65' 00"	8' 08"
Danicia	8991774	TB	1943	DE	240*	110' 02"	26' 04"	14' 08"

    Built: Ira S. Bushey and Sons Inc., Brooklyn, NY; inactive at Escanaba, MI
    (USCGC Chinook [WYT / WYTM-96] '44-'86, Tracie B '86-'98)

Erika Kobasic	8654235	TB	1939	DE	226*	110' 00"	25' 01"	14' 03"

    Built: Gulfport Shipbuilding, Port Arthur, TX (USCGC Arundel [WYT / WYTM-90] '39-'84, Karen Andrie '84-'90)

Escort		TB	1969	D	26*	50' 00"	14' 00"	6' 03"

    Built: Jakobson Shipyard, Oyster Bay, NY

Krystal		TB	1954	D	23*	45' 02"	12' 08"	6' 00"

    Built: Roamer Boat Co., Holland, MI (ST-2168 '54-'62, Thunder Bay '62-'02)

Nickelena	8654247	TB	1973	D	240*	109' 00"	30' 07"	15' 08"

    Built: Marinette Marine Corp., Marinette, WI (USS Chetek [YTB-827] '73-'96, Chetek '96-'00, Koziol '00-'08)

Tug Mississippi and Hon. James L. Oberstar leave Ironhead Marine at Toledo, Ohio. (Paul C. LaMarre III)

Michipicoten on the Calumet River. (Christine Douglas 2-christine-douglas.pixels.com)

Fleet Name / Vessel Name	Vessel IMO #	Vessel Type	Year Built	Engine Type	Cargo Cap. or Gross*	Overall Length	Vessel Breadth	Vessel Depth

BAY CITY BOAT LINES LLC, BAY CITY, MI *(baycityboatlines.com)*

Islander		ES	1946	D	39*	53' 04"	19' 09"	5' 04"
Princess Wenonah		ES	1954	D	96*	64' 09"	31' 00"	7' 03"

Built: Sturgeon Bay Shipbuilding Co., Sturgeon Bay, WI (William M. Miller '54-'98)

BAY SHIPBUILDING CO., DIV. OF FINCANTERI MARINE GROUP LLC., STURGEON BAY, WI
(bayshipbuildingcompany.com)

Bayship		TB	1943	D	19*	45' 00"	12' 04"	5' 03"

Built: Sturgeon Bay Shipbuilding Co., Sturgeon Bay, WI (Sturshipco)

BAYSAIL, BAY CITY, MI *(baysailbaycity.org)*

Appledore IV		2S/ES	1989	W/D	48*	85' 00"	18' 08"	8' 08"
Built: Treworgy Yachts, Palm Coast, FL								
Appledore V		2S/ES	1992	W/D	34*	65' 00"	14' 00"	8' 06"

Built: Treworgy Yachts, Palm Coast, FL (Westwind, Appledore)

BEAUSOLEIL FIRST NATION TRANSPORTATION, CHRISTIAN ISLAND, ON *(chimnissing.ca)*

Indian Maiden		PA/CF	1987	D	91.5*	73' 06"	23' 00"	8' 00"
Sandy Graham		PA/CF	1957	D	212*	125' 07"	39' 09"	8' 00"

Built: Barbour Boat Works Inc., New Bern, NC

BEAVER ISLAND BOAT CO., CHARLEVOIX, MI *(bibco.com)*

Beaver Islander		PF/CF	1963	D	95*	96' 03"	27' 02"	8' 03"
Built: Sturgeon Bay Shipbuilding, Sturgeon Bay, WI								
Emerald Isle {2}	8967840	PF/CF	1997	D	95*	130' 00"	38' 00"	12' 00"

Built: Washburn & Doughty Associates Inc., East Boothbay, ME

BLOUNT SMALL SHIP ADVENTURES, WARREN, RI *(blountsmallshipadventures.com)*

Grande Caribe	8978631	PA	1997	D	97*	182' 07"	39' 01"	9' 10"
Grande Mariner	8978643	PA	1998	D	97*	182' 07"	39' 01"	9' 10"
Niagara Prince	8978629	PA	1994	D	99*	174' 00"	40' 00"	9' 00"

BLUE HERON CO. LTD., TOBERMORY, ON *(blueheronco.com)*

Blue Heron V		ES	1983	D	24*	54' 06"	17' 05"	7' 02"
Flowerpot		ES	1978	D	39*	47' 02"	15' 08"	5' 06"
Flowerpot Express		ES	2011	D	59*	49' 07"	16' 05"	1' 25"
Great Blue Heron		ES	1994	D	112*	79' 00"	22' 00"	6' 05"

Calumet negotiates the Cuyahoga River at Cleveland, Ohio. (Kate White)

Fleet Name Vessel Name	Vessel IMO #	Vessel Type	Year Built	Engine Type	Cargo Cap. or Gross*	Overall Length	Vessel Breadth	Vessel Depth

BLUEWATER FERRY CO., SOMBRA, ON (bluewaterferry.com)

Daldean		CF	1951	D	145*	75' 00"	35' 00"	7' 00"
Built: Erieau Shipbuilding & Drydock Co. Ltd., Erieau, ON								
Ontamich		CF	1939	D	55*	65' 00"	28' 10"	8' 06"
Built: Champion Auto Ferries, Harsens Island, MI (Harsens Island '39-'73)								

BRIGANTINE INC., KINGSTON, ONT. (brigantine.ca)

St. Lawrence II		TV	1954	W/D	34*	72' 00"	15' 00"	8' 06"

BUFFALO DEPARTMENT OF PUBLIC WORKS, BUFFALO, NY (emcotter.com)

Edward M. Cotter		FB	1900	D	208*	118' 00"	24' 00"	11' 06"
Built: Crescent Shipbuilding, Elizabeth, NJ (W. S. Grattan 1900-'53, Firefighter '53-'54)								

BUFFALO RIVER HISTORY TOURS, BUFFALO, NY (buffaloriverhistorytours.com)

Harbor Queen		PA	2016	D	48*	63' 00"	24' 00"	10' 00"

BUFFALO SAILING ADVENTURES INC., BUFFALO, NY (spiritofbuffalo.com)

Spirit of Buffalo		2S/ES	1992	D/W	34*	73' 00"	15' 06"	7' 02"
Built: Rover Marine Lines, Norfolk, VA (Jolly Rover '92-'09)								

BUSCH MARINE INC., CARROLLTON, MI (buschmarine.com)

BMT 3		DB	1965	B	280*	120' 01"	36' 01"	7' 06"
Edwin C. Busch		TB	1935	D	18*	42' 06"	11' 11"	5' 00"
Built: Manitowoc Shipbuilding Co., Manitowoc, WI (Paul L. Luedtke '35-'02, Joanne '02-'09)								
Gregory J. Busch	5156725	TB	1919	D	299*	151' 00"	27' 06"	14' 07"
Built: Whitney Bros. Co., Superior, WI (Humaconna '19-'77)								
STC 2004		TK	1963	B	1,230*	250' 00"	50' 00"	12' 00"

C

CALUMET RIVER FLEETING INC., CHICAGO, IL (calumetriverfleeting.com)

Aiden William		TB	1954	D	120*	82' 00"	23' 06"	9' 09"
Built: Defoe Shipbuilding Co., Bay City, MI (John A. McGuire '54-'87, William Hoey {1} '87-'94, Margaret Ann '94-'08, Steven Selvick '08-'14)								
Audrie S		TW	1956	D	268*	102' 00"	28' 00"	8' 00"
Built: Calumet Shipyard & Drydock Co., Chicago, IL (Cindy Jo '56-'66, Katherine L. '66-'93, Daryl C. Hannah '93-'12)								

Tug Stormont passes Baie Comeau near Detroit. (Christopher Dark)

Fleet Name / Vessel Name	Vessel IMO #	Vessel Type	Year Built	Engine Type	Cargo Cap. or Gross*	Overall Length	Vessel Breadth	Vessel Depth
John Marshall	7223261	TB	1972	D	199*	111' 00"	30' 00"	9' 07"
Built: Main Iron Works, Houma, LA (Miss Lynn '72-'78, Newpark Sunburst '78-'82, Gulf Tempest '82-'89, Atlantic Tempest '89-'89, Catherine Turecamo '89-'14)								
John M. Selvick	8993370	TB	1898	D	256*	118' 00"	24' 03"	16' 00"
Built: Chicago Shipbuilding Co., Chicago, IL (Illinois {1} 1898-'41, John Roen III '41-'74)								
Kimberly Selvick		TW	1975	D	93*	57' 07"	28' 00"	10' 00"
Built: Grafton Boat Co., Grafton, IL (Scout '75-'02)								
Nathan S		TB	1951	D	144*	84' 01"	23' 06"	9'06"
Built: Ira S. Bushey & Sons Inc., Brooklyn, NY (Huntington '51-'05, Spartacus '05-'06, Huntington '06-'08)								
Niki S		TW	1971	D	39*	42' 00"	18' 00"	6' 00"
Built: Scully Bros. Boat Builders, Morgan City, LA (Miss Josie '71-'79, Matador VI '79-'08)								
Terry D		TB	1954	D	76*	66' 00"	19' 00"	9' 00"
(Sanita '54-'77, Soo Chief '77-'81, Susan M. Selvick '81-'96, Nathan S. '96-'02, John M. Perry '02-'08, Zuccolo '08-'12, Carla Selvick '12-'14)								

CANADA STEAMSHIP LINES INC., MONTREAL, QC – DIVISION OF THE CSL GROUP INC. (cslships.com)

Atlantic Huron {2}	8025680	SU	1984	D	34,860	736' 07"	77' 11"	46' 04"
Built: Collingwood Shipyards, Collingwood, ON; converted to a self-unloader in '89 and widened 3' in '03 at Port Weller Dry Docks, St. Catharines, ON (Prairie Harvest '84-'89, Atlantic Huron {2} '89-'94, Melvin H. Baker II {2} '94-'97)								
Baie Comeau {3}	9639892	SU	2013	D	37,690	739' 10"	77' 11"	48' 05"
Built: Chengxi Shipyard Co. Ltd., Jiangyin City, China								
Baie St. Paul {2}	9601027	SU	2012	D	37,690	739' 10"	77' 11"	48' 05"
Built: Chengxi Shipyard Co. Ltd., Jiangyin City, China								
Cedarglen {2}	5103974	BC	1959	D	29,518	730' 00"	75' 09"	40' 04"
Built: Schlieker-Werft, Hamburg, Germany; rebuilt, lengthened with a new forebody at Davie Shipbuilding Co., Lauzon, QC, in '77 ([**Stern Section**] Ems Ore '59-'76, [**Fore Section**] Montcliffe Hall '76-'88, Cartierdoc '88-'02)								
CSL Assiniboine	7413218	SU	1977	D	36,768	739' 10"	78' 00"	48' 05"
Built: Davie Shipbuilding Co., Lauzon, QC; rebuilt with a new forebody at Port Weller Dry Docks, St. Catharines, ON, in '05; repowered in '15 (Jean Parisien '77-'05)								
CSL Laurentien	7423108	SU	1977	D	37,795	739' 10"	78' 00"	48' 05"
Built: Collingwood Shipyards, Collingwood, ON; rebuilt with new forebody in '01 at Port Weller Dry Docks, St. Catharines, ON; repowered in '15 (**Stern section:** Louis R. Desmarais '77-'01)								
CSL Niagara	7128423	SU	1972	D	37,694	739' 10"	78' 00"	48' 05"
Built: Collingwood Shipyards, Collingwood, ON; rebuilt with a new forebody in '99 at Port Weller Dry Docks, St. Catharines, ON (Stern section: J. W. McGiffin '72-'99)								
CSL St-Laurent	9665281	BC	2014	D	35,529	739' 10"	77' 11"	48' 05"
Built: Yangfan Shipbuilding Co. Ltd., Zhoushan City, China								

Wilfred Sykes greeted 2016 with a fresh paint job.
(Peter Groh)

Fleet Name / Vessel Name	Vessel IMO #	Vessel Type	Year Built	Engine Type	Cargo Cap. or Gross*	Overall Length	Vessel Breadth	Vessel Depth
CSL Tadoussac	6918716	SU	1969	D	30,051	730' 00"	77' 11"	41' 11"

Built: Collingwood Shipyards, Collingwood, ON; rebuilt with new mid-body, widened 3' at Port Weller Dry Docks, St. Catharines, ON, in '01; spent '15-'16 laid up at Thunder Bay, ON (Tadoussac {2} '69-'01)

2020

CSL Welland	9665279	BC	2014	D	35,529	739' 10"	77' 11"	48' 05"

Built: Yangfan Shipbuilding Co. Ltd., Zhoushan City, China

Frontenac {5}	6804848	SU	1968	D	26,822	729' 07"	75' 00"	39' 08"

Built: Davie Shipbuilding Co., Lauzon, QC; converted to a self-unloader by Collingwood Shipyards, Collingwood, ON, in '73

Oakglen {3}	7901148	BC	1980	D	35,067	729' 11"	75' 10"	47' 01"

Built: Boelwerf Vlaanderen Shipbuilding N.V., Temse, Belgium (Federal Danube '80-'95, Lake Ontario '95-'09)

Pineglen {2}	8409331	BC	1985	D	33,197	736' 07"	75' 11"	42' 00"

Built: Collingwood Shipyards, Collingwood, ON (Paterson '85-'02)

Rt. Hon. Paul J. Martin	7324405	SU	1973	D	37,694	739' 07"	77' 11"	48' 04"

*Built: Collingwood Shipyards, Collingwood, ON; rebuilt with a new forebody in '00 at Port Weller Dry Docks, St. Catharines, ON (**Stern section:** H. M. Griffith '73-'00)*

Salarium	7902233	SU	1980	D	35,123	730' 00"	75' 11"	46' 06"

Built: Collingwood Shipyards, Collingwood, ON (Nanticoke '80-'09)

Spruceglen {2}	8119261	BC	1983	D	33,824	730' 01"	75' 09"	48' 00"

Built: Govan Shipyards, Glasgow, Scotland
(Selkirk Settler '83-'91, Federal St. Louis '91-'91, Federal Fraser {2} '91-2001, Fraser '01-'02)

Thunder Bay {2}	9601039	SU	2013	D	37,690	739' 10"	77' 11"	48' 05"

Built: Chengxi Shipyard Co. Ltd., Jiangyin City, China

Whitefish Bay {2}	9639880	SU	2013	D	37,690	739' 10"	77' 11"	48' 05"

Built: Chengxi Shipyard Co. Ltd., Jiangyin City, China

CANADIAN COAST GUARD (FISHERIES AND OCEANS CANADA), OTTAWA, ON *(www.ccg-gcc.gc.ca)*
CENTRAL AND ARCTIC REGION, MONTREAL, QC

Cape Chaillon, Cape Commodore, Cape Discovery, Cape Dundas, Cape Hearne,								
Cape Providence, Cape Rescue,		SR	2004	D	34*	47' 09"	14' 00"	4' 05"
Cape Lambton, Cape Mercy, Thunder Cape		SR	2000	D	34*	47' 09"	14' 00"	4' 05"
Cape Storm		SR	1999	D	34*	47' 09"	14' 00"	4' 05"
Caporal Kaeble V	9586045	PV	2012	D	253*	141' 07"	22' 09"	9' 09"
Caribou Isle		BT	1985	D	92*	75' 06"	19' 08"	7' 04"
Constable Carrière	9586069	PV	2012	D	253*	141' 07"	22' 09"	9' 09"
Corporal Teather C.V.	9586057	PV	2012	D	253*	141' 07"	22' 09"	9' 09"
Cove Isle		BT	1980	D	80*	65' 07"	19' 08"	7' 04"
Griffon	7022887	IB	1970	D	2,212*	234' 00"	49' 00"	21' 06"

Built: Davie Shipbuilding Co., Lauzon, QC

Fleetmates Ojibway and Tecumseh in the Welland Canal. *(Paul Beesley)*

Fleet Name / Vessel Name	Vessel IMO #	Vessel Type	Year Built	Engine Type	Cargo Cap. or Gross*	Overall Length	Vessel Breadth	Vessel Depth
Kelso		RV	2009	D	63*	57' 07"	17' 01"	4' 09"
Built: ABCO Industries Ltd., Lunenburg, NS								
Limnos	6804903	RV	1968	D	489*	147' 00"	32' 00"	12' 00"
Built: Port Weller Dry Docks, St. Catharines, ON								
Private Robertson VC	9586033	PV	2012	D	253*	141' 07"	22' 09"	9' 09"
Built: Irving Shipbuilding Inc., Halifax, NS								
Samuel Risley	8322442	IB	1985	D	1,988*	228' 09"	47' 01"	21' 09"
Built: Vito Steel Boat & Barge Construction Ltd., Delta, BC								
QUEBEC REGION, QUÉBEC, QC *(Vessels over 100' only have been listed)*								
Amundsen	7510846	IB	1978	D	5,910*	295' 09"	63' 09"	31' 04"
Built: Burrard Dry Dock Co., North Vancouver, BC (Sir John Franklin '78-'03)								
Des Groseilliers	8006385	IB	1983	D	5,910*	322' 07"	64' 00"	35' 06"
Built: Port Weller Dry Docks, St. Catharines, ON								
F. C. G. Smith	8322686	SV	1985	D	439*	114' 02"	45' 11"	11' 02"
Built: Georgetown Shipyard, Georgetown, PEI								
Martha L. Black	8320432	IB	1986	D	3,818*	272' 04"	53' 02"	25' 02"
Built: Versatile Pacific Shipyards, Victoria, BC								
Pierre Radisson	7510834	IB	1978	D	5,910*	322' 00"	62' 10"	35' 06"
Built: Burrard Dry Dock Co., North Vancouver, BC								
Tracy	6725432	BT	1968	D	837*	181' 01"	38' 00"	16' 00"
Built: Port Weller Dry Docks, St. Catharines, ON								

CANAMAC CRUISES, TORONTO, ON *(canamac.com)*

Stella Borealis		ES	1989	D	356*	118 '00"	26' 00"	7' 00"
Built: Duratug Shipyard & Fabricating Ltd., Port Dover, ON								

CARGILL GRAIN CO. LTD., BAIE COMEAU, QC
   MANAGED BY GROUPE OCÉAN INC., QUÉBEC, QC

Pointe Comeau	7520322	TB	1976	D	391*	99' 09"	36' 01"	12' 01"
Built: Marystown Shipyard Ltd., Marystown, NL								

CARMEUSE NORTH AMERICA (ERIE SAND AND GRAVEL CO.), PITTSBURGH, PA *(carmeusena.com)*

J. S. St. John	5202524	SC	1945	D	415*	174' 00"	31' 09"	15' 00"
Built: Smith Shipyards & Engineering Corp., Pensacola, FL (USS YO-178 '45-'51, Lake Edward '51-'67)								

CAUSLEY MARINE CONTRACTING LLC, BAY CITY, MI

Jill Marie		TB	1891	D	24*	60' 00"	12' 06"	6' 00"
Built: Cleveland Shipbuilding Co., Cleveland, OH (Cisco 1891-1952, Capama-S '52-'07)								

CEMBA MOTOR SHIPS LTD., PELEE ISLAND, ON

Cemba		TK	1960	D	17*	50' 00"	15' 06"	7' 06"

CENTRAL MARINE LOGISTICS INC., GRIFFITH, IN *(centralmarinelogistics.com)*

Edward L. Ryerson	5097606	BC	1960	T	27,500	730' 00"	75' 00"	39' 00"
Built: Manitowoc Shipbuilding Co., Manitowoc, WI; in long-term lay-up at Superior, WI, since May 2009								
Joseph L. Block	7502320	SU	1976	D	37,200	728' 00"	78' 00"	45' 00"
Built: Bay Shipbuilding Co., Sturgeon Bay, WI								
Wilfred Sykes	5389554	SU	1949	T	21,500	678' 00"	70' 00"	37' 00"
Built: American Shipbuilding Co., Lorain, OH; converted to a self-unloader by Fraser Shipyards, Superior, WI, in '75								

CENTRAL MICHIGAN UNIVERSITY, COLLEGE OF SCIENCE & TECHNOLOGIES, MOUNT PLEASANT, MI

Chippewa		RV	2013	D	17*	34' 09"	12' 00"	6' 03"

CHAMPION MARINE INC., ALGONAC, MI

Champion		CF	1941	D	69*	65' 00"	25' 09"	5' 08"
Middle Channel		CF	1997	D	81*	79' 00"	30' 00"	6' 05"
North Channel		CF	1967	D	67*	75' 00"	30' 04"	6' 01"
South Channel		CF	1973	D	94*	79' 00"	30' 03"	6' 01"

CHARITY ISLAND TRANSPORT INC., AU GRES, MI *(charityisland.net)*

North Star		PA	1949	D	14*	50' 05"	14' 06"	3' 06"

CHARLEVOIX COUNTY TRANSPORTATION AUTHORITY, CHARLEVOIX, MI

Charlevoix {1}		CF	1926	D	43*	47' 00"	30' 00"	3' 08"

CHICAGO DEPARTMENT OF WATER MANAGEMENT, CHICAGO, IL

James J. Versluis		TB	1957	D	126*	83' 00"	22' 00"	11' 02"
Built: Sturgeon Bay Shipbuilding Co., Sturgeon Bay, WI								

Fleet Name Vessel Name	Vessel IMO #	Vessel Type	Year Built	Engine Type	Cargo Cap. or Gross*	Overall Length	Vessel Breadth	Vessel Depth
CHICAGO FIRE DEPARTMENT, CHICAGO, IL								
Christopher Wheatley		FB	2011	D	300*	90' 00"	25' 00"	12' 02"
Built: Hike Metal Products Ltd., Wheatley, ON								
Victor L. Schlaeger		FB	1949	D	350*	92' 06"	24' 00"	11' 00"
CHICAGO'S FIRST LADY CRUISES, CHICAGO, IL (cruisechicago.com)								
Chicago's Classic Lady		ES	2014	D	93*	98' 00"	32' 00"	6' 02"
Chicago's Fair Lady		ES	1979	D	82*	72' 04"	23' 01"	7' 01"
Chicago's First Lady		ES	1991	D	62*	96' 00"	22' 00"	9' 00"
Chicago's Leading Lady		ES	2011	D	92*	92' 07"	32' 00"	6' 09"
Chicago's Little Lady		ES	1999	D	70*	69' 02"	22' 08"	7' 00"
CHICAGO FROM THE LAKE LTD., CHICAGO, IL (chicagoline.com)								
Ft. Dearborn		ES	1985	D	72*	64' 10"	22' 00"	7' 03"
Innisfree		ES	1980	D	35*	61' 09"	15' 06"	5' 07"
Marquette {6}		ES	1957	D	39*	50' 07"	15' 00"	5' 05"
CITY OF TORONTO, TORONTO, ON (toronto.ca/parks)								
Ned Hanlan II		TB	1966	D	22*	41' 06"	14' 01"	5' 05"
Built: Erieau Shipbuilding & Drydock Co. Ltd., Erieau, ON								
Ongiara	6410374	PA/CF	1963	D	180*	78' 00"	12' 04"	9' 09"
Built: Russel Brothers Ltd., Owen Sound, ON								
Sam McBride		PF	1939	D	387*	129' 00"	34' 11"	6' 00"
Built: Toronto Dry Dock Co. Ltd., Toronto, ON								
Thomas Rennie		PF	1951	D	387*	129' 00"	32' 11"	6' 00"
Built: Toronto Dry Dock Co. Ltd., Toronto, ON								
Trillium		PF	1910	R	564*	150' 00"	30' 00"	8' 04"
Built: Poulson Iron Works, Toronto, ON; last sidewheel-propelled vessel on the Great Lakes								
William Inglis		PF	1935	D	238*	99' 00"	24' 10"	6' 00"
Built: John Inglis Co. Ltd., Toronto, ON (Shamrock {2} '35-'37)								
CJC CRUISES INC., GRAND LEDGE, MI (detroitprincess.com)								
Detroit Princess		PA	1993	D	1,430*	222' 00"	62' 00"	11' 01"
Built: Leevac Shipyards Inc., Jennings, LA (Players Riverboat Casino II '93-'04)								
CLEARWATER MARINE LLC, HOLLAND, MI (clearwatermarinellc.com)								
G.W. Falcon		TB	1936	D	22*	49' 07"	13' 08"	6' 02"
Built: Fred E. Alford, South Haven, MI (J.W. Walsh, Anna Marie)								
CLEVELAND FIRE DEPARTMENT, CLEVELAND, OH								
Anthony J. Celebrezze		FB	1961	D	42*	66' 00"	17' 00"	5' 00"
Built: Paasch Marine Services Inc., Erie, PA								
CLINTON RIVER CRUISE CO., MOUNT CLEMENS, MI (clintonrivercruisecompany.com)								
Captain Paul II		PA	1960	D	14*	44' 07"	11' 00"	4' 00"
Clinton		PA	1949	D	10*	63' 07"	15' 03"	4' 08"
Clinton Friendship		PA	1984	D	43*	64' 08"	22' 00"	4' 05"
CONSTRUCTION POLARIS INC., L'ANCIENNE-LORETTE, QC (constructionpolaris.com)								
Point Viking	5118840	TB	1962	D	207*	98' 05"	27' 10"	13' 05"
Built: Davie Shipbuilding Co., Lauzon, QC (Foundation Viking '62-'75)								
COOPER MARINE LTD., SELKIRK, ON								
Ella G. Cooper		PB	1972	D	21*	43' 00"	14' 00"	6' 05"
Janice C. No. 1		TB	1980	D	33*	57' 00"	20' 00"	6' 00"
J. W. Cooper		PB	1984	D	25*	48' 00"	14' 07"	5' 00"
Kimberley A. Cooper		TB	1974	D	17*	40' 00"	13' 05"	4' 05"
Mrs. C.		PB	1991	D	26*	50' 00"	14' 05"	4' 05"
Stacey Dawn		TB	1993	D	14*	35' 09"	17' 04"	3' 05"
Wilson T. Cooper		DB	2009		58*	56' 08"	23' 06"	5' 08"
CORPORATION OF THE TOWNSHIP OF FRONTENAC ISLANDS, WOLFE ISLAND, ON								
Howe Islander		CF	1946	D	13*	53' 00"	12' 00"	3' 00"
Built: Canadian Dredge & Dock Co. Ltd., Kingston, ON								
Simcoe Islander		PF	1964	D	24*	47' 09"	18' 00"	3' 06"
Built: Canadian Dredge & Dock Co. Ltd., Kingston, ON								

Fleet Name Vessel Name	Vessel IMO #	Vessel Type	Year Built	Engine Type	Cargo Cap. or Gross*	Overall Length	Vessel Breadth	Vessel Depth
COBBY MARINE (1985) INC., KINGSVILLE, ON								
Vida C.		TB	1960	D	17*	46'03"	15'05"	3'02"
CROISIÈRES AML INC., QUÉBEC, QC *(croisieresaml.com)*								
AML Levant	9056404	ES	1991	D	380*	112'07"	29'0"	10'02"
Built: Goelette Marie Clarisse Inc., LaBaleine, QC (Famille Dufour)								
AML Suroît		ES	2002	D	171*	82'00"	27'00"	6'00"
Built: RTM Construction, Petite Rivière-St-François, QC (Le Coudrier de l'Isle '02-'14)								
AML Zephyr		ES	1992	D	171*	82'00"	27'00"	6'00"
Built: Katamarine International, Paspebiac, QC (Le Coudrier de l'Anse '92-'14)								
Cavalier Maxim	5265904	ES	1962	D	752*	191'02"	42'00"	11'07"
Built: John I. Thornycroft & Co., Wollston, Southampton, England (Osborne Castle '62-'78, Le Gobelet D' Argent '78-'88, Gobelet D' Argent '88-'89, Le Maxim '89-'93)								
Grand Fleuve		ES	1987	D	499*	145'00"	30'00"	5'06"
Built: Kanter Yacht Co., St. Thomas, ON								
Louis Jolliet	5212749	ES	1938	R	2,436*	170'01"	70'00"	17'00"
Built: Davie Shipbuilding Co., Lauzon, QC								
CROISIÈRES M/S JACQUES-CARTIER INC., TROIS-RIVIERES, QC *(msjacquescartier.com)*								
Jacques Cartier		ES	1924	D	589*	132'05"	35'00"	10'00"
Built: Davie Shipbuilding Co., Lauzon, QC (rebuilt '75, '17)								
CRUISE TORONTO INC., TORONTO ON *(cruisetoronto.com)*								
Obsession III		ES	1967	D	160*	66'00"	25'00"	6'01"
Built: Halter Marine, New Orleans, LA (Mystique)								
CTMA GROUP (NAVIGATION MADELEINE INC.), CAP-AUX-MEULES, QC *(ctma.ca)*								
C.T.M.A. Vacancier	7310260	PA/RR	1973	D	11,481*	388'04"	70'02"	43'06"
Built: J.J. Sietas KG Schiffswerft, Hamburg, Germany (Aurella '80-'82, Saint Patrick II '82-'98, Egnatia II '98-'00, Ville de Sete '00-'01, City of Cork '01-'02)								
C.T.M.A. Voyageur	7222229	PA/RR	1972	D	4,526*	327'09"	52'06"	31'07"
Built: Trosvik Versted A/S, Brevik, Norway (Anderida '72-'81, Truck Trader '81-'84, Sealink '84-'86, Mirela '86-'86)								
Madeleine	7915228	PA	1981	D	10,024*	381'04"	60'06"	41'00"
Built: Verolme Cork Dockyard Ltd., Cobh, Ireland (Isle of Inishturk)								

D

DAN MINOR & SONS INC., PORT COLBORNE, ON								
Andrea Marie I		TB	1986	D	87*	75'02"	24'07"	7'03"

Canadian cargo vessel Claude A. Desgagnés on Lake Ontario. (Jeff Cameron)

Fleet Name Vessel Name	Vessel IMO #	Vessel Type	Year Built	Engine Type	Cargo Cap. or Gross*	Overall Length	Vessel Breadth	Vessel Depth
Jeanette M.		TB	1981	D	31*	70' 00"	20 01'	6' 00"
Susan Michelle		TB	1995	D	89*	79' 10"	20' 11"	6' 02"
Welland		TB	1954	D	94*	86' 00"	20' 00"	8' 00"

DANN MARINE TOWING, CHESAPEAKE CITY, MD *(dannmarine.com)*

Calusa Coast	7942295	TB	1978	D	186*	110' 00"	30' 01"	11' 00"

Built: Bollinger Shipyards, Lockport, LA (Marc G., Katrina G.); paired with barge Delaware

Delaware	1588255	TK	2006	B	98*	292' 00"	60' 00"	24' 00"

Vessel owned by Kirby Offshore Marine Operating LLC, Houston, TX

Zeus	9506071	TB	1964	D	98*	104' 02"	29' 03"	13' 05"

Built: Houma Shipbuilding Co., Houma, LA; paired with barge Robert F. Deegan

DEAN CONSTRUCTION CO. LTD., BELLE RIVER, ON *(deanconstructioncompany.com)*

Americo Dean		TB		D	15*	45' 00"	15' 00"	5' 00"
Annie M. Dean		TB	1981	D	58*	50' 00"	19' 00"	5' 00"
Bobby Bowes		TB	1944	D	11*	37' 04"	10' 02"	3' 06"
Canadian Jubilee		DR	1978	B	896*	149' 09"	56' 01"	11' 01"
Neptune III		TB	1939	D	23*	53' 10"	15' 06"	5' 00"

DEAN MARINE & EXCAVATING INC., MOUNT CLEMENS, MI *(deanmarineandexcavating.com)*

Andrew J.		TB	1950	D	25*	47' 00"	15' 07"	8' 00"

Built: J.F. Bellinger & Sons, Jacksonville, FL

Kimberly Anne		TB	1965	D	65*	55' 02"	18' 08"	8' 00"

Built: Main Iron Works, Houma, LA (Lady Lisa, Lucy, Mrs. Alma)

DMC MARINE LLC, HILLSIDE, NJ

Cheyenne	6515851	TB	1965	D	146*	84' 05"	25' 03"	12' 06"

Built: Ira S. Bushey and Sons Inc., Brooklyn, NY (Glenwood '65-'70)

DETROIT CITY FIRE DEPARTMENT, DETROIT, MI

Curtis Randolph		FB	1979	D	85*	77' 10"	21' 06"	9' 03"

Built: Peterson Builders Inc., Sturgeon Bay, WI

DEWEY LEASING LLC, ROCHESTER, NY

Ronald J. Dahlke		TB	1903	D	58*	63' 04"	17' 06"	9' 00"

Built: Johnston Bros., Ferrysburg, MI (Bonita '03-'14, Chicago Harbor No. 4 '14-'60, Eddie B. '60-'69, Seneca Queen '69-'70, Ludington '70-'96, Seneca Queen '96-'04)

DIAMOND JACK'S RIVER TOURS, DETROIT, MI *(diamondjack.com)*

Diamond Belle		ES	1958	D	93*	93' 06"	25' 00"	7' 00"

Built: Hans Hansen Welding Co., Toledo, OH (Mackinac Islander {2} '58-'90, Sir Richard '90-'91)

Ojibway overtakes Paul R. Tregurtha at dusk. (Roger LeLievre)

-43

Diamond Jack		ES	1955	D	82*	72' 00"	25' 00"	7' 03"
Built: Christy Corp., Sturgeon Bay, WI (Emerald Isle {1} '55–'91)								
Diamond Queen		ES	1956	D	94*	92' 00"	25' 00"	7' 02"
Built: Marinette Marine Corp., Marinette, WI (Mohawk '56–'96)								

DISCOVERY WORLD AT PIER WISCONSIN, MILWAUKEE, WI (discoveryworld.org)

Denis Sullivan	1100209	TV/ES	2000	W/D	99*	138' 00"	22' 08"	10' 06"
Built: Wisconsin Lake Schooner, Milwaukee, WI								

DONJON MARINE CO. INC., HILLSIDE, NJ (donjon.com)

Elizabeth Anna		TB	1958	D	37*	53' 08"	17' 00"	5' 07"
Built: Diesel Shipbuilding Co., Jacksonville, FL (Catherine M. Brown '58–'11, Bear '11–'14); tug is stationed at Erie, PA								

DONKERSLOOT MARINE DEVELOPMENT CORP., NEW BUFFALO, MI (donkerslootmarine.com)

Miss Jamie Lynn		DR	1989	D	254*	120' 00"	34' 00"	5' 06"

DUC D' ORLEANS CRUISE BOAT, CORUNNA, ON (ducdorleans.com)

Duc d' Orleans II		ES	1987	D	120*	71' 03	23' 02"	7' 07"
Built: Blount Marine Corp., Warren, RI (Spirit of Newport '87–'06)								

DUNDEE ENERGY LTD., TORONTO, ON (eurogascorp.com)

Vessels are engaged in oil and gas exploration on Lake Erie

Dr. Bob	8771992	DV	1973	B	1,022*	160' 01"	54' 01"	11' 01"
Built: Cenac Shipyard Co. Inc., Houma, LA (Mr. Chris '73–'03)								
J.R. Rouble	8767020	DV	1958	D	562*	123' 06"	49' 08"	16' 00"
Built: American Marine Machinery Co., Nashville, TN (Mr. Neil)								
Miss Libby		DV	1972	B	924*	160' 01"	54' 01"	11' 01"
Built: Service Machine & Shipbuilding Corp., Morgan City, LA								
Sarah No. 1		TB	1969	D	43*	72' 01"	17' 03"	6' 08"
Built: Halter Marine, New Orleans, LA (Auries)								
Timesaver II		DB	1964	B	510*	91' 08"	70' 08"	9' 01"
Russel Bros. Ltd., Owen Sound, ON								

DUROCHER MARINE, DIV. OF KOKOSING CONSTRUCTION CO., CHEBOYGAN, MI (kokosing.biz)

Champion {3}		TB	1974	D	125*	75' 00"	23' 05"	9' 05"
Built: Service Machine & Shipbuilding Co., Amelia, LA								
General {2}		TB	1954	D	119*	71' 00"	19' 06"	10' 00"
Built: Missouri Valley Bridge & Iron Works, Leavenworth, KS (U. S. Army ST-1999 '54–'61, USCOE Au Sable '61–'84, Challenger {3} '84–'87)								
Joe Van		TB	1955	D	32*	57' 09"	15' 00"	7' 00"
Built: W.J. Hingston, Buffalo, NY								

Baie Comeau below the Ambassador Bridge at Detroit. (Neil Schultheiss)

Fleet Name Vessel Name	Vessel Type	Vessel IMO #	Year Built	Engine Type	Cargo Cap. or Gross*	Overall Length	Vessel Breadth	Vessel Depth
Nancy Anne	TB		1969	D	73*	60' 00"	20' 00"	8' 00"
Built: Houma Shipbuilding Co., Houma, LA								
Ray Durocher	TB		1943	D	20*	45' 06"	12' 05"	7' 06"
Valerie B.	TB		1981	D	101*	65' 00"	25' 06"	10' 00"
Built: Rayco Shipbuilders & Repairers, Bourg, LA (Mr. Joshua, Michael Van)								

E

EASTERN UPPER PENINSULA TRANSPORTATION AUTHORITY, SAULT STE. MARIE, MI *(eupta.net)*

Drummond Islander III	CF		1989	D	96*	108' 00"	37' 00"	7' 02"
Built: Moss Point Marine Inc., Escatawpa, MS								
Drummond Islander IV	CF		2000	D	97*	148' 00"	40' 00"	12' 00"
Built: Basic Marine Inc., Escanaba, MI								
Neebish Islander II	CF		1946	D	90*	89' 00"	25' 09"	5' 08"
Built: Lock City Machine/Marine, Sault Ste. Marie, MI (Sugar Islander '46-'95)								
Sugar Islander II	CF		1995	D	90*	114' 00"	40' 00"	10' 00"
Built: Basic Marine Inc., Escanaba, MI								

ECOMARIS, MONTREAL, QC *(ecomaris.org)*

Roter Sand	TV/2S		1999	W/D	28*	65' 02"	17' 07"	8' 03"

EMPRESS OF CANADA ENTERPRISES LTD., TORONTO, ON *(empressofcanada.com)*

Empress of Canada	ES		1980	D	399*	116' 00"	28' 00"	6' 06"
Built: Hike Metal Products, Wheatley, ON (Island Queen V {2} '80-'89)								

ENTERPRISE MARISSA INC., QUEBEC, QC

Cap Brulé	TB			D	12*	39' 09"	10' 00"	2' 00"
Soulanges	TB		1905	D	72*	77' 00"	17' 00"	8' 00"
Built: Cie Pontbriand Ltée., Sorel, QC (Dandy '05-'39)								

EQUIPMENTS VERREAULT INC., LES MÉCHINS, QC

Epinette II	TB		1965	D	75*	61' 03"	20' 01"	8' 05"
Built: Russel Brothers Ltd., Owen Sound, ON								
Grande Baie	TT		1972	D	194*	86' 06"	30' 00"	12' 00"
Built: Prince Edward Island Lending Authority, Charlottetown, PEI								

ERIE ISLANDS PETROLEUM INC., PUT-IN-BAY, OH *(putinbayfuels.com)*

Cantankerus	TK		1955	D	43*	56' 00"	14' 00"	6' 06"
Built: Marinette Marine Corp., Marinette, WI								

Tug Sharon M. 1 in the Welland Canal. (Matt Miner)

Fleet Name / Vessel Name	Vessel IMO #	Vessel Type	Year Built	Engine Type	Cargo Cap. or Gross*	Overall Length	Vessel Breadth	Vessel Depth

ESSROC CANADA INC., PICTON, ON
VESSELS MANAGED BY McKEIL MARINE LTD., HAMILTON, ON

Metis	5233585	CC	1956	B	5,800	331'00"	43'09"	26'00"

Built: Davie Shipbuilding Co., Lauzon, QC; lengthened 72', deepened 3'6" in '59 and converted to a self-unloading cement barge in '91 by Kingston Shipbuilding & Dry Dock Co., Kingston, ON

Stephen B. Roman	6514900	CC	1965	D	7,600	488'09"	56'00"	35'06"

Built: Davie Shipbuilding Co., Lauzon, QC; converted to a self-unloading cement carrier by Collingwood Shipyards, Collingwood, ON, in '83 (Fort William '65-'83)

F-G

FITZ SUSTAINABLE FORESTRY MANAGEMENT LTD., MANITOWANING, ON

Wyn Cooper		TB	1973	D	25*	48'00"	13'00"	4'00"

FRASER SHIPYARDS INC., SUPERIOR, WI (frasershipyards.com)

FSY II		TB	2013	D	32*	45'00"	13'00"	6'05"
FSY III		TB	1959	D	30*	47'04"	13'00"	6'06"

(Susan A. Fraser '59-'78, Maxine Thompson '78-'14)

GAELIC TUGBOAT CO., DETROIT, MI

Marysville		TK	1973	B	1,136*	200'00"	50'00"	12'06"

(N.M.S. No. 102 '73-'81)

Patricia Hoey {2}	5285851	TB	1949	D	146*	88'06"	25'06"	11'00"

Built: Alexander Shipyard Inc., New Orleans, LA (Propeller '49-'82, Bantry Bay '82-'91)

Shannon	8971669	TB	1944	D	145*	101'00"	25'08"	13'00"

Built: Consolidated Shipbuilding Corp., Morris Heights, NY (USS Connewango [YT / YTB / YTM-388] '44-'77)

William Hoey	5029946	TB	1951	D	149*	88'06"	25'06"	11'00"

Built: Alexander Shipyard Inc., New Orleans, LA (Atlas '51-'84, Susan Hoey {1} '84-'85, Atlas '85-'87, Carolyn Hoey '87-'13)

GAFCO CORP., GROSSE POINTE FARMS, MI

Linnhurst		TB	1930	D	11*	37'05"	10'05"	4'08"

Built: Great Lakes Engineering Works, Ecorse, MI (G.L.E. WKS, Toledoan, Grosse Ile)

GALCON MARINE LTD., TORONTO, ON (galconmarine.com)

Barney Drake		TB	1954	D	10*	31'02"	9 05"	3'04"

Built: Toronto Dry Dock Co Ltd., Toronto ON (T.T.&S. No. 9)

Kenteau		TB	1937	D	15*	54'07"	16'04"	4'02"

Built: George Gamble, Port Dover, ON

Patricia D		TB	1958	D	12*	38'08"	12'00"	3'08"

Built: Toronto Drydock Co. Ltd., Toronto, ON (Big Chief III)

William Rest		TB	1961	D	62*	65'00"	18'06"	10'06"

Built: Erieau Shipbuilding & Drydock Co. Ltd., Erieau, ON

GANANOQUE BOAT LINE LTD., GANANOQUE, ON (ganboatline.com)

Thousand Islander	7227346	ES	1972	D	200*	96'11"	22'01"	5'05"
Thousand Islander II	7329936	ES	1973	D	200*	99'00"	22'01"	5'00"
Thousand Islander III	8744963	ES	1975	D	376*	118'00"	28'00"	6'00"
Thousand Islander IV	7947984	ES	1976	D	347*	110'09"	28'04"	10'08"
Thousand Islander V	8745187	ES	1979	D	246*	88'00"	24'00"	5'00"

GANNON UNIVERSITY, ERIE, PA (gannon.edu)

Environaut		RV	1950	D	18*	48'00"	13'00"	4'05"

GENESIS ENERGY, HOUSTON, TX (genesisenergy.com)

Genesis Victory	8973942	TB	1981	D	398*	105'00"	34'00"	17'00"

Built: Halter Marine, New Orleans, LA (Eric Candies '81-'05, Huron Service '05-'15)

GM 6506		TK	2007	B	5,778*	345'06"	60'00"	29'00"

Built: Bollinger Marine Fabricators, Amelia, LA; paired with the tug Genesis Victory

GEO. GRADEL CO., TOLEDO, OH (geogradelco.com)

George Gradel		TB	1956	D	128*	84'00"	26'00"	9'02"

Built: Parker Brothers & Co. Inc., Houston, TX (Harbor Queen '56-'76, St. John '76-'16)

John Francis		TB	1965	D	99*	75'00"	22'00"	9'00"

Built: Bollinger Shipbuilding Inc., Lockport, LA (Dad '65-'98, Creole Eagle '98-'03)

Mighty Jake		TB	1969	D	15*	36'00"	12'03"	7'03"

Fleet Name / Vessel Name	Vessel IMO #	Vessel Type	Year Built	Engine Type	Cargo Cap. or Gross*	Overall Length	Vessel Breadth	Vessel Depth
Mighty Jessie		TB	1954	D	57*	61' 02"	18' 00"	7' 03"
Mighty Jimmy		TB	1945	D	34*	56' 00"	15' 10"	6' 05"
Mighty John III		TB	1962	D	24*	45' 00"	15' 00"	5' 10"
(Niagara Queen '62-'99)								
Norman G		DB	2016	B	578*	141' 01"	54' 00"	10' 00"
Pioneerland		TB	1943	D	53*	58' 00"	16' 08"	8' 00"
Prairieland		TB	1955	D	35*	49' 02"	15' 02"	6' 00"
Timberland		TB	1946	D	20*	41' 03"	13' 01"	7' 00"

GILLEN MARINE CONSTRUCTION LLC, MEQUON, WI (gillenmarine.com)

Kristin J.		TB	1963	D	60*	52' 06"	19' 01"	7' 04"

Built: St. Charles Steel Works, Thibodaux, LA (Jason A. Kadinger '63-'06)

GOODTIME CRUISE LINE INC., CLEVELAND, OH (goodtimeiii.com)

Goodtime III		ES	1990	D	95*	161' 00"	40' 00"	11' 00"

Built: Leevac Shipyards Inc., Jennings, LA

GRAND PORTAGE / ISLE ROYALE TRANSPORTATION LINE, WHITE BEAR LAKE, MN (isleroyaleboats.com)

Sea Hunter III		ES	1985	D	47*	65' 00"	16 00"	7' 05"
Voyageur II		ES	1970	D	40*	63' 00"	18' 00"	5' 00"

GRAND RIVER NAVIGATION CO. – SEE LOWER LAKES TRANSPORTATION CO.

GRAND VALLEY STATE UNIVERSITY, ANNIS WATER RESOURCES, MUSKEGON, MI (gvsu.edu/wri)

D. J. Angus		RV	1986	D	16*	45' 00"	14' 00"	4' 00"
W. G. Jackson		RV	1996	D	80*	64' 10"	20' 00"	5' 00"

GRAVEL & LAKE SERVICES LTD., THUNDER BAY, ON

Peninsula		TB	1944	D	261*	111' 00"	27' 00"	13' 00"

Built: Montreal Drydock Ltd., Montreal, QC (HMCS Norton [W-31] '44-'45, W.A.C. 1 '45-'46)

Wolf River		BC	1956	D	5,880	349' 02"	43' 07"	25' 04"

Built: Port Weller Dry Docks, Port Weller, ON; last operated in 1998; in long-term layup at Thunder Bay, ON
(Tecumseh {2} '56-'67, New York News {3} '67-'86, Stella Desgagnés '86-'93, Beam Beginner '93-'95)

GREAT LAKES DOCK & MATERIALS LLC, MUSKEGON, MI (greatlakesdock.com)

Duluth		TB	1954	D	87*	70' 01"	19' 05"	9' 08"

Built: Missouri Valley Bridge & Iron Works, Leavenworth, KS (U. S. Army ST-2015 '54-'62)

Ethan George		TB	1940	D	27*	42' 05"	12' 08"	6' 06"

Built: Sturgeon Bay Shipbuilding, Sturgeon Bay, WI (Holland, Captain Roy)

Fischer Hayden		TB	1967	D	64*	54' 00"	22' 01"	7' 01"

Built: Main Iron Works Inc., Houma, LA (Gloria G. Cheramie, Joyce P. Crosby)

Sarah B.		TB	1953	D	23*	45' 00"	13' 00"	7' 00"

Built: Nashville Bridge Co., Nashville, TN (ST-2161 '53-'63, Tawas Bay '63-'03)

GREAT LAKES ENVIRONMENTAL RESEARCH LABORATORY, ANN ARBOR, MI (www.glerl.noaa.gov)

Huron Explorer		RV	1979	D	15*	41' 00"	14' 08"	4' 08"
Laurentian		RV	1974	D	129*	80' 00"	21' 06"	11' 00"
Shenehon		SV	1953	D	90*	65' 00"	17' 00"	6' 00"

GREAT LAKES FLEET INC., DULUTH, MN (KEY LAKES INC., MANAGER) (keyship.com)

Arthur M. Anderson	5025691	SU	1952	T	25,300	767' 00"	70' 00"	36' 00"

Built: American Shipbuilding Co., Lorain, OH; lengthened 120' in '75 and converted to a self-unloader in '82 at Fraser Shipyards, Superior, WI

Cason J. Callaway	5065392	SU	1952	T	25,300	767' 00"	70' 00"	36' 00"

Built: Great Lakes Engineering Works, River Rouge, MI; lengthened 120' in '74 and converted to a self-unloader in '82 at Fraser Shipyards, Superior, WI

Edgar B. Speer	7625952	SU	1980	D	73,700	1,004' 00"	105' 00"	56' 00"

Built: American Shipbuilding Co., Lorain, OH

Edwin H. Gott	7606061	SU	1979	D	74,100	1,004' 00"	105' 00"	56' 00"

Built: Bay Shipbuilding Co., Sturgeon Bay, WI; converted from shuttle self-unloader to deck-mounted self-unloader at Bay Shipbuilding, Sturgeon Bay, WI, in '96

Great Republic	7914236	SU	1981	D	25,600	634' 10"	68' 00"	39' 07"

Built: Bay Shipbuilding Co., Sturgeon Bay, WI (American Republic '81-'11)

John G. Munson {2}	5173670	SU	1952	D	25,550	768' 03"	72' 00"	36' 00"

Built: Manitowoc Shipbuilding Co., Manitowoc, WI; lengthened 102' at Fraser Shipyards, Superior, WI, in '76; repowered in '16

Fleet Name / Vessel Name	Vessel IMO #	Vessel Type	Year Built	Engine Type	Cargo Cap. or Gross*	Overall Length	Vessel Breadth	Vessel Depth
Philip R. Clarke	5277062	SU	1952	T	25,300	767' 00"	70' 00"	36' 00"

Built: American Shipbuilding Co., Lorain, OH; lengthened 120' in '74 and converted to a self-unloader in '82 at Fraser Shipyards, Superior, WI

Presque Isle {2}	7303877	IT	1973	D	1,578*	153' 03"	54' 00"	31' 03"

Built: Halter Marine, New Orleans, LA; paired with the self-unloading barge Presque Isle

Presque Isle {2}		SU	1973	B	57,500	974' 06"	104' 07"	46' 06"

Built: Erie Marine Inc., Erie, PA

[ITB Presque Isle OA dimensions together]					1,000' 00"	104' 07"	46' 06"	
Roger Blough	7222138	SU	1972	D	43,900	858' 00"	105' 00"	41' 06"

Built: American Shipbuilding Co., Lorain, OH

GREAT LAKES GROUP, CLEVELAND, OH *(thegreatlakesgroup.com)*

THE GREAT LAKES TOWING CO., CLEVELAND, OH – DIVISION OF THE GREAT LAKES GROUP

Fleet Name / Vessel Name	Vessel IMO #	Vessel Type	Year Built	Engine Type	Cargo Cap. or Gross*	Overall Length	Vessel Breadth	Vessel Depth
Arizona		TB	1931	D	98*	74' 08"	19' 09"	11' 06"
Arkansas {2}		TB	1909	D	97*	74' 08"	19' 09"	11' 06"
(Yale '09-'48)								
California		TB	1926	DE	97*	74' 08"	19' 09"	11' 06"
Cleveland		TB	2017	D	N/A*	65' 08"	24' 00"	11' 00"

Built: Great Lakes Shipyard, Cleveland, OH; this is the first of 10 new tugs being built for Great Lakes service

Colorado		TB	1928	D	98*	78' 08"	20' 00"	12' 04"
Erie		TB	1971	D	243*	102' 03"	29' 00"	16' 03"
(YTB 810 {Anoka} '71-'15)								
Favorite		FD	1983			90' 00"	50' 00"	5' 00"
Florida		TB	1926	D	99*	71' 00"	20' 02"	11' 02"
(Florida '26-'83, Pinellas '83-'84)								
Huron	8980907	TB	1974	D	243*	102' 03"	29' 00"	16' 03"
(YTB 833 {Shabonee} '74-'02, Daniel McAllister '02-'15)								
Idaho		TB	1931	DE	98*	78' 08"	20' 00"	12' 04"
Illinois {2}		TB	1914	D	98*	71' 00"	20' 00"	12' 05"
Indiana		TB	1911	DE	97*	74' 08"	19' 09"	11' 06"
Iowa		TB	1915	D	97*	74' 08"	19' 09"	11' 06"
Kansas		TB	1927	D	97*	74' 08"	19' 09"	11' 06"
Kentucky {2}		TB	1929	D	98*	78' 08"	20' 00"	12' 04"
Louisiana		TB	1917	D	97*	74' 08"	19' 09"	11' 06"
Maine {1}		TB	1921	D	96*	71' 00"	20' 01"	11' 02"
(Maine {1} '21-'82, Saipan '82-'83, Hillsboro '83-'84)								
Massachusetts		TB	1928	D	98*	78' 08"	20' 00"	12' 04"
Michigan	6604016	TB	1965	D	148*	75' 05"	24' 00"	8' 06"
(Vincent J.Robin IV, Betty Smith, Seacor Enterprise '91-'97, Leo '97-'98, Ybor '98-'99, Capt. Sweet '99-'01, Susan McAllister '01-'15)								
Milwaukee		DB	1924	B	1,095	172' 00"	40' 00"	11' 06"
Minnesota		TB	1911	D	98*	78' 08"	20' 00"	12' 04"
Mississippi		TB	1916	DE	97*	74' 08"	19' 09"	11' 06"
Missouri {2}		TB	1927	D	149*	88' 04"	24' 06"	12' 03"
(Rogers City {1} '27-'56, Dolomite {1} '56-'81, Chippewa {7} '81-'90)								
Nebraska		TB	1929	D	98*	78' 08"	20' 00"	12' 05"
New Jersey		TB	1924	D	98*	78' 08"	20' 00"	12' 04"
(New Jersey '24-'52, Petco-21 '52-'53)								
New York		TB	1913	D	98*	78' 08"	20' 00"	12' 04"
North Carolina {2}		TB	1952	DE	145*	87' 09"	24' 01"	10' 07"
(Limestone '52-'83, Wicklow '83-'90)								
North Dakota		TB	1910	D	97*	74' 08"	19' 09"	11' 06"
(John M. Truby '10-'38)								
Ohio {3}	6507440	TB	1903	D	194*	101' 02"	26' 00"	13' 07"

Built: Great Lakes Towing Co., Chicago, IL (M.F.D. No. 15 '03-'52, Laurence C. Turner '52-'73)

Oklahoma		TB	1913	DE	97*	74' 08"	19' 09"	11' 06"
(T. C. Lutz {2} '13-'34)								
Ontario		TB	1964	D	243*	102' 03"	29' 00"	16' 03"
(YTB 770 {Dahlonega} '64-'01, Jeffrey K. McAllister '01-'15)								
Pennsylvania {3}		TB	1911	D	98*	78' 08"	20' 00"	12' 04"
Rhode Island		TB	1930	D	98*	78' 08"	20' 00"	12' 04"
South Carolina		TB	1925	D	102*	79' 06"	21' 01"	11' 03"
(Welcome {2} '25-'53, Joseph H. Callan '53-'72, South Carolina '72-'82, Tulagi '82-'83)								

Tanker Jana Desgagnés on the Seaway. *(Alain Gindroz)*

Algomarine on her last trip before heading for scrap in the spring of 2016. Here, she's meeting Arthur M. Anderson on the St. Clair River. *(Wade P. Streeter)*

Superior {3}		TB	1912	D	147*	82' 00"	22' 00"	10' 07"
(Richard Fitzgerald '12-'46)								
Texas		TB	1916	DE	97*	74' 08"	19' 09"	11' 06"
Vermont		TB	1914	D	98*	71' 00"	20' 00"	12' 05"
Virginia {2}		TB	1914	DE	97*	74' 08"	19' 09"	11' 06"
Washington		TB	1925	DE	97*	74' 08"	19' 09"	11' 06"
Wisconsin {4}		TB	1897	D	105*	83' 00"	21' 02"	9' 06"
(America {3}, Midway)								
Wyoming		TB	1929	D	104*	78' 08"	20' 00"	12' 04"

GREAT LAKES MARITIME ACADEMY, TRAVERSE CITY, MI *(nmc.edu/maritime)*

Anchor Bay		TV	1953	D	23*	45' 00"	13' 00"	7' 00"
Built: Roamer Boat Co., Holland, MI (ST-2158 '53-'62)								
Northwestern {2}		TV	1969	D	12*	55' 00"	15' 00"	6' 06"
Built: Paasch Marine Services Inc., Erie, PA (USCOE North Central '69-'98)								
State of Michigan	8835451	TV	1985	D	1,914*	224' 00"	43' 00"	20' 00"
Built: Tacoma Boatbuilding Co., Tacoma, WA (USNS Persistent '85-'98, USCG Persistent '98-'02)								

GREAT LAKES OFFSHORE SERVICES INC., PORT DOVER, ON

H. H. Misner		TB	1946	D	28*	66' 09"	16' 04"	4' 05"

GREAT LAKES SCHOONER CO., TORONTO, ON *(greatlakesschooner.com)*

Challenge		ES	1980	W/D	76*	96' 00"	16' 06"	8' 00"
Kajama		ES	1930	W/D	263*	128' 09"	22' 09"	11' 08"

GREAT LAKES SCIENCE CENTER, ANN ARBOR, MI *(glsc.usgs.gov)*

Arcticus		RV	2014	D	148*	77' 03"	26' 11"	11' 00"
Kaho		RV	2011	D	55*	70' 02"	18' 00"	
Kiyi		RV	1999	D	290*	107' 00"	27' 00"	12' 02"
Muskie		RV	2011	D	55*	70' 02"	18' 00"	
Sturgeon		RV	1977	D	325*	100'00"	25' 05"	10' 00"

GREAT LAKES SHIPWRECK HISTORICAL SOCIETY, SAULT STE. MARIE, MI *(shipwreckmuseum.com)*

David Boyd		RV	1982	D	26*	47' 00"	17' 00"	3' 00"*

GROUPE DESGAGNÉS INC., QUÉBEC CITY, QC *(groupedesgagnes.com)*

OPERATED BY SUBSIDIARY TRANSPORT DESGAGNÉS

Amelia Desgagnés	7411167	GC	1976	D	7,349	355' 00"	49' 00"	30' 06"
Built: Collingwood Shipyards, Collingwood, ON (Soodoc {2} '76-'90)								
Anna Desgagnés	8600507	RR	1986	D	17,850	569' 03"	75' 07"	44' 11"
Built: Kvaerner Warnow Werft GmbH, Rostock, Germany (Truskavets '86-'96, Anna Desgagnés '96-'98, PCC Panama '98-'99)								
Camilla Desgagnés	8100595	GC	1982	D	6,889	ww436' 04"	67' 07"	46' 03"
Built: Kroeger Werft GmbH & Co. KG, Rendsburg, Germany (Camilla 1 '82-'04)								
Claude A. Desgagnés	9488059	GC	2011	D	12,671	454' 05"	69' 11"	36' 01"
Built: Sanfu Ship Engineering, Taizhou Jiangsu, China (Elsborg '11-'12)								
Rosaire A. Desgagnés	9363534	GC	2007	D	12,575	453' 00"	68' 11"	36' 01"
Built: Quingshan/Jiangdong/Jiangzhou Shipyards, Jiangzhou, China (Beluga Fortification '07-'07)								
Sedna Desgagnés	9402093	GC	2009	D	12,413	456' 00"	68' 11"	36' 01"
Built: Quingshan/Jiangdong/Jiangzhou Shipyards, Jiangzhou, China (Beluga Festivity '09-'09)								
Vectis Castle	9626168	BC	2013	D	10,150	406' 08"	57' 01"	37' 05"
Built: Jiangsu Yangzijiang Shipyard Co. Ltd., Jingjiang City, China								
Zélada Desgagnés	9402081	GC	2008	D	12,413	453' 00"	68' 11"	36' 01"
Built: Quingshan/Jiangdong/Jiangzhou Shipyards, Jiangzhou, China (Beluga Freedom '09-'09)								

THE FOLLOWING VESSELS CHARTERED TO PETRO-NAV INC., MONTREAL, QC, A SUBSIDIARY OF GROUPE DESGAGNÉS INC.

Damia Desgagnés	9766437	TK	2016	D	15,182	442' 11"	77' 01"	37' 01"
Built: Besiktas Gemi Insa A.S., Istanbul, Turkey								
Dara Desgagnés	9040089	TK	1992	D	10,511	405' 10"	58' 01"	34' 09"
Built: MTW Shipyard, Wismar, Germany (Elbestern '92-'93, Diamond Star, '93-'10)								
Esta Desgagnés	9040077	TK	1992	D	10,511	405' 10"	58' 01"	34' 09"
Built: MTW Shipyard, Wismar, Germany (Emsstern '92-'92, Emerald Star '92-'10)								
Jana Desgagnés	9046564	TK	1993	D	10,511	405' 10"	58' 01"	34' 09"
Built: MTW Shipyard, Wismar, Germany (Jadestern '93-'94, Jade Star '94-'10)								
Maria Desgagnés	9163752	TK	1999	D	13,199	393' 08"	68' 11"	40' 05"
Built: Qiuxin Shipyard, Shanghai, China (Kilchem Asia '99-'99)								

Fleet Name / Vessel Name	Vessel IMO #	Vessel Type	Year Built	Engine Type	Cargo Cap. or Gross*	Overall Length	Vessel Breadth	Vessel Depth
Mia Desgagnés	9772278	TK	2016	D	15,182	442' 11"	77' 01"	37' 01"

Built: Besiktas Gemi Insa A.S., Istanbul, Turkey

Sarah Desgagnés	9352171	TK	2007	D	18,000	483'11"	73' 06"	41' 04"

Built: Gisan Shipyard, Tuzla, Turkey (Besiktas Greenland '07-'08)

THE FOLLOWING VESSELS CHARTERED TO RELAIS NORDIK INC., RIMOUSKI, QC (relaisnordik.com)
A SUBSIDIARY OF GROUPE DESGAGNÉS INC.

Bella Desgagnés	9511519	PF/RR	2012	D	1,054	312' 00"	63' 06"	22' 08"

Built: Brodogradil Kraljevica d.d., Kraljevica, Croatia

Nordik Express	7391290	GC/CF	1974	D	1,697	219' 11"	44' 00"	16' 01"

Built: Todd Pacific Shipyards Corp., Seattle, WA (Theriot Offshore IV '74-'77, Scotoil 4 '77-'79, Tartan Sea '79-'87)

TRANSPORT MARITIME ST-LAURENT INC., A SUBSIDIARY OF GROUPE DESGAGNÉS INC.

Espada Desgagnés	9334698	TK	2006	D	42,810*	750' 00	105' 08"	67' 01"

Built: Brodosplit, Split, Croatia (Stena Poseidon '06-'14)

Laurentia Desgagnés	9334703	TK	2007	D	42,810*	750' 00	105' 08"	67' 01"

Built: Brodosplit, Split, Croatia (laid down as Neste Polaris, Palva '07-'14)

GROUPE OCÉAN INC., QUÉBEC, QC (groupocean.com)

Fleet Name / Vessel Name	Vessel IMO #	Vessel Type	Year Built	Engine Type	Cargo Cap. or Gross*	Overall Length	Vessel Breadth	Vessel Depth
Andre H.	5404172	TB	1963	D	317*	126' 00"	28' 06"	12' 10"

Built: Davie Shipbuilding Co., Lauzon, QC (Foundation Valiant '63-'73, Point Valiant {1} '73-'95)

Avantage	6828882	TB	1969	D	362*	116' 10"	32' 09"	16' 03"

Built: J. Boel En Zonen, Temse, Belgium (Sea Lion '69-'97)

Basse-Cote	8644620	DB	1932	B	400	201' 00"	40' 00"	12' 00"

Built: Department of Marine and Fisheries Government Shipyard, Sorel, QC (Louis D. '32-'93)

Duga	7530030	TB	1977	D	382*	114' 02"	32' 10"	16' 05"

Built: Langsten Slip & Båtbyggeri A/S, Lansten, Norway

Escorte	8871027	TT	1964	D	120*	85' 00"	23' 07"	7' 05"

Built: Jakobson Shipyard, Oyster Bay, NY (USS Menasha [YTB / YTM-773, YTM-761] '64-'92, Menasha {1} '92-'95)

Jerry G.	8959788	TB	1960	D	202*	91' 06"	27' 03"	12' 06"

Built: Davie Shipbuilding Co., Lauzon, QC

Josee H.		PB	1961	D	66*	63' 50"	16' 02"	9' 50"

Built: Ferguson Industries Ltd., Pictou, NS (Le Bic '61-'98)

Kim R.D.		TB	1954	D	36*	48' 08"	14' 01"	5' 01

Built: Port Dalhousie Shipyard Co., Port Dalhousie, ON (Constructor '54-'86)

La Prairie	7393585	TB	1975	D	110*	73' 09"	25' 09"	11' 08"

Built: Georgetown Shipyard, Georgetown, PEI

Le Phil D.		TB	1961	D	38*	56' 01"	16' 00"	5' 08"

Built: Russel Brothers Ltd., Owen Sound, ON (Expanse)

Mega	7347641	TB	1975	D	768*	125' 03"	42' 03"	22' 09"

Built: Oy Wartsila AB, Helsinki, Finland; mated with articulated barge Motti

Motti	9072434	DB	1993	B	5,195*	403' 04"	78' 02"	7' 07"

Built: Kvaerner Masa Yards, Turku, Finland

Océan Abys	8644644	DB	1948	B	1,000	140' 00"	40' 00"	9' 00"

Built: Marine Industries Ltd., Sorel, QC (Omni No. 1 '48-'94)

Océan Arctique	9261607	TB	2005	TB	512*	102' 08"	39' 05"	17' 00"

Built: Industries Ocean Inc., Ile-Aux-Coudres, QC (Stevns Arctic '05-'13)

Océan A. Simard	8000056	TT	1980	D	286*	92' 00"	34' 00"	13' 07"

Built: Georgetown Shipyards Ltd., Georgetown, PEI (Alexis-Simard '80-'11)

Océan Basques	7237212	TB	1972	D	396*	98' 04"	32' 08"	16' 04"

Built: Canadian Shipbuilding & Engineering Co., Collingwood, ON (Pointe Aux-Basques '72-'13)

Océan Bertrand Jeansonne	9521526	TB	2008	D	402*	94' 05"	36' 05"	17' 02"

Built: East Isle Shipyard, Georgetown, PEI

Océan Bravo	7025279	TB	1970	D	320*	110' 00"	28' 06"	17' 00"

Built: Davie Shipbuilding Co., Lauzon, QC (Takis V. '70-'80, Donald P '80-'80, Nimue '80-'83, Donald P. '83-'98)

Océan Cape Crow		TB	1951		14*	37' 08"	10' 05"	5' 00"

Built: Russel-Hipwell Engines, Owen Sound, ON (Cape Crow '51-'16)

Océan Charlie	7312024	TB	1973	D	448*	123' 02"	31' 07"	16' 01"

Built: Davie Shipbuilding Co., Lauzon, QC (Leonard W. '73-'98)

Océan Cote-Nord			2001		79*	75' 01"	18' 00"	10' 06"

Built: Industries Ocean Inc., Ile-Aux-Coudres, QC (Cote-Nord '01-'14)

Océan Delta	7235707	TB	1973	D	722*	136' 08"	35' 08"	22' 00"

Built: Ulstein Mek. Verksted A.S., Ulsteinvik, Norway (Sistella '73-'78, Sandy Cape '78-'80, Captain Ioannis S. '80-'99)

Océan Echo II	6913091	AT	1969	D	438*	104' 08"	34' 05"	18' 00"

Built: Port Weller Dry Docks, Port Weller, ON (Atlantic '69-'75, Laval '75-'96)

Fleet Name / Vessel Name	Vessel IMO #	Vessel Type	Year Built	Engine Type	Cargo Cap. or Gross*	Overall Length	Vessel Breadth	Vessel Depth
Océan Express		PB	1999	D	29*	47' 02"	14' 00"	7' 05"
Built: Industries Ocean Inc., Charlevoix, QC (H-2000 '99-'00)								
Océan Georgie Bain	9553892	TB	2009	D	204*	75' 02"	29' 09"	12' 09"
Built: Industries Ocean Inc., Ile-Aux-Coudres, QC								
Océan Golf	5146354	TB	1959	D	159*	103' 00"	25' 10"	11' 09"
Built: P.K. Harris & Sons, Appledore, England (launched as Stranton; Helen M. McAllister '59-'97)								
Océan Guide		PB	2001	D	29*	47' 02"	14' 00"	7' 05"
Built: Industries Ocean Inc., Charlevoix, QC								
Océan Henry Bain	9420916	TB	2006	D	402*	94' 08"	30' 01"	14' 09"
Built: East Isle Shipyard, Georgetown, PEI								
Océan Hercule	7525346	TB	1976	D	448*	120' 00"	32' 00"	19' 00"
(Stril Pilot '76-'81, Spirit Sky '81-'86, Ireland '86-'89, Irelandia '89-'95, Charles Antoine '95-'97)								
Océan Intrepide	9203423	TT	1998	D	302*	80' 00"	30' 01"	14' 09"
Built: Industries Ocean Inc., Ile-Aux-Coudres, QC								
Océan Jupiter	9220160	TT	1998	D	302*	80' 00"	30' 01"	14' 09"
Built: Industries Ocean Inc., Ile-Aux-Coudres, QC								
Océan K. Rusby	9345556	TB	2005	D	402*	94' 08"	30' 01"	14' 09"
Built: East Isle Shipyard, Georgetown, PEI								
Océan Lima		TB	1977	D	15*	34' 02"	11' 08"	4' 00"
(VM/S St. Louis III '77-'10)								
Océan Maisonneuve		SV	1974	D	56*	58' 03"	20' 03"	6' 05"
Built: Fercraft Marine, St. Catherine d'Alexandrie, QC (VM/S Maisonneuve '74-'16)								
Océan Pierre Julien	9688142	TB	2013	D	204*	75' 01"	30' 01"	12' 09"
Built: Industries Ocean Inc., Ile-Aux-Coudres, QC								
Océan Raymond Lemay	9420904	TB	2006	D	402*	94' 08"	30' 01"	14' 09"
Built: East Isle Shipyard, Georgetown, PEI								
Océan Ross Gaudreault	9542221	TB	2011	D	402*	94' 04"	36' 05"	17' 00"
Built: East Isle Shipyard, Georgetown, PEI								

Paul R. Tregurtha greets the day at Duluth, Minn. (Paul Scinocca)

Fleet Name Vessel Name	Vessel IMO #	Vessel Type	Year Built	Engine Type	Cargo Cap. or Gross*	Overall Length	Vessel Breadth	Vessel Depth
Océan Sept-Iles	7901162	TB	1980	D	427*	98' 04"	36' 01"	13' 01"
Built: Canadian Shipbuilding & Engineering Co., Collingwood, ON (Pointe Sept-Iles '80-'13)								
Océan Serge Genois	9553907	TB	2010	D	204*	75' 01"	30' 01"	12' 09"
Built: Industries Ocean Inc., Ile-Aux-Coudres, QC								
Océan Stevns	9224960	TB	2002	D	512*	102' 08"	39' 05"	17' 00"
Built: Industries Ocean Inc., Ile-Aux-Coudres, QC (Stevns Ocean '02-'13)								
Océan Taiga	9679488	TB	2016	D	710*	112' 00"	42' 06"	26' 07"
Built: Industries Ocean Inc., Ile-Aux-Coudres, QC								
Océan Traverse Nord	9666534	DR	2012	B	1,165*	210' 00"	42' 06"	14' 07"
Built: Industries Ocean Inc., Ile-Aux-Coudres, QC								
Océan Tundra	9645504	TB	2013	D	710*	118' 01"	42' 03"	22' 09"
Built: Industries Ocean Inc., Ile-Aux-Coudres, QC								
Océan Yvan Desgagnés	9542207	TB	2010	D	402*	94' 04"	36' 05"	17' 00"
Built: East Isle Shipyard, Georgetown, PEI								
Omni-Atlas	8644668	CS	1913	B	479*	133' 00"	42' 00"	10' 00"
Built: Sir William Arrol & Co. Ltd., Glasgow, Scotland								
Omni-Richelieu	6923084	TB	1969	D	144*	83' 00"	24' 06"	13' 06"
Built: Pictou Industries Ltd., Pictou, NS (Port Alfred II '69-'82)								
R. F. Grant		TB	1934	D	78*	71' 00"	17' 00"	8' 00"
Service Boat No. 1		PB	1965	D	55*	57' 08"	16' 01"	7' 06"
Service Boat No. 2		TB	1934	D	78*	65' 02"	17' 00"	8' 01"
Service Boat No. 4		PB	1959	D	26*	39' 01"	14' 02"	6' 03"

GROUPE RIVERIN MARITIME INC., SAGUENAY, QC

Jean-Joseph	8817382	GC	1990	D	1,999*	257' 08	41' 00"	21' 06"
Built: Ferus Smit, Westerbroek, Netherlands (Bothniaborg '90-'04, Westerborg '04-'06, Maple '06-'08, Myras '08-'13, Hav Sund '13-'15)								

H

HAMILTON PORT AUTHORITY, HAMILTON, ON *(hamiltonport.ca)*

Fleet Name / Vessel Name	Vessel IMO #	Vessel Type	Year Built	Engine Type	Cargo Cap. or Gross*	Overall Length	Vessel Breadth	Vessel Depth
Judge McCombs		TB	1948	D	10*	33' 01"	10' 03"	4' 00"

Built: Northern Shipbuilding & Repair Co. Ltd., Bronte, ON (Bronte Sue '48–'50)

HAMILTON HARBOUR QUEEN CRUISES, HAMILTON, ON *(hamiltonharbourqueen.ca)*

Hamilton Harbour Queen		ES	1956	D	252*	100' 00"	40' 00"	4' 05"

Built: Russel-Hipwell Engines, Owen Sound, ON (Johnny B. '56–'89, Garden City '89–'00, Harbour Princess '00–'05)

HARBOR LIGHT CRUISE LINES INC., TOLEDO, OH *(sandpiperboat.com)*

Sandpiper		ES	1984	D	37*	65' 00"	16' 00"	3' 00"

HARBOR BOAT CRUISE CO., TORONTO, ON *(rivergambler.ca)*

River Gambler		ES	1992	D	332*	100' 06"	16' 00"	4' 07"

Built: Jacques Beauchamp, Windsor, ON

HERITAGE MARINE, KNIFE RIVER, MN *(heritagemarinetug.com)*

Edward H.	8651879	TB	1944	D	142*	86' 00"	23' 00"	10' 03"

Built: Equitable Equipment Co., Madisonville, LA (ST-707 '44–'60, Forney '60–'07)

Helen H.	8624670	TB	1967	D	138*	82' 03"	26' 08"	10' 05"

Built: Bludworth Shipyard, Corpus Christi, TX (W. Douglas Masterson '67–'11)

Nancy J.	6504838	TB	1964	D	186*	92' 17"	29' 05"	14' 00"

Built: Main Iron Works, Houma, La (Horace, Point Comfort–'14)

Nels J.	5126615	TB	1958	D	194*	103' 00"	26 06"	12' 00"

Built: Gulfport Shipbuilding Co., Port Arthur, TX (Gatco Alabama, Ares)

HORNBLOWER NIAGARA CRUISES, NIAGARA FALLS, ON *(niagaracruises.com)*
VESSELS OWNED BY HORNBLOWER CANADA CO., NIAGARA FALLS, ON

Niagara Guardian		PA	2013	D	38*	68' 09"	15' 07"	7' 05"
Niagara Thunder		PA	2014	D	185*	83' 02"	35' 09"	8' 09"
Niagara Wonder		PA	2014	D	185*	83' 02"	35' 09"	8' 09"

HORNE TRANSPORTATION LTD., WOLFE ISLAND, ON *(wolfeisland.com/ferry.php)*

William Darrell		CF	1952	D	66*	66' 00"	28' 00"	6' 00"

HUFFMAN EQUIPMENT RENTAL INC., EASTLAKE, OH

Benjamin Ridgway		TW	1969	D	51*	53' 00"	18' 05"	7' 00"
Bert Huffman		TW	1979	D	34*	38' 00"	13' 06"	5' 02"
Hamp Thomas		TB	1968	D	22*	43' 00"	13' 00"	4' 00"
Paddy Miles		TB	1934	D	16*	45' 04"	12' 04"	4' 07"

HURON LADY II INC., PORT HURON, MI *(huronlady.com)*

Huron Lady II		ES	1993	D	82*	65' 00"	19' 00"	10' 00"

(Lady Lumina '93–'99)

HYDRO-QUEBEC, MONTREAL, QC

Des Chenaux		TB	1953	D	46*	51' 08"	16' 00"	7' 08"

Built: Chantiers Manseau Ltd., Sorel, QC

R.O. Sweezy		TB	1991	D	29*	41' 09"	14' 00"	5' 07"

Built: Jean Fournier, Quebec City, QC (Citadelle I '91–'92)

I

INFINITY AND OVATION YACHT CHARTERS LLC, ST. CLAIR SHORES, MI *(infinityandovation.com)*

Infinity		PA	2001	D	82*	117' 00"	22' 00"	6' 00"
Ovation		PA	2005	D	97*	138' 00"	27' 00"	7' 00"

INLAND LAKES MANAGEMENT INC., ALPENA, MI

Alpena {2}	5206362	CC	1942	T	13,900	519' 06"	67' 00"	35' 00"

Built: Great Lakes Engineering Works, River Rouge, MI; shortened by 120' and converted to a self-unloading cement carrier at Fraser Shipyards, Superior, WI, in '91 (Leon Fraser '42–'91)

J.A.W. Iglehart	5139179	CC	1936	T	12,500	501' 06"	68' 03"	37' 00"

Built: Sun Shipbuilding and Drydock Co., Chester, PA; converted from a saltwater tanker to a self-unloading cement carrier at American Shipbuilding Co., South Chicago, IL , in '65; last operated Oct. 29, 2006; in use as a cement storage/transfer vessel at Superior, WI (Pan Amoco '36–'55, Amoco '55–'60, H. R. Schemm '60–'65)

Fleet Name / Vessel Name	Vessel IMO #	Vessel Type	Year Built	Engine Type	Cargo Cap. or Gross*	Overall Length	Vessel Breadth	Vessel Depth
Paul H. Townsend	5272050	CC	1945	D	7,850	447' 00"	50' 00"	29' 00"

Built: Consolidated Steel Corp., Wilmington, DE; converted from a saltwater cargo vessel to a self-unloading cement carrier at Bethlehem Steel Co., Shipbuilding Div., Hoboken, NJ, and Calumet Shipyard, Chicago, IL, in '52-'53; lengthened at Great Lakes Engineering Works, Ashtabula, OH, in '58; last operated Dec. 5, 2005; in long-term lay-up at Muskegon, MI (USNS Hickory Coll '45-'46, USNS Coastal Delegate '46-'52)

S.T. Crapo	5304011	CC	1927	B	8,900	402' 06"	60' 03"	29' 00"

Built: Great Lakes Engineering Works, River Rouge, MI; last operated Sept. 4, 1996; in use as a cement storage and transfer vessel at Green Bay, WI

INLAND SEAS EDUCATION ASSOCIATION, SUTTONS BAY, MI (schoolship.org)

Inland Seas		RV	1994	W	41*	61' 06"	17' 00"	7' 00"
Utopia		RV	1946	W	49*	65' 0"	18' 00"	6' 08"

INLAND TUG & BARGE LTD., BROCKVILLE, ON

Katanni		TB	1991	D	19*	34' 08"	14' 05"	5' 05"

INTERLAKE STEAMSHIP CO., MIDDLEBURG HEIGHTS, OH (interlakesteamship.com)

Dorothy Ann	8955732	AT/TT	1999	D	1,090*	124' 03"	44' 00"	24' 00"

Built: Bay Shipbuilding Co., Sturgeon Bay, WI; paired with self-unloading barge Pathfinder

Herbert C. Jackson	5148417	SU	1959	D	24,800	690' 00"	75' 00"	37' 06"

Built: Great Lakes Engineering Works, River Rouge, MI; converted to a self-unloader at Defoe Shipbuilding Co., Bay City, MI, in '75; repowered in '16

Hon. James L. Oberstar	5322518	SU	1959	D	31,000	806' 00"	75' 00"	37' 06"

Built: American Shipbuilding Co., Lorain, OH; lengthened 96' in '72; converted to a self-unloader in '81 at Fraser Shipyards, Superior, WI; repowered in '09 (Shenango II '59-'67, Charles M. Beeghly '67-'11)

James R. Barker	7390260	SU	1976	D	63,300	1,004' 00"	105' 00"	50' 00"

Built: American Shipbuilding Co., Lorain, OH

John Sherwin {2}	5174428	BC	1958	B	31,500	806' 00"	75' 00"	37' 06"

Built: American Steamship Co., Lorain, OH; lengthened 96' at Fraser Shipyards, Superior, WI, in '73; last operated Nov. 16, 1981; in long-term lay-up at DeTour, MI

Kaye E. Barker	5097450	SU	1952	D	25,900	767' 00"	70' 00"	36' 00"

Built: American Shipbuilding Co., Toledo, OH; lengthened 120' at Fraser Shipyards, Superior, WI, in '76; converted to a self-unloader at American Shipbuilding Co., Toledo, OH, in '81; repowered in '12 (Edward B. Greene '52-'85, Benson Ford {3} '85-'89)

Lee A. Tregurtha	5385625	SU	1942	D	29,360	826' 00"	75' 00"	39' 00"

Built: Bethlehem Shipbuilding and Drydock Co., Sparrows Point, MD; converted from a saltwater tanker to a Great Lakes bulk carrier in '61; lengthened 96' in '76 and converted to a self-unloader in '78, all at American Shipbuilding Co., Lorain, OH; repowered in '06 (laid down as Mobiloil; launched as Samoset; USS Chiwawa [AO-68] '42-'46, Chiwawa '46-'61, Walter A. Sterling '61-'85, William Clay Ford {2} '85-'89)

Mesabi Miner	7390272	SU	1977	D	63,300	1,004' 00"	105' 00"	50' 00"

Built: American Shipbuilding Co., Lorain, OH

Pathfinder {3}	5166768	SU	1953	B	10,577	606' 00"	70' 03"	36' 03"

Built: Great Lakes Engineering Works, River Rouge, MI; converted from a powered vessel to a self-unloading barge at Bay Shipbuilding Co., Sturgeon Bay, WI, in '98 (J. L. Mauthe '53-'98)

Paul R. Tregurtha	7729057	SU	1981	D	68,000	1,013' 06"	105' 00"	56' 00"

Built: American Shipbuilding Co., Lorain, OH; this is the largest vessel on the lakes (William J. DeLancey '81-'90)

INTERLAKE LEASING III – A SUBSIDIARY OF INTERLAKE STEAMSHIP CO.

Stewart J. Cort	7105495	SU	1972	D	58,000	1,000' 00"	105' 00"	49' 00"

Built: Erie Marine Inc., Erie, PA; built for Bethlhem Steel Corp., this was the Great Lakes' first 1,000-footer   2020

ISLAND FERRY SERVICES CORP., CHEBOYGAN, MI

Polaris		PF	1952	D	99*	60' 02"	36' 00"	8' 06"

ISLE ROYALE LINE INC., COPPER HARBOR, MI (isleroyale.com)

Isle Royale Queen IV		PA/PK	1980	D	93*	98' 09"	22' 01"	7' 00"

J-K

J&J MARINE LTD., LASALLE, ON (jjmarine.com)

Howard W. Fitzpatrick		TB	1971	D	97*	78' 00"	20' 05"	4' 09"

J.W. WESTCOTT CO., DETROIT, MI (jwwestcott.com)

Joseph J. Hogan		MB	1957	D	16*	40' 00"	12' 05"	5' 00"

(USCOE Ottawa '57-'95)

Fleet Name / Vessel Name	Vessel IMO #	Vessel Type	Year Built	Engine Type	Cargo Cap. or Gross*	Overall Length	Vessel Breadth	Vessel Depth
J. W. Westcott II		MB	1949	D	14*	46' 01"	13' 03"	4' 05"

Built: Paasch Marine Service, Erie, PA; floating post office has its own U.S. ZIP code, 48222

JEFF FOSTER, SUPERIOR, WI

Sundew		IB	1944	DE	1,025*	180' 00"	37' 05"	17' 04"

Built: Marine Ironworks and Shipbuilding Corp., Duluth, MN; former U.S. Coast Guard cutter WLB-404 was decommissioned in 2004 and turned into a marine museum; vessel was returned to private ownership in 2009

JUBILEE QUEEN CRUISE LINES, TORONTO, ON (jubileequeencruises.ca)

Jubilee Queen		ES	1986	D	269*	122' 00"	23' 09"	5' 05"

(Pioneer Princess III '86-'89)

K & S MARITIME LLC, HOLLAND, MI

Bonnie G. Selvick		TB	1981	D	45*	57' 08"	17' 00"	6' 01"

(Captain Robbie '81-'90, Philip M. Pearse '90-'97, Chris Ann '97-'09)

Lake Trader		DB	1982	B	2,262*	240' 00"	72' 00"	17' 00"

Built: Forked Island Shipyard Inc., Abbeville, LA (TJ 2501, Primary 1)

KEHOE MARINE CONSTRUCTION CO., LANSDOWNE, ON (kehoemarine.com)

Halton		TB	1942	D	15*	42' 08"	14' 00"	5' 08"

Built: Muir Bros. Dry Dock Co. Ltd., Port Dalhousie, ON

Houghton		TB	1944	D	15*	45' 00"	13' 00"	6' 00"

Built: Port Houston Iron Works, Houston, TX

KELLEYS ISLAND BOAT LINES, MARBLEHEAD, OH (kelleysislandferry.com)

Carlee Emily		PA/CF	1987	D	98*	101' 00"	34' 06"	10' 00"

Built: Blount Marine Corp., Warren, RI (Endeavor '87-'02)

Juliet Alicia		PA/CF	1969	D	95*	88' 03"	33' 00"	6' 08"

Built: Blount Marine Corp., Warren, RI (Kelley Islander)

Shirley Irene		PA/CF	1991	D	68*	160' 00"	46' 00"	9' 00"

Built: Ocean Group Shipyard, Bayou La Batre, AL

KINDRA LAKE TOWING LP, CHICAGO, IL (kindralake.com)

Buckley		TW	1958	D	94*	95' 00"	26' 00"	11' 00"

Built: Parker Bros. Shipyard, Houston, TX (Linda Brooks '58-'67, Eddie B. {2} '67-'95)

Donald C.	8841967	TB	1962	D	198*	91' 00"	29' 00"	11' 06"

Built: Main Iron Works Inc., Houma, LA (Donald C. Hannah '62-'09)

Ellie		TB	1970	D	29*	39' 07"	16' 00"	4' 06"

Built: Big River Shipbuilding Inc., Vicksburg, MS (Miss Bissy '09)

Morgan		TB	1974	D	134*	90' 00"	30' 00"	10' 06"

Built: Peterson Builders Inc., Sturgeon Bay, WI (Donald O'Toole '74-'86, Bonesey B. '86-'95)

Old Mission		TB	1945	D	94*	85' 00"	23' 00"	10' 04"

Built: Sturgeon Bay Shipbuilding, Sturgeon Bay, WI (U. S. Army ST-880 '45-'47, USCOE Avondale '47-'64, Adrienne B. '64-'95)

Tanner		TW	1977	D	62*	56' 06"	22' 03"	6' 06"

Built: Thrift Shipbuilding Inc., Sulphur, LA; Owned by Jamattca, Downers Grove, IL (J.H. Tanner 76-'00)

KING CO. (THE), HOLLAND, MI

Barry J		TB	1943	D	26*	46' 00"	13' 00"	7' 00"

Built: Sturgeon Bay Shipbuilding & Dry Dock Co., Sturgeon Bay, WI

Buxton II		DR	1976	B	147*	130' 02"	28' 01"	7' 00"

Built: Barbour Boat Works Inc., Holland, MI

Carol Ann		TB	1981	D	86*	61' 05"	24' 00"	8' 07"

Built: Rodriguez Boat Builders, Bayou La Batre, AL

John Henry		TB	1954	D	66*	65' 04"	19' 04"	9' 06"

Missouri Valley Steel, Leavenworth, KS (U. S. Army ST-2013 '54-'80)

Julie Dee		TB	1937	D	64*	68' 08"	18' 01"	7' 06"

Herbert Slade, Beaumont, TX (Dernier, Jerry O'Day, Cindy B)

Matt Allen		TB	1961	D	146*	80' 04"	24' 00"	11' 03"

Nolty Theriot Inc., Golden Meadow, LA (Gladys Bea '61-'73, American Viking '73-'83, Maribeth Andrie '83-'05)

Miss Edna		TB	1935	D	13*	36' 08"	11' 02"	4' 08"

Levingston Shipbuilding, Orange, TX

KINGSTON 1,000 ISLANDS CRUISES, KINGSTON, ON (1000islandscruises.on.ca)

Island Belle I		ES	1988	D	150*	65' 00"	22' 00"	8' 00"

(Spirit of Brockville '88-'91)

L

LAFARGE CANADA INC., MISSISSAUGA, ON
THE FOLLOWING VESSEL MANAGED BY ALGOMA CENTRAL CORP.

English River	5104382	CC	1961	D	7,450	404' 03"	60' 00"	36' 06"

Built: Canadian Shipbuilding and Engineering Ltd., Collingwood, ON; converted to a self-unloading cement carrier by Port Arthur Shipbuilding, Port Arthur (now Thunder Bay), ON, in '74

LAFARGE NORTH AMERICA INC., BINGHAM FARMS, MI (lafargenorthamerica.com)
THE FOLLOWING VESSELS MANAGED BY ANDRIE INC., MUSKEGON, MI (andrie.com)

G. L. Ostrander	7501106	AT	1976	D	198*	140' 02"	40' 01"	22' 03"

Built: Halter Marine, New Orleans, LA; paired with barge Integrity (Andrew Martin '76-'90, Robert L. Torres '90-'94, Jacklyn M '94-'04)

Innovation	9082336	CC	2006	B	7,320*	460' 00"	70' 00"	37' 00"

Built: Bay Shipbuilding Co., Sturgeon Bay, WI

Integrity	8637213	CC	1996	B	14,000	460' 00"	70' 00"	37' 00"

Built: Bay Shipbuilding Co., Sturgeon Bay, WI

Samuel de Champlain	7433799	AT	1975	D	299*	140' 02"	39' 02"	20' 00"

Built: Mangone Shipbuilding, Houston, TX; paired with barge Innovation (Musketeer Fury '75-'78, Tender Panther '78-'79, Margarita '79-'83, Vortice '83-'99, Norfolk '99-'06)

LAKE ERIE ISLAND CRUISES LLC, SANDUSKY, OH (goodtimeboat.com)

Goodtime I		ES	1960	D	81*	111' 00"	29' 08"	9' 05"

Built: Blount Marine Corp., Warren, RI

LAKE EXPRESS LLC, MILWAUKEE, WI (lake-express.com)

Lake Express	9329253	PA/CF	2004	D	96*	179' 02"	57' 07"	16' 00"

Built: Austal USA, Mobile, AL; high-speed ferry service from Milwaukee, WI, to Muskegon, MI; capacity is 250 passengers, 46 autos

LAKE MICHIGAN CARFERRY SERVICE INC., LUDINGTON, MI (ssbadger.com)

Badger	5033583	PA/CF	1953	S	4,244*	410' 06"	59' 06"	24' 00"

Built: Christy Corp., Sturgeon Bay, WI; traditional ferry service from Ludington, MI, to Manitowoc, WI; capacity is 520 passengers, 180 autos; vessel is the last coal-fired steamship on the Great Lakes

Spartan		PA/CF	1952	S	4,244*	410' 06"	59' 06"	24' 00"

Built: Christy Corp., Sturgeon Bay, WI; last operated Jan. 20, 1979; in long-term lay-up at Ludington, MI

LAKE MICHIGAN CONTRACTORS INC., HOLLAND, MI (lakemicontractors.com)

Defiance		TW	1965	D	39*	48' 00"	18' 00"	6' 03"
James Harris		TW	1943	D	18*	41' 09"	12' 05"	5' 00"

LAKEHEAD TUG BOATS INC., THUNDER BAY, ON (steven-lecuyer.squarespace.com)

George N. Carleton		TB	1943	D	97*	82' 00"	21' 00"	11' 00"

Built: Russel Brothers Ltd., Owen Sound, ON (HMCS Glenlea [W-25] '43-'45, Bansaga '45-'64)

Robert John		TB	1945	D	98*	82' 00"	20' 01"	11' 00"

Built: Canadian Dredge & Dock Co., Kingston, ON (HMCS Gleneagle [W-40] '45-'46, Bansturdy '46-'65)

Teclutsa		TB	1973	D	235*	102' 85"	30' 00"	15' 00"

Built: Marinette Marine Ltd., Marinette, WI (YTB-822 – USS Pawhuska '73-'95)

LAKES PILOTS ASSOCIATION, PORT HURON, MI (lakespilots.com)

Huron Belle		PB	1979	D	38*	50' 00"	15' 07"	7' 09"

Built: Gladding-Hearn Shipbuilding, Somerset, MA; vessel offers pilot service at Detroit, MI

Huron Maid		PB	1977	D	26*	46' 00"	12' 05"	3' 05"

Built: Hans Hansen Welding Co., Toledo, OH; vessel offers pilot service at Port Huron, MI

Huron Spirit		PB	2016	D	47*	52' 05"	16' 07"	8' 01"

Built: Gladding Hearn Shipbuilding, Somerset, MA; vessel offers pilot service at Port Huron, MI

LAMBTON MARINE LTD., PORT LAMBTON, ON

Mary Ellen I		TB	2008	D	18*	41' 08"	14' 02"	7' 0

LAURENTIAN PILOTAGE AUTHORITY, MONTREAL, QC (pilotagestlaurent.gc.ca)

Grandes Eaux		PB	2008	D	63*	62' 06"	17' 02"	9' 05
Taukamaim		PB	2012	D	82*	72' 01"	19' 05"	10' 05

LEGEND CRUISES LLC, STURGEON BAY, WI *(ridethefireboat.com)*

Fred A. Busse		ES	1937	D	99*	92' 00"	22' 04"	9' 06"

Built: Defoe Boat & Motor Works, Bay City, MI; former Chicago fireboat offers cruises at Sturgeon Bay, WI

LOWER LAKES TOWING LTD., PORT DOVER, ON *(randlogisticsinc.com)*
A SUBSIDIARY OF RAND LOGISTICS INC., NEW YORK, NY

Cuyahoga	5166392	SU	1943	D	15,675	620' 00"	60' 00"	35' 00"

Built: American Shipbuilding Co., Lorain, OH; converted to a self-unloader by Manitowoc Shipbuilding Co., Manitowoc, WI, in '74; repowered in '01 (J. Burton Ayers '43–'95)

Kaministiqua	8119285	BC	1983	D	34,500	730' 01"	75' 09"	48' 00"

Built: Govan Shipyards, Glasgow, Scotland (Saskatchewan Pioneer '83–'95, Lady Hamilton '95–'06, Voyageur Pioneer '06–'08)

Manitoba {3}	6702301	BC	1967	D	19,093	607' 09"	62' 00"	36' 00"

Built: Collingwood Shipyards, Collingwood, ON; (Mantadoc '67–'02, Teakglen '02–'05, Maritime Trader '05–'11)

Manitoulin {6}	8810918	SU	1991	D	25,000	662' 09"	77' 09"	44' 11"

Former saltwater tanker rebuilt for Great Lakes service in 2015 with a new self-unloading bow section.
***Bow section** built 2014-15 at Chengxi Shipyards, Jiangyin, China. **Stern section** built in 1991 at Uljanik Shipyard, Pula, Croatia. (Trelsi '91–'01, Euro Swan '01–'11, Lalandia Swan '11–'15)*

Michipicoten {2}	5102865	SU	1952	D	22,300	698' 00"	70' 00"	37' 00"

Built: Bethlehem Shipbuilding & Drydock Co., Sparrows Point, MD; lengthened 72' by American Shipbuilding Co., S. Chicago, IL, in '57; converted to a self-unloader by American Shipbuilding Co., Toledo, OH, in '80; repowered in '11 (Elton Hoyt 2nd '52–'03)

Mississagi	5128467	SU	1943	D	15,800	620' 06"	60' 00"	35' 00"

Built: Great Lakes Engineering Works, River Rouge, MI; converted to a self-unloader by Fraser Shipyards, Superior, WI, in '67; repowered in '85 (Hill Annex '43–'43, George A. Sloan '43–'01)

Ojibway	5105831	BC	1952	D	20,668	642' 03"	67' 00"	35' 00"

Built: Defoe Shipbuilding Co., Bay City, MI; repowered in '05 (Charles L. Hutchinson {3} '52–'62, Ernest R. Breech '62–'88, Kinsman Independent '88–'05, Voyageur Independent '05–'08)

Robert S. Pierson	7366403	SU	1974	D	19,650	630' 00"	68' 00"	36' 11"

Built: American Shipbuilding Co., Lorain, OH (Wolverine {2} '74–'08)

Saginaw {3}	5173876	SU	1953	D	20,200	639' 03"	72' 00"	36' 00"

Built: Manitowoc Shipbuilding Co., Manitowoc, WI, repowered in '08 (John J. Boland {3} '53–'99)

Tecumseh {2}	7225855	BC	1973	D	29,510	641' 00"	78' 00"	45' 03

Built: Lockheed Shipbuilding & Construction Co., Seattle, WA (Sugar Islander '73–'96, Islander '96–'96, Judy Litrico '96–'06, Tina Litrico '06–'11)

Fleetmates Lee A. Tregurtha and Herbert C. Jackson at the ore dock in Marquette, Mich. (Rod Burdick)

Fleet Name / Vessel Name	Vessel IMO #	Vessel Type	Year Built	Engine Type	Cargo Cap. or Gross*	Overall Length	Vessel Breadth	Vessel Depth

GRAND RIVER NAVIGATION CO., NEW YORK, NY – AFFILIATE OF LOWER LAKES TOWING LTD.

Fleet Name / Vessel Name	IMO #	Type	Built	Engine	Cargo/Gross	Length	Breadth	Depth
Ashtabula	8637495	SU	1982	B	17,982	610' 01"	78' 01"	49' 08"

Built: Bay Shipbuilding Co., Sturgeon Bay, WI (Mary Turner '82-'12)

| **Calumet** {3} | 7329314 | SU | 1973 | D | 19,650 | 630' 00" | 68' 00" | 36' 11" |

Built: American Shipbuilding Co., Lorain, OH (William R. Roesch '73-'95, David Z. Norton {3} '95-'07, David Z. '07-'08)

| **CTC No. 1** | | CC | 1943 | R | 16,300 | 620' 06" | 60' 00" | 35' 00" |

Built: Great Lakes Engineering Works, River Rouge, MI; last operated Nov. 12, 1981; former cement storage/transfer vessel is laid up at South Chicago, IL; may be returned to service at a future date (Launched as McIntyre; Frank Purnell {1} '43-'64, Steelton {3} '64-'78, Hull No. 3 '78-'79, Pioneer {4} '79-'82)

| **Defiance** | 8109761 | ATB | 1982 | D | 196* | 145' 01" | 44' 00" | 21' 00 |

Built: Marinette Marine Corp., Marinette, WI; paired with barge Ashtabula (April T. Beker '82-'87, Beverly Anderson '82-'12)

| **Invincible** | 7723819 | ATB | 1979 | D | 180* | 100' 00" | 35' 00" | 22' 06" |

Built: Atlantic Marine Inc., Fort George Island, FL (R. W. Sesler '79-'91)

| **James L. Kuber** | 5293341 | SU | 1953 | B | 25,500 | 703' 08" | 70' 00" | 36' 00" |

Built: Great Lakes Engineering Works, River Rouge, MI; lengthened 120' by Fraser Shipyards, Superior, WI, in '75; converted to a self-unloader by Bay Shipbuilding, Sturgeon Bay, WI, in '83; converted to a barge by the owners in '07 (Reserve '53-'08)

| **Lewis J. Kuber** | 5336351 | SU | 1952 | B | 22,300 | 616' 10" | 70' 00" | 37' 00" |

Built: Bethlehem Steel Corp., Sparrows Point, MD; lengthened 72' by American Shipbuilding, South Chicago, IL, in '58; converted to a self-unloader by Fraser Shipyards, Superior, WI, in '80; converted to a barge by Erie Shipbuilding, Erie, PA, in '06; (Sparrows Point '52-'90, Buckeye {3} '90-'06)

| **Manistee** | 5294307 | SU | 1943 | D | 14,900 | 620' 06" | 60' 03" | 35' 00" |

Built: Great Lakes Engineering Works, River Rouge, MI; converted to a self-unloader by Manitowoc Shipbuilding Co., Manitowoc, WI, in '64; repowered in '76; entered long-term lay-up at Toledo, Ohio, in December 2015; (launched as Adirondack, Richard J. Reiss {2} '43-'86, Richard Reiss '86-'05)

| **Manitowoc** | 7366398 | SU | 1973 | D | 19,650 | 630' 00" | 68' 00" | 36' 11" |

Built: American Shipbuilding Co., Lorain, OH (Paul Thayer '73-'95, Earl W. Oglebay '95-'07, Earl W. '07-'08)

| **Olive L. Moore** | 8635227 | AT | 1928 | D | 524* | 125' 00" | 39' 02" | 13' 09" |

Built: Manitowoc Shipbuilding Co., Manitowoc, WI; paired with barge Lewis J. Kuber (John F. Cushing '28-'66, James E. Skelly '66-'66)

| **Victory** | 8003292 | TB | 1980 | D | 194* | 140' 00" | 43' 01" | 18' 00" |

Built: McDermott Shipyard Inc., Amelia, LA; paired with barge James L. Kuber

Evans Spirit on a calm morning in the Welland Canal. (Ted Wilush)

Fleet Name / Vessel Name	Vessel IMO #	Vessel Type	Year Built	Engine Type	Cargo Cap. or Gross*	Overall Length	Vessel Breadth	Vessel Depth
LUEDTKE ENGINEERING CO., FRANKFORT, MI *(luedtke-eng.com)*								
Alan K. Luedtke		TB	1944	D	149*	86' 04"	23' 00"	10' 03"
Built: Allen Boat Co., Harvey, LA (U. S. Army ST-527 '44-'55, USCOE Two Rivers '55-'90)								
Ann Marie		TB	1954	D	81*	71' 00"	19' 05"	9' 06"
Built: Smith Basin & Drydock, Pensacola, FL (ST-9684 '54- '80, Lewis Castle '80-'97, Apache '97-'01)								
Chris E. Luedtke		TB	1936	D	18*	42' 05"	11' 09"	5' 00"
Erich R. Luedtke		TB	1939	D	18*	42' 05"	11' 09"	5' 00"
Gretchen B		TB	1943	D	18*	41' 09"	12' 05"	6' 00"
Karl E. Luedtke		TB	1928	D	32*	55' 02"	14' 09"	6' 00"
Built: Leathem D. Smith Dock Co., Sturgeon Bay, WI								
Krista S		TB	1954	D	93*	67' 09"	20' 01"	7' 07"
Built: Pascagoula, MS (Sea Wolf '54-'01, Jimmy Wray '01-'08)								
Kurt R. Luedtke		TB	1956	D	95*	72' 00"	22' 06"	7' 06"
Built: Lockport Shipyard, Lockport, LA (Jere C. '56-'90)								
Paul L. Luedtke		TB	1988	D	97*	75' 00"	26' 00"	9' 06"
Built: Terrebonne Shipbuilders Inc., Houma, LA (Edward E. Gillen III '88-'13)								

M

Fleet Name / Vessel Name	Vessel IMO #	Vessel Type	Year Built	Engine Type	Cargo Cap. or Gross*	Overall Length	Vessel Breadth	Vessel Depth
MCM MARINE INC., SAULT STE. MARIE, MI *(mcmmarine.com)*								
Beaver State		TB	1935	D	18*	43' 06"	12' 00"	5' 02"
Drummond Islander II		TB	1961	D	97*	65' 00"	36' 00"	9' 00"
Madison		TB	1975	D	17*	33' 08"	13' 05"	4' 07"
Mohawk		TB	1945	D	46*	65' 00"	19' 00"	10' 06"
No. 55		DR	1927	DE	721*	165' 00"	42' 08"	12' 00"
No. 56		DS	1928	DE	1,174*	165' 00"	42' 04"	15' 07"
Peach State		TB	1961	D	19*	42' 01"	12' 04"	5' 03"
Sioux		DS	1954	B	504*	120' 00"	50' 00"	10' 00"
The company also operates two small towboats, Kelli Anne and Tammy; details unavailable								
MacDONALD MARINE LTD., GODERICH, ON *(mactug.com)*								
Debbie Lyn		TB	1950	D	10*	45' 00"	14' 00"	10' 00"
Built: Matheson Boat Works, Goderich, ON (Skipper '50-'60)								
Donald Bert		TB	1953	D	11*	45' 00"	14' 00"	10' 00"
Built: Matheson Boat Works, Goderich, ON								
Dover		TB	1931	D	70*	84' 00"	17' 00"	6' 00"
Built: Canadian Mead-Morrison Co. Ltd., Welland, ON (Earleejune, Iveyrose)								
Ian Mac		TB	1955	D	12*	45' 00"	14' 00"	10' 00"
Built: Matheson Boat Works, Goderich, ON								
MADELINE ISLAND FERRY LINE INC., LaPOINTE, WI *(madferry.com)*								
Bayfield {2}		PA/CF	1952	D	83*	120' 00"	43' 00"	10' 00"
Built: Chesapeake Marine Railway, Deltaville, VA (Charlotte '52-'99)								
Island Queen {2}		PA/CF	1966	D	90*	75' 00"	34' 09"	10' 00"
Madeline		PA/CF	1984	D	94*	90' 00"	35' 00"	8' 00"
Nichevo II		PA/CF	1962	D	89*	65' 00"	32' 00"	8' 09"
MAID OF THE MIST STEAMBOAT CO. LTD., NIAGARA FALLS, ON *(maidofthemist.com)*								
Maid of the Mist VI		ES	1990	D	155*	78' 09"	29' 06"	7' 00"
Maid of the Mist VII		ES	1997	D	160*	80' 00"	30' 00"	7' 00"
MALCOLM MARINE, ST. CLAIR, MI *(malcolmmarine.com)*								
Capt. Keith		TB	1955	D	39*	53' 03"	15' 06"	6' 04"
Built: Diamond Manufacturing, Savannah GA (Richard Merritt '55-'13)								
Debbie Lee		TB	1955	D	13*	32' 00"	11' 00"	4' 04"
Manitou {2}	8971695	TB	1942	D	199*	110' 00"	26' 02"	15' 06"
Built: U.S. Coast Guard, Curtis Bay, MD (USCGC Manitou [WYT-60] '43-'84)								
MANITOU ISLAND TRANSIT, LELAND, MI *(manitoutransit.com)*								
Manitou Isle		PA/PK	1946	D	39*	52' 00"	14' 00"	8' 00"
(Namaycush '46-'59)								
Mishe Mokwa		PA/CF	1966	D	49*	65' 00"	17' 06"	8' 00"

Fleet Name / Vessel Name	Vessel IMO #	Vessel Type	Year Built	Engine Type	Cargo Cap. or Gross*	Overall Length	Vessel Breadth	Vessel Depth
MARINE RECYCLING CORP., PORT COLBORNE & PORT MAITLAND, ON (marinerecycling.ca)								
Charlie E.		TB	1943	D	32*	63' 00"	16' 06"	7' 06"
Built: W.F. Kolbe & Co. Ltd., Port Dover, ON (Kolbe '43-'86, Lois T. '86-'02)								
MARINE SERVICES INC., DETROIT, MI								
Tenacious	5238004	TB	1960	D	149*	79' 01"	25' 06"	12' 06"
Built: Ingalls Shipbuilding Corp., Pascagoula, MS (Mobil 8 '60-'91, Tatarrax '91-'93, Nan McKay '93-'95)								
MARINE TECH LLC, DULUTH, MN (marinetechduluth.com)								
Callie M.		TB	1910	D	51*	64' 03"	16' 09"	8' 06"
Built: Houma Shipbuilding Co., Houma, LA (Chattanooga '10-'79, Howard T. Hagen '79-'94, Nancy Ann '94-'01)								
Dean R. Smith		DR	1985	B	338*	120' 00"	48' 00"	7' 00"
(No. 2 '85-'94, B. Yetter '94-'01)								
Miss Laura		TB	1943	D	146*	81' 01"	24' 00"	9' 10"
Built: Lawley & Son Corp., Neponset, MA (DPC-3 '43-'46, DS-43 '46-'50, Fresh Kills '50-'69, Richard K. '69-'93, Leopard '93-'03)								
MARIPOSA CRUISE LINE LTD., TORONTO, ON (mariposacruises.com)								
Capt. Matthew Flinders	8883355	ES	1982	D	746*	144' 00"	40' 00"	8' 06"
Built: North Arm Slipway Pty. Ltd., Port Adelaide, Australia								
Klancy II		ES	1989	D	124*	60' 02"	20' 00"	8' 02"
Northern Spirit I	8870073	ES	1983	D	489*	136' 00"	31' 00"	9' 00"
Built: Blount Marine Corp., Warren, RI (New Spirit '83-'89, Pride of Toronto '89-'92)								
Oriole	8800054	ES	1987	D	200*	75' 00"	23' 00"	9' 00"
Rosemary		ES	1960	D	52*	68' 00"	15' 06"	6' 08"
Showboat		ES	1988	D	135*	74' 00"	21' 00"	4' 00"
MARTIN GAS & OIL INC., BEAVER ISLAND, MI								
Petroqueen		TK	2015	B		70' 00"	24' 00"	8' 00"
Shamrock		TB	1933	D	60*	64' 00"	18' 00"	7' 03"
MAXIMUS CORP., BLOOMFIELD HILLS, MI (boblosteamers.com)								
Ste. Claire		PA	1910	R	870*	197' 00"	65' 00"	14' 00"
Built: Toledo Ship Building Co., Toledo, OH; former Detroit to Bob-Lo Island passenger steamer last operated Sept. 2, 1991; undergoing restoration at Detroit, MI								
McASPHALT MARINE TRANSPORTATION LTD., TORONTO, ON (mcasphalt.com)								
Everlast	7527332	ATB	1976	D	1,361*	143' 04"	44' 04"	21' 04"
Built: Hakodate Dock Co., Hakodate, Japan; paired with barge Norman McLeod (Bilibino '77-'96)								
John J. Carrick	9473444	TK	2008	B	11,613	407' 06"	71' 07"	30' 00"
Built: Penglai Bohai Shipyard Co. Ltd., Penglai, China								
Leo A. McArthur	9473262	ATB	2009	D	1,299	122' 00"	44' 03"	26' 02
Built: Penglai Bohai Shipyard Co. Ltd., Penglai, China; paired with barge John J. Carrick (Victorious '09-'17)								
Norman McLeod	8636219	TK	2001	B	6,809*	379' 02"	71' 06"	30' 02"
Built: Jinling Shipyard, Nanjing, China								
McKEIL MARINE LTD., BURLINGTON, ON (mckeil.com)								
Alouette Spirit	8641537	DB	1969	B	10,087*	425' 01"	74' 02"	29' 05"
Built: Gulfport Shipbuilding Co., Port Arthur, TX (KTC 135 '69-'04, Lambert's Spirit '04-'05)								
Ardita	9347023	BC	2007	D	14,650	459' 02"	68' 11"	34' 0"
Built: Royal Niestern Sander, Delfzijl, The Netherlands								
Beverly M 1	9084047	TB	1994	D	450*	114' 06"	34' 04"	17' 04"
Built: Imamura Shipbuilding, Kure, Japan (Shek O, Hunter, Pacific Typhoon)								
Blain M	7907099	RV	1981	D	925*	165' 05"	36' 00"	19' 09"
Built: Ferguson Industries, Picton, ON (Wilfred Templeman '81-'11)								
Bonnie B III	7017662	TB	1969	D	308*	107' 00"	32' 00"	18' 00"
(Esso Oranjestad '69-'85, Oranjestad '85-'86, San Nicolas '86-'87, San Nicolas I '87-'88)								
Carrol C. 1	7017674	TB	1969	D	307*	107' 00"	32' 00"	18' 00"
Built: Gulfport Shipbuilding Corp., Port Arthur, TX (Esso San Nicolas '69-'86, San Nicolas '86-'87, Carrol C '87-'88)								
Evans McKeil	8983416	TB	1936	D	284*	110' 06"	25' 06"	14' 08"
Built: Panama Canal Co., Balboa, Panama (Alhajuela '36-'70, Barbara Ann {2} '70-'89)								
Evans Spirit	9327774	GC	2007	D	14,650	459' 02"	68' 11"	34' 09"
Built: Royal Niestern Sander, Delfzijl, Netherlands (Spavalda '07-'16)								
Florence M	5118797	TB	1961	D	236*	90' 00"	28' 08"	11' 04
Built: P.K.Harris, Appledore, England (Foundation Vibert '61-'73, Point Vibert '73-'06)								
Florence Spirit	9314600	BC	2004	D	13,988	477' 07"	69' 07"	37' 01"
Built: Kyokuyo Shipyard Corp., Shimonoseki, Japan (Arklow Willow '04-'16)								

Fleet Name Vessel Name	Vessel IMO #	Vessel Type	Year Built	Engine Type	Cargo Cap. or Gross*	Overall Length	Vessel Breadth	Vessel Depth
Huron Spirit	8646642	SU	1995	B	4,542*	328' 01"	82' 25"	23 06"
Built: Jiangdu Shipyard, Tiangsu Province, China (Mulege '95-'14)								
Jarrett M	5030086	TB	1945	D	96*	82' 00"	20' 00"	10' 00"
Built: Russel Brothers Ltd., Owen Sound, ON (Atomic '45-'06)								
Lambert Spirit	8641525	TB	1968	B	9,645	400' 01"	70' 02"	27' 06"
Built: Avondale Shipyards Inc., Avondale, LA (KTC 115 '68-'06)								
Leonard M.	8519215	TB	1986	D	457*	103' 07"	36' 01"	19' 02"
Built: McTay Marine, Bromborough, England (Point Halifax '86-'12)								
Lois M.	9017616	TT	1991	D	453*	35' 09"	11' 65"	5' 07"
Built: Matsuura Tekko Zosen, Higashino, Japan (Lambert '91-'14)								
Niagara Spirit	8736021	DB	1984	D	9,164*	340' 01"	78' 02"	19' 06"
Built: FMC Corp., Portland, OR (Alaska Trader '84-'99, Timberjack '99-'08)								
Nunavut Spirit	8636673	DB	1983	B	6,076*	400' 00"	105' 00"	20' 06"
Built: FMC Corp., Portland, OR (Barge 5001)								
Salvor	5427019	TB	1963	D	407*	120' 00"	31' 00"	18' 06"
Built: Jakobson Shipyard, Oyster Bay, NY (Esther Moran '63-'00)								
Sharon M I	9084059	TB	1993	D	450*	107' 04"	34' 04"	17' 03"
Built: Inamura Shipbuilding, Kure, Japan (Mai Po, Pacific Tempest)								
Stormont	8959893	TB	1953	D	108*	80' 00"	20' 00"	15' 00"
Built: Canadian Dredge & Dock Co., Kingston, ON								
S/VM 86		DB	1958	B	487*	168' 01"	40' 00"	10' 00"
Built: Canadian Shipbuilding & Engineering Ltd., Collingwood, ON (S.L.S. 86)								
Tim McKeil	9017604	TB	1991	D	453*	107' 07"	34' 04"	17' 03"
Built: Matsuura Tekko Zosen, Higashino, Japan (Pannawonica 1 '91-'14)								
Tobias	9642253	DB	2012	B	8,870*	393' 09"	105' 07"	26' 07"
Built: Damen Shipyards Gorinchem, Gorinchem, Netherlands								
Tony MacKay	7227786	TB	1973	D	366*	117' 00"	30' 02"	14' 05"
Built: Richard Dunston Ltd., Hessle, England (Point Carroll '73-'01)								
Viateur's Spirit		DB	2004	D	253*	141' 01"	52' 03"	5' 01"
Built: Port Weller Dry Dock, Port Weller, ON (Traverse René Lavasseur '04-'06)								
Wilf Seymour	5215789	TB	1961	D	442*	122' 00"	31' 00"	17' 00"
Built: Gulfport Shipbuilding, Port Arthur, TX (M. Moran '61-'70, Port Arthur '70-'72, M. Moran '72-'00, Salvager '00-'04)								
Wyatt M.	8974178	TB	1948	D	123*	85' 00"	20' 00"	10' 00"
Built: Russel Brothers Ltd., Owen Sound, ON (P. J. Murer '48-'81, Michael D. Misner '81-'93, Thomas A. Payette '93-'96, Progress '96-'06)								

The Richardson International Ltd. grain terminal at Thunder Bay, Ont., hosts Kaministiqua. (Chris Mazzella)

Fleet Name / Vessel Name	Vessel IMO #	Vessel Type	Year Built	Engine Type	Cargo Cap. or Gross*	Overall Length	Vessel Breadth	Vessel Depth
MAMMOET-McKEIL LTD., AYR, ON – A SUBSIDIARY OF McKEIL MARINE LTD.								
Dowden Spirit		DB	2014	B	2,130*	250' 02"	72' 01"	16' 04"
Built: Glovertown Shipyards Ltd., Glovertown, NL								
Glovertown Spirit	9662174	DB	2012	B	2,073*	243' 07"	77' 02"	14' 09"
Built: Damen Shipyards Gorichem, Netherlands								
MM Newfoundland		DB	2011	B	2,165*	260' 00"	72' 00"	16' 01"
Built: Signal International, Pascagoula, MS								
MONTREAL BOATMEN LTD., PORT COLBORNE, ON – A SUBSIDIARY OF McKEIL MARINE LTD.								
Aldo H.		PB	1979	D	37*	56' 04"	15' 04"	6' 02"
Boatman No. 3		PB	1965	D	13*	33' 08"	11' 00"	6' 00"
Boatman No. 6		PB	1979	D	39*	56' 07"	18' 07"	6' 03"
Primrose		DR	1915	D	916*	136' 06"	42' 00"	10' 02"
McMULLEN & PITZ CONSTRUCTION CO., MANITOWOC, WI (mcmullenandpitz.net)								
Dauntless		TB	1937	D	25*	52' 06"	15' 06"	5' 03"
McNALLY INTERNATIONAL INC., HAMILTON, ON (mcnallycorp.com)								
A SUBSIDIARY OF WEEKS MARINE INC., CRANFORD, NJ								
Bagotville		TB	1964	D	65*	65' 00"	18' 05"	8' 03"
Built: Verreault Navigation, Les Méchins, QC								
Beaver Delta II		TB	1959	D	14*	35' 08"	12' 00"	4' 04"
Built: Allied Builders Ltd., Vancouver, BC (Halcyon Bay)								
Beaver Gamma		TB	1960	D	17*	37' 01"	12' 09"	6' 00"
Built: Diesel Sales & Service Ltd., Burlington, ON (Burlington Bertie)								
Beaver Kay		GC	1953	B	614*	115' 01"	60' 00"	9' 05"
Built: George T. Davie & Sons Ltd., Lauzon, QC (YD 251 '53-'96)								
Canadian		DR	1954	B	1,087*	173' 08"	49' 08"	13' 04"
Built: Port Arthur Shipbuilding Co. Ltd., Port Arthur (Thunder Bay), ON								
Canadian Argosy		DS	1978	B	951*	149' 09"	54' 01"	10' 08"
Cargo Carrier I		DB	1969	B	196*	89' 09"	29' 09"	8' 05"
Built: Halifax Shipyards Ltd., Halifax, NS								
Cargo Master		CS	1964	B	562*	136' 00"	50' 00"	9' 00"
Built: Canadian Shipbuilding & Engineering Ltd., Collingwood, ON								
Carl M.		TB	1957	D	21*	47' 00"	14' 06"	6' 00"
Dapper Dan		TB	1948	D	21*	41' 03"	12' 07"	5' 09"

Algoma Enterprise on the Calumet River. (Christine Douglas, 2-christine-douglas.pixels.com)

Fleet Name Vessel Name	Vessel IMO #	Vessel Type	Year Built	Engine Type	Cargo Cap. or Gross*	Overall Length	Vessel Breadth	Vessel Depth
D.L. Stanyer		TB	2014	D	14*	40' 03"	11' 08"	6' 02"
Built: Chantier Naval Forillon, Gaspé, QC								
F. R. McQueen		DB	1959	B	180*	79' 09"	39' 09"	5' 07"
Built: Manitowoc Engineering Corp., Manitowoc, WI								
Handy Andy		DB	1925	B	313*	95' 09"	43' 01"	10' 00"
Idus Atwell		DS	1962	B	366*	100' 00"	40' 00"	8' 05"
Built: Dominion Bridge Co. Ltd., Toronto, ON								
Island Sauvage		DB	1969	D	381*	86' 03"	61' 04"	9' 03"
Built: Halifax Shipyards Ltd., Halifax, NS (Cargo Carrier II)								
J.F. Whalen		TB	2014	D	14*	40' 03"	11' 08"	6' 02"
Built: Chantier Naval Forillon, Gaspé, QC								
Jamie L.		TB	1988	D	25*	36' 04"	14' 07"	5' 09"
(Baie Ste-Anne '88-'96, T-1 '96-'98, Baie Ste-Anne II '98-'05)								
John Holden		DR	1954	B	148*	89' 08"	30' 01"	6' 02"
Built: McNamara Construction Co. Ltd., Toronto, ON								
Lac Como		TB	1944	D	63*	65' 00"	16' 10"	7' 10"
Built: Canadian Bridge Co., Walkerville, ON (Tanac 74 '44-'64)								
Lac Vancouver		TB	1943	D	65*	60' 09"	16' 10"	7' 08"
Built: Central Bridge Co., Trenton, ON (Vancouver '43-'74)								
Maggie Girl		TB	1972	D	72*	72' 07	17' 04	8' 05
Built: Alloy Manufacturing Ltd., Lachine, QC (Advent)								
Mister Joe		TB	1964	D	70*	61' 00"	19' 00"	7' 02"
Built: Russel Brothers Ltd., Owen Sound, ON (Churchill River '64-'01)								
Oshawa		TB	1969	D	24*	42' 09"	13' 08"	5' 04"
Paula M.		TB	1959	D	12*	48' 02"	10' 05"	3' 01"
Sandra Mary		TB	1962	D	97*	80' 00"	21' 00"	10' 09"
Built: Russel Brothers Ltd., Owen Sound, ON (Flo Cooper '62-'00)								
Whitby		TB	1978	D	24*	42' 19"	13' 08"	6' 05"
William B. Dilly		DR	1957	B	473*	116' 00"	39' 10"	9' 01"
Built: Canadian Shipbuilding & Engineering Ltd., Collingwood, ON								
Willmac		TB	1959	D	16*	40' 00"	13' 00"	3' 07"

MERCURY CRUISES, CHICAGO, IL (mercuryskylinecruiseline.com)

Skyline Queen		ES	1959	D	45*	61' 05"	16' 10"	6' 00"

MICHELS CORPORATION, BROWNSVILLE, WI (michels.us)

Edith J.		TB	1962	D	18*	43' 02"	13' 00"	5' 04"

MICHIGAN DEPARTMENT OF NATURAL RESOURCES, LANSING, MI (michigan.gov/dnr)

Channel Cat		RV	1968	D	24*	46' 00"	13' 06"	4' 00"
Lake Char		RV	2006	D	26*	56' 00"	16' 00"	4' 05"
Steelhead		RV	1967	D	70*	63' 00"	16' 04"	6' 06"
Tanner		RV	2016	D	26*	57' 00"	16' 00"	4' 05"

MICHIGAN TECHNOLOGICAL UNIVERSITY, HOUGHTON, MI (mtu.edu/greatlakes/fleet/agassiz)

Agassiz		RV	2002	D	14*	36' 00"	13' 00"	4' 00"

MIDLAND TOURS INC., PENETANGUISHENE, ON (midlandtours.com)

Miss Midland	7426667	ES	1974	D	106*	68' 07"	19' 04"	6' 04"
Serendipity Princess		ES	1992	D	93*	64' 09"	23' 00"	4' 07"

MIDWEST MARITIME CORP., MILWAUKEE, WI

Leona B.		TB	1972	D	99*	59' 08"	24' 01"	10' 03"
(Kings Squire '72-'89, Juanita D. '78-'89, Peggy Ann '89-'93, Mary Page Hannah {2} '93-'04)								

MILLER BOAT LINE, PUT-IN-BAY, OH (millerferry.com)

Islander {3}		PA/CF	1983	D	92*	90' 03"	38' 00"	8' 03"
Put-in-Bay {3}		PA/CF	1997	D	97*	136 00"	38' 06"	9' 06"
Built: Sturgeon Bay Shipbuilding Co., Sturgeon Bay, WI; lengthened by 40' at Cleveland, OH, in '09								
South Bass		PA/CF	1989	D	95*	96' 00"	38' 06"	9' 06"
Wm. Market		PA/CF	1993	D	95*	96' 00"	38' 06"	8' 09"
Built: Peterson Builders Inc., Sturgeon Bay, WI								

MILWAUKEE BOAT LINE LLC, MILWAUKEE, WI (mkeboat.com)

Iroquois		PA	1922	D	91*	61' 09"	21' 00"	6' 04"
Vista King		ES	1978	D	60*	78' 00"	23' 00"	5' 02"
Voyageur		PA	1988	D	94*	67' 02"	21' 00"	7' 04"

Fleet Name / Vessel Name	Vessel IMO #	Vessel Type	Year Built	Engine Type	Cargo Cap. or Gross*	Overall Length	Vessel Breadth	Vessel Depth

MILWAUKEE HARBOR COMMISSION, MILWAUKEE, WI *(city.milwaukee.gov/port)*

Harbor Seagull		TB	1961	D	23*	44' 05"	16' 04"	5' 00"
Joey D.		TB	2011	D	65*	60' 00"	20' 06"	6' 06"

MILWAUKEE RIVER CRUISE LINE, MILWAUKEE, WI *(edelweissboats.com)*

Edelweiss II		ES	1989	D	95*	73' 08"	20' 00"	2' 08"
Harbor Lady		ES	1996	D	76*	80' 08"	20' 00"	6' 00"
Lakeside Spirit		ES	1992	D	25*	63' 00"	15' 00"	4' 00"

MINISTRY OF TRANSPORTATION, DOWNSVIEW, ON *(mto.gov.on.ca)*

Frontenac II	5068875	PA/CF	1962	D	666*	181' 00"	45' 00"	10' 00"
Built: Chantier Maritime de Saint-Laurent, Saint-Laurent, QC (Charlevoix {2} '62-'92)								
Frontenac Howe Islander		PF/CF	2004	D	130*	100' 00"	32' 03"	5' 05"
Built: Heddle Marine Service Inc., Hamilton, ON								
Glenora	5358074	PA/CF	1952	D	189*	127' 00"	33' 00"	9' 00"
Built: Erieau Shipbuilding & Drydock Co. Ltd., Erieau, ON (The St. Joseph Islander '52-'74)								
Jiimaan	9034298	PA/CF	1992	D	2,807*	176' 09"	42' 03"	13' 06"
Built: Port Weller Drydock, Port Weller, ON								
Pelee Islander	5273274	PA/CF	1960	D	334*	145' 00"	32' 00"	10' 00"
Built: Erieau Shipbuilding & Drydock Co. Ltd., Erieau, ON								
Quinte Loyalist	5358062	PA/CF	1954	D	204*	127' 00"	32' 00"	8' 00"
Built: Erieau Shipbuilding & Drydock Co. Ltd., Erieau, ON								
Wolfe Islander III	7423079	PA/CF	1975	D	985*	205' 00"	68' 00"	6' 00"
Built: Port Arthur Shipbuilding Co., Port Arthur, ON								

MONTREAL PORT AUTHORITY, MONTREAL, QC *(port-montreal.com)*

Denis M		TB	1942	D	21*	46' 07"	12' 08"	4' 01"
Built: Russel Brothers Ltd., Owen Sound, ON (Marcel D.)								
Maisonneuve	7397749	TB	1972	D	84*	63' 10"	20' 07"	9' 03"
Built: Fercraft Marine Inc., Ste. Catherine D'Alexandrie, QC								

MUNISING BAY SHIPWRECK TOURS INC., MUNISING, MI *(shipwrecktours.com)*

Miss Munising		ES	1967	D	50*	60' 00"	14' 00"	4' 04"

MUSIQUE AQUATIQUE CRUISE LINES INC., TORONTO, ON *(citysightseeingtoronto.com)*

Harbour Star		ES	1978	D	45*	63' 06"	15' 09"	3' 09"
(K. Wayne Simpson '78-'95)								

MUSKOKA STEAMSHIP & HISTORICAL SOCIETY, GRAVENHURST, ON *(segwun.com)*

Segwun		PA	1887	R	308*	128' 00"	24' 00"	7' 06"
Built: Melancthon Simpson, Toronto, ON (Nipissing {2} 1887-'25)								
Wenonah II	8972003	PA	2001	D	447*	127' 00"	28' 00"	6' 00"
Built: McNally Construction Inc., Belleville, ON								

MYSTIC BLUE CRUISES INC., CHICAGO, IL *(mysticbluecruises.com)*

Mystic Blue		PA	1998	D	97*	138' 09"	36' 00"	10' 05"
Built: Chesapeake Shipbuilding Corp., Salisbury, MD								

N

NADRO MARINE SERVICES LTD., PORT DOVER, ON *(nadromarine.com)*

Ecosse	8624682	TB	1979	D	142*	91' 00"	26' 00"	8' 06"
Built: Hike Metal Products Ltd., Wheatley, ON (R & L No. 1 '79-'96)								
Intrepid III		TB	1976	D	39*	66' 00"	17' 00"	7' 06"
Built: Halter Marine Ltd., Chalmette, LA								
Lac St-Jean		DB	1971	B	771*	150' 00"	54' 09"	10' 06"
Built: Canadian Vickers Ltd., Montreal, QC								
Molly M. 1	5118838	TB	1962	D	207*	98' 06"	27' 10"	12' 02"
Built: Davie Shipbuilding Co., Lauzon, QC (Foundation Vigour '62-'74, Point Vigour '74-'07)								
Seahound		TB	1941	D	57*	65' 00"	18' 00"	8' 00"
Built: Equitable Equipment Co., New Orleans, LA ([Unnamed] '41-'56, Sea Hound '56-'80, Carolyn Jo '80-'00)								
Vac		TB	1942	D	36*	65' 00"	20' 04"	4' 03"
Built: George Gamble, Port Dover, ON								
Vigilant I	8994178	TB	1944	D	111*	79' 06"	20' 11"	10' 02"
Built: Russell Brothers Ltd., Owen Sound, ON (HMCS Glenlivet [W-43] '44-'75, Glenlivet II '75-'77, Canadian Franko '77-'82, Glenlivet II '82-'00)								

Fleet Name / Vessel Name	Vessel IMO #	Vessel Type	Year Built	Engine Type	Cargo Cap. or Gross*	Overall Length	Vessel Breadth	Vessel Depth

NAUTICA QUEEN CRUISE DINING, CLEVELAND, OH *(nauticaqueen.com)*

Nautica Queen		ES	1981	D	95*	124' 00"	31' 02"	8' 09"

Built: Blount Marine Corp., Warren, RI (Bay Queen '81-'85, Arawanna Queen '85-'88, Star of Nautica '88-'92)

NAUTICAL ADVENTURES, TORONTO, ON *(nauticaladventure.com)*

Empire Sandy	5071561	ES/3S	1943	D/W	338*	140' 00"	32' 08"	14' 00"

Built: Clellands Ltd., Wellington Quay-on-Tyne, England (Empire Sandy '43-'48, Ashford '48-'52, Chris M. '52-'79)

Wayward Princess		ES	1976	D	325*	92' 00"	26' 00"	10' 00"

Built: Marlin Yacht Co., Summerstown, ON (Cayuga II '76-'82)

NEAS (NUNAVUT EASTERN ARCTIC SHIPPING), MONTREAL, QC *(neas.ca)*

Vessels offer service between St. Lawrence River ports and the Canadian Arctic between July and November

Avataq	8801618	GC	1989	D	9,653	370' 07"	62' 00"	37' 00"

Built: Miho Shipbuilding Co. Ltd., Shimizu Shizuoka Prefecture, Japan; operated by Spliethoff's, Amsterdam, Netherlands (Poleca, Mekhanik Volkosh, Tiger Speed, Lootsgracht)

Mitiq	9081306	GC	1995	D	12,754	447' 04"	62' 00"	38' 03"

Built: Frisian Shipbuilding Welgelegen B.V., Harlingen, Netherlands; operated by Spliethoff's, Amsterdam, Netherlands (Emmagracht '95-'13)

Qamutik	9081289	GC	1995	D	12,760	446' 00"	62' 00"	38' 02"

Built: Frisian Shipbuilding Welgelegen B.V., Harlingen, Netherlands; operated by Spliethoff's, Amsterdam, Netherlands (Edisongracht)

Umiavut	8801591	GC	1988	D	9,653	370' 07"	63' 01"	37' 00"

Built: Miho Shipbuilding Co. Ltd., Shimizu Shizuoka Prefecture, Japan; operated by Spliethoff's, Amsterdam, Netherlands (Completed as Newca; Kapitan Silin '88-'92, Lindengracht '92-'00)

NEW YORK POWER AUTHORITY, LEWISTON, NY

Breaker		IB/TB	1962	D	29*	43' 03"	14' 03"	5' 00"
Daniel Joncaire		IB/TB	1979	D	25*	43' 03"	15' 00"	5' 00"
Joncaire II		IB/TB	2015	D	47*	45' 00"	19' 07"	6' 01"
William H. Latham		IB/TB	1987	D	77*	61' 00"		

NEW YORK DEPARTMENT OF ENVIRONMENTAL CONSERVATION, LAKE ONTARIO UNIT, ALBANY, NY

Seth Green		RV	1984	D	50*	47' 00"	17' 00"	8' 00"

The sun rises over Lee A. Tregurtha at Sault Ste. Marie. (Glenn Blaszkiewicz)

Fleet Name Vessel Name	Vessel IMO #	Vessel Type	Year Built	Engine Type	Cargo Cap. or Gross*	Overall Length	Vessel Breadth	Vessel Depth

NEW YORK STATE MARINE HIGHWAY TRANSPORTATION CO., TROY, NY (nysmarinehighway.com)

Benjamin Elliot		TB	1960	D	27*	47' 07"	15' 02"	7' 02

Built: Gladding-Hearn Shipbuilding, Somerset, MA (El-Jean)

Margot	5222043	TB	1958	D	141*	90' 00"	25' 00"	10' 00"

Built: Jakobson Shipyard, Oyster Bay, NY (Jolene Rose, Margot Moran)

NORTH CHANNEL TRANSPORT LLC., ALGONAC, MI

Islander {2}		PA/CF	1967	D	38*	41' 00"	15' 00"	3' 06"

NORTH SHORE SCENIC CRUISES, SILVER BAY, MN (scenicsuperior.com)

Wenonah		ES	1960	D	91*	70' 07"	19' 04"	9' 07"

(Jamaica '60-'64)

NORTHERN MARINE TRANSPORTATION INC., SAULT STE. MARIE, MI

Linda Jean		PB	1950	D	17*	38' 00"	10' 00"	5' 00"
Soo Pilot		PB	1976	D	22*	41' 03"	13' 06"	5' 09"

O-P

OAK GROVE & MARINE TRANSPORTATION INC., CLAYTON, NY

Maple Grove		PK	1954	D	55*	73' 07"	20' 00"	9' 00"

(LCM 8168)

OFFSHORE DREDGING & CONSTRUCTION INC., MUSKEGON, MI (offshoredredging.com)

Andrew J.		TB	1972	D	31*	43' 08"	14' 03"	7' 05"

OHIO DEPARTMENT OF NATURAL RESOURCES, COLUMBUS, OH (dnr.state.oh.us)

Explorer II		RV	1999	D		53' 00"	15' 05"	4' 05"
Grandon		RV	1990	D	47*	47' 00"	16' 00"	5' 05"

OLSON DREDGE & DOCK CO., ALGONAC, MI

John Michael		TB	1913	D	41*	55' 04"	15' 01"	7' 06"

Built: Cowles Shipyard Co., Buffalo, NY (Colonel Ward, Ross Coddington, Joseph J. Olivieri)

Tugs BeeJay and John R. Asher at Marquette, Mich. *(Rod Burdick)*

Fleet Name / Vessel Name	Vessel IMO #	Vessel Type	Year Built	Engine Type	Cargo Cap. or Gross*	Overall Length	Vessel Breadth	Vessel Depth
OLYMPIA CRUISE LINE INC., THORNHILL, ON *(torontocruises.com)*								
Enterprise 2000		ES	1998	D	370*	121' 06"	35' 00"	6' 00"
ONTARIO MINISTRY OF NATURAL RESOURCES, PETERBOROUGH, ON *(mnr.gov.on.ca)*								
Erie Explorer		RV	1981	D	72*	53' 05"	20' 01"	4' 08"
Built: Hopper Fisheries Ltd., Port Stanley, ON (Janice H.X. '81-'97)								
Huron Explorer I		RV	2010	D	112*	62' 00"	21' 03"	6' 00"
Built: Hike Metal Products Ltd., Wheatley, ON								
Keenosay		RV	1957	D	68*	51' 04"	20' 07"	2' 07"
Built: S.G. Powell Shipyard Ltd., Dunnville, ON								
Nipigon Osprey		RV	1990	D	33*	42' 04"	14' 09"	6' 08"
Built: Kanter Yachts Corp., St. Thomas, ON								
Ontario Explorer		RV	2009	D	84*	64' 09"	21' 03"	6' 00"
Built: Hike Metal Products Ltd., Wheatley, ON								
ONTARIO POWER GENERATION INC., TORONTO, ON								
Niagara Queen II		IB	1992	D	58*	56' 01"	18' 00"	6' 08"
Built: Hike Metal Products Ltd., Wheatley, ON								
OWEN SOUND TRANSPORTATION CO. LTD., OWEN SOUND, ON *(ontarioferries.com)*								
Chi-Cheemaun	7343607	PA/CF	1974	D	6,991*	365' 05"	61' 00"	21' 00"
Built: Canadian Shipbuilding and Engineering Ltd., Collingwood, ON								
PERE MARQUETTE SHIPPING CO., LUDINGTON, MI *(pmship.com)*								
Pere Marquette 41	5073894	SU	1941	B	3,413*	403' 00"	58' 00"	23' 05"
Built: Manitowoc Shipbuilding Co., Manitowoc, WI; converted from powered train/car ferry to a self-unloading barge in '97 (City of Midland 41 '41-'97)								
Undaunted	8963210	AT	1943	DE	569*	143' 00"	38' 00"	18' 00"
Built: Gulfport Boiler/Welding, Port Arthur, TX; paired with barge Pere Marquette 41 (USS Undaunted [ATR-126, ATA-199] '44-'63, USMA Kings Pointer '63-'93, Krystal K. '93-'97)								
PICTURED ROCKS CRUISES INC., MUNISING, MI *(picturedrocks.com)*								
Grand Island {2}		ES	1989	D	52*	68' 00"	16' 01"	7' 01"
Grand Portal		ES	2004	D	76*	64' 08"	20' 00"	8' 04"
Miners Castle		ES	1974	D	82*	68' 00"	16' 06"	6' 04"
Miss Superior		ES	1984	D	83*	68' 00"	16' 09"	10' 04"
Pictured Rocks		ES	1972	D	53*	55' 07"	13' 07"	4' 04"
Pictured Rocks Express		ES	1988	D	90*	82' 07"	28' 06"	4' 04"
PLAUNT TRANSPORTATION CO. INC., CHEBOYGAN, MI *(bbiferry.com)*								
Kristen D		CF	1987	D	83*	94' 11"	36' 00"	4' 06"
PORT CITY CRUISE LINE INC., NORTH MUSKEGON, MI *(portcityprincesscruises.com)*								
Port City Princess		ES	1966	D	79*	64' 09"	30' 00"	5' 06"
Built: Blount Marine Corp., Warren, RI (Island Queen {1} '66-'87)								
PORTOFINO ON THE RIVER, WYANDOTTE, MI *(portofinoontheriver.com)*								
Friendship		ES	1968	D	76*	85' 00"	23' 04"	7' 03"
Built: Hike Metal Products Ltd., Wheatley, ON (Peche Island V '68-'71, Papoose V '71-'82)								
Portofino		ES	1997	D	76*	80' 08"	20' 00"	6' 00"
Built: Skipper Liner, LaCrosse, WI (Island Girl X, Naples Royal Princess, Romantics, Infinity, The Jude Thaddeus, Infinity, Jacksonville Princess II, Miami Magic)								
PRESQUE ISLE BOAT TOURS, ERIE, PA *(piboattours.com)*								
Lady Kate {2}		ES	1952	D	11*	59' 03"	15' 00"	3' 09"
(G.A. Boeckling II, Cedar Point III, Island Trader '89-'97)								
PURE MICHIGAN BOAT CRUISES LLC, MUNISING, MI *(puremichiganboatcruises.com)*								
Isle Royale Queen III		PA	1959	D	88*	74' 03"	18' 04"	6' 05"
Built: T.D. Vinette Co., Escanaba, MI (Isle Royale Queen II)								
PURVIS MARINE LTD., SAULT STE. MARIE, ON *(purvismarine.com)*								
Adanac III		TB	1913	D	108*	80' 03"	19' 03"	9' 10"
Built: Western Drydock & Shipbuilding Co., Port Arthur, ON (Edward C. Whalen '13-'66, John McLean '66-'95)								
Anglian Lady	5141483	TB	1953	D	398*	132' 00"	31' 00"	14' 00"
Built: John I. Thornecroft & Co., Southampton, England (Hamtun '53-'72, Nathalie Letzer '72-'88)								

Great Republic unloading on the Rouge River at Detroit. (Kevin Pollock – skylitphoto.com)

Algorail framed by cables. (Alain Gindroz)

Fleet Name / Vessel Name	Vessel IMO #	Vessel Type	Year Built	Engine Type	Cargo Cap. or Gross*	Overall Length	Vessel Breadth	Vessel Depth
Avenger IV	5401297	TB	1962	D	291*	120' 00"	30' 00"	19' 00"
Built: Cochrane & Sons Ltd., Selby, Yorkshire, England (Avenger '62-'85)								
G.L.B. No. 2		DB	1953	B	3,215	240' 00"	50' 00"	12' 00"
Built: Ingalls Shipbuilding Corp., Birmingham, AL (Jane Newfield '53-'66, ORG 6502 '66-'75)								
Malden		DB	1946	B	1,075	150' 00"	41' 09"	10' 03"
Built: Russel Brothers Ltd., Owen Sound, ON								
Martin E. Johnson		TB	1959	D	26*	47' 00"	16' 00"	7' 00"
Osprey		TB	1944	D	36*	45' 00"	13' 06"	7' 00"
PML 357		DB	1932	B	363*	138' 00"	38' 00"	11' 00"
PML 2501		TK	1980	B	1,954*	302' 00"	52' 00"	17' 00"
PML 9000		DB	1968	B	4,285*	400' 00"	76' 000"	20' 00"
Built: Bethlehem Steel – Shipbuilding Division, San Francisco, CA (Palmer '68-'00)								
PML Alton		DB	1933	B	150	93' 00"	30' 00"	8' 00"
Built: McClintic- Marshall, Sturgeon Bay, WI								
PML Ironmaster		DB	1962	D	7,437*	360' 00"	75' 000"	25' 00"
Built: Yarrows Ltd., Esquimalt, BC (G.T. Steelmaster, Ceres, American Gulf VII, Seaspan 241, G.T. Ironmaster)								
PML Tucci		CS	1958	B	601*	150' 00"	52' 00"	10' 00"
Built: Calumet Shipyard & Drydock Co., Chicago, IL (MCD '58-'73, Minnesota '73-'88, Candace Andrie '88-'08)								
PML Tucker		DS	1971	B	477*	140' 00"	50' 00"	9' 00"
Built: Twin City Shipyard, St. Paul, MN (Illinois '71-'02, Meredith Andrie '02-'08)								
Provider		TW	1954	D	38*	38' 00"	12' 05"	5' 03"
Built: Marinette Marine Corp., Marinette, WI (T.T. Youngfelt '54-'16)								
Reliance	7393808	TB	1974	D	708*	148' 03"	35' 07"	21' 07"
Built: Ulstein Hatlo A/S, Ulsteinvik, Norway (Sinni '74-'81, Irving Cedar '81-'96, Atlantic Cedar '96-'02)								
Rocket		TB	1901	D	40*	73' 00"	16' 00"	7' 00"
Built: Buffalo Shipbuilding Co., Buffalo, NY								
Tecumseh II		DB	1976	B	2,500	180' 00"	54' 00"	12' 00"
Wilfred M. Cohen	7629271	TB	1947	D	284*	102' 06"	28' 00"	15' 00"
Built: Newport News Shipbuilding and Drydock Co., Newport News, VA (A. T. Lowmaster '48-'75)								
W. I. Scott Purvis	5264819	TB	1938	D	203*	96' 00"	26' 00"	10' 00"
Built: Marine Industries, Sorel, QC (Orient Bay '38-'75, Guy M. No. 1 '75-'90)								
W.J. Isaac Purvis	318726	TB	1962	D	71*	72' 00"	19' 00"	12' 00"
Built: McNamara Marine Ltd., Toronto, ON (Angus M. '62-'92, Omni Sorel '92-'02, Joyce B. Gardiner '02-'09)								
W. J. Ivan Purvis	5217218	TB	1938	D	190*	100' 00"	26' 00"	10' 00"
Built: Marine Industries, Sorel, QC (Magpie '38-'66, Dana T. Bowen '66-'75)								
Built: Collingwood Shipyards, Collingwood, ON; in long-term lay-up at Sault Ste. Marie, ON, since 2008								

PUT-IN-BAY BOAT LINE CO., PORT CLINTON, OH *(jet-express.com)*

Jet Express		PF/CA	1989	D	93*	92' 08"	28' 06"	8' 04"
Jet Express II		PF/CA	1992	D	85*	92' 06"	28' 06"	8' 04"
Jet Express III		PF/CA	2001	D	70*	78' 02"	27' 06"	8' 02"
Jet Express IV		PF/CA	1995	D	71*	77' 02"	28' 05"	7' 07"

Q-R

QUEBEC PORT AUTHORITY, QUÉBEC, QC *(portquebec.ca)*

Le Cageux		TB	2011	D	24*	42' 06"	16' 01"	7' 07"

QUYON FERRY, QUYON, QC *(quyonferry.com)*

Grant Beattie (The)		PF	2013		235*	&&115' 00"	46' 00"	7' 05"

RDK LLC, HOLLAND, MI

Mary E. Hannah		TB	1945	D	612*	149' 00"	33' 00"	16' 00"
Built: Marietta Manufacturing, Marietta, GA (U. S. Army LT-821 '45-'47, Brooklyn '47-'66, Lee Reuben '66-'75)								

RIO TINTO-ALCAN INC., LA BAIE, QC *(riotintoalcan.com)*

Fjord Éternité	9364348	TT	2006	D	381*	94' 00"	36' 05"	16' 04"
Built: East Isle Shipyard, Georgetown, PEI (Stevns Icecap '06-'07, Svitzer Nanna '07-'11, Stevns Icecap '10-'11)								
Fjord Saguenay	9351012	TT	2006	D	381*	94' 00"	36' 05"	16' 04"
Built: East Isle Shipyard, Georgetown, PEI (Stevns Iceflower '06-'07, Svitzer Njord '07-'09, Stevns Iceflower '09-'09)								

ROCKPORT BOAT LINE LTD., ROCKPORT, ON *(rockportcruises.com)*

Chief Shingwauk		ES	1965	D	109*	70' 00"	24' 00"	4' 06"
Ida M.		ES	1970	D	29*	55' 00"	14' 00"	3' 00"

Fleet Name Vessel Name	Vessel IMO #	Vessel Type	Year Built	Engine Type	Cargo Cap. or Gross*	Overall Length	Vessel Breadth	Vessel Depth
Ida M. II		ES	1973	D	121*	63' 02"	22' 02"	5' 00"
Sea Prince II		ES	1978	D	172*	83' 00"	24' 02"	6' 08"

ROEN SALVAGE CO., STURGEON BAY, WI *(roensalvage.com)*

Chas. Asher		TB	1967	D	39*	49' 02"	17' 06"	6' 10"
Built: Sturgeon Bay Shipbuilding Co., Sturgeon Bay, WI								
John R. Asher		TB	1943	D	93*	68' 09"	20' 00"	8' 00"
Built: Platzer Boat Works, Houston, TX (U. S. Army ST-71 '43-'46, Russell 8 '46-'64, Reid McAllister '64-'67, Donegal '67-'85)								
Louie S.		TB	1956	D	10*	37' 00"	12' 00"	4' 05"
Spuds		TB	1944	D	19*	42' 00"	12' 05"	5' 04"
Stephan M. Asher		TB	1954	D	60*	65' 00"	19' 01"	5' 04"
Built: Burton Shipyard Inc., Port Arthur, TX (Captain Bennie '54-'82, Dumar Scout '82-'87)								
Timmy A.		TB	1953	D	12*	33' 06"	10' 08"	5' 02"

RYBA MARINE CONSTRUCTION CO., CHEBOYGAN, MI *(rybamarine.com)*

Amber Mae		TB	1922	D	67*	65' 00"	14' 01"	10' 00"
Built: Glove Shipyard Inc., Buffalo, NY (E. W. Sutton '22-'52, Venture '52- '00)								
Kathy Lynn	8034887	TB	1944	D	140*	85' 00"	24' 00"	9' 06"
Built: Decatur Iron & Steel Co., Decatur, AL (U. S. Army ST-693 '44-'79, Sea Islander '79-'91)								
Rochelle Kaye		TB	1963	D	52*	51' 06"	19' 04"	7' 00"
Built: St. Charles Steel Works Inc., Thibodeaux, LA (Jaye Anne '63-?, Katanni ?-'97)								
Thomas R. Morrish		TB	1980	D	88*	64' 00"	14' 05"	8' 06"
Built: Houma Shipbuilding Co., Houma, LA. (Lady Ora '80-'99, Island Eagle '99-'04, Captain Zeke '01-'14)								

S

SAIL DOOR COUNTY, SISTER BAY, WI *(saildoorcounty.com)*

Edith M. Becker		PA	1984	D/W	22*	62' 00"	24' 00"	8' 06"

SAND PRODUCTS CORP., MUSKEGON, MI

LAKE SERVICE SHIPPING, MUSKEGON, MI

McKee Sons	5216458	SU	1945	B	19,900	579' 02"	71' 06"	38' 06"
Built: Sun Shipbuilding and Drydock Co., Chester, PA; converted from saltwater vessel to a self-unloading Great Lakes bulk carrier by Maryland Drydock, Baltimore, MD, in '52; completed as a self-unloader by Manitowoc Shipbuilding Co., Manitowoc, WI, in '53; converted to a self-unloading barge by Upper Lakes Towing, Escanaba, MI, in '91; laid up at Erie, PA 2012-14 and Muskegon, MI, since Dec. 20, 2014 (USNS Marine Angel '45-'52)								

MICHIGAN-OHIO BARGE LLC, MUSKEGON, MI

Cleveland Rocks		CC	1957	B	6,280*	390' 00"	71' 00"	27' 00"
Built: Todd Shipyards Corp., Houston, TX (M-211 '57-'81, Virginia '81-'88, C-11 '88-'93, Kellstone 1 '93-'04)								

PORT CITY MARINE SERVICES, MUSKEGON, MI

Bradshaw McKee	7644312	ATB	1977	D	174*	121' 06"	34' 06"	18' 02"
Built: Toche Enterprises Inc., Ocean Springs, MS; paired with barge St. Marys Conquest (Lady Elda '77-'78, Kings Challenger '78-'78, ITM No. 1 '78-'81, Kings Challenger '81-'86, Susan W. Hannah '86-'11)								
Colleen McAllister	7338872	TB	1967	D	194*	124' 00"	31' 06"	13' 08
Built: Gulfport Shipbuilding Corp., Port Arthur, TX (Ellena Hicks '67-'03)								
Katie G. McAllister	7046089	TB	1966	D	194*	124' 00"	31' 06"	13' 08
Built: Gulfport Shipbuilding Corp., Port Arthur, TX (Libby Black '67-'03)								
Prentiss Brown	7035547	TB	1967	D	197*	123' 05"	31' 06"	19' 00"
Built: Gulfport Shipbuilding, Port Arthur, TX; paired with barge St. Marys Challenger (Betty Culbreath '67-'03, Micheala McAllister '03-'09)								
St. Marys Challenger	5009984	CC	1906	B	N/A	N/A	56' 00"	31' 00"
Built: Great Lakes Engineering Works, Ecorse, MI; repowered in '50; converted to a self-unloading cement carrier by Manitowoc Shipbuilding Co., Manitowoc, WI, in '67; converted to a barge by Bay Shipbuilding Co., Sturgeon Bay, WI, over the winter of 2013-'14 (William P. Snyder '06-'26, Elton Hoyt II {1} '26-'52, Alex D. Chisholm '52-'66, Medusa Challenger '66-'99, Southdown Challenger '99-'04)								
St. Marys Conquest	5015012	CC	1937	B	8,500	437' 06"	55' 00"	28' 00"
Built: Manitowoc Shipbuilding Co., Manitowoc, WI; converted from a powered tanker to a self-unloading cement barge by Bay Shipbuilding, Sturgeon Bay, WI, in '87 (Red Crown '37-'62, Amoco Indiana '62-'87, Medusa Conquest '87-'99, Southdown Conquest '99-'04)								

SEA SERVICE LLC, SUPERIOR, WI *(seaservicellc.com)*

Sea Bear		PB	1959	D	28*	45' 08"	13' 08"	7' 00"

Fleet Name Vessel Name	Vessel IMO #	Vessel Type	Year Built	Engine Type	Cargo Cap. or Gross*	Overall Length	Vessel Breadth	Vessel Depth
SEAWAY MARINE GROUP LLC, CLAYTON, NY *(seawaymarinegroup.com)*								
Seaway Supplier		GC	1952	D	97*	73' 06"	21' 00"	9' 04"
SELVICK MARINE TOWING CORP., STURGEON BAY, WI								
Cameron O		TB	1955	D	26*	50' 00"	15' 00"	7' 03"
Built: Peterson Builders Inc., Sturgeon Bay, WI (Escort II '55-'06)								
Donny S	7436234	TB	1950	DE	461*	143' 00"	33' 01"	14' 06"
Built: Levingston Shipbuilding, Orange, TX (U. S. Army ATA-230 '49-'72, G. W. Codrington '72-'73, *William P. Feeley {2} '73-'73, William W. Stender '73-'78, Mary Page Hannah '78-'14)*								
Jimmy L		TB	1939	D	148*	110' 00"	25' 00"	13' 00"
Built: Defoe Shipbuilding Co., Bay City, MI (USCGC Naugatuck [WYT / WYTM-92] '39-'80, Timmy B. '80-'84)								
Sharon M. Selvick		TB	1945	D	28*	45' 05"	12' 10"	7' 01"
Built: Kewaunee Shipbuilding & Engineering, Kewaunee, WI (USACE Judson)								
Susan L		TB	1944	D	133*	86' 00"	23' 00"	10' 04"
Built: Equitable Equipment Co., New Orleans, LA (U. S. Army ST-709 '44-'47, USCOE Stanley '47-'99)								
William C. Gaynor	8423818	TB	1956	D	187*	94' 00"	27' 00"	11' 09"
Built: Defoe Shipbuilding Co., Bay City, MI (William C. Gaynor '56-'88, Captain Barnaby '88-'02)								
William C. Selvick	5322623	TB	1944	D	142*	85' 00"	23' 00"	9' 07"
Built: Platzer Boat Works, Houston, TX (U. S. Army ST-500 '44-'49, Sherman H. Serre '49-'77)								
SERVICE WELDING & SHIPBUILDING LLC, LEMONT, IL								
Alice E		TB	1950	D	183*	100' 00"	26' 00"	9' 00"
Built: St. Louis Shipbuilding, St. Louis, MO (L. L. Wright '50-'55, Martin '55-'74, Mary Ann '74-'77, Judi C. '77-'94)								
Daniel E		TW	1967	D	70*	70' 00"	18' 06"	6' 08"
Built: River Enterprises Inc., Morris, IL (Foster M. Ford '67-'84)								
David E		TW	1952	D	236*	95' 00"	30' 00"	8' 06"
Built: Sturgeon Bay Shipbuilding & Drydock Co., Sturgeon Bay, WI (Irving Crown '52-'01)								
Derek E		TB	1907	D	85*	72' 06"	20' 01"	10' 06"
Built: Benjamin T. Cowles, Buffalo, NY (John Kelderhouse '07-'13, Sachem '13-'90)								
Lisa E		TB	1963	D	75*	65' 06"	20' 00"	8' 06"
Built: Main Iron Works Inc., Houma, LA (Dixie Scout '63-'90)								
SHELL CANADA LIMITED, CALGARY, AB								
Juno Marie	9301641	RT	2004	D	2,191	262' 05"	45' 04"	
Built: Miura Shipbuilding, Saiki, Japan; stationed at Montreal, QC (Alios Apollo '04-'10, Elin Apollo '10-'12, Milo '12-'16)								
SHEPLER'S MACKINAC ISLAND FERRY, MACKINAW CITY, MI *(sheplersferry.com)*								
Capt. Shepler		PF	1986	D	71*	84' 00"	21' 00"	7' 10"
Felicity		PF	1972	D	65*	65' 00"	18' 01"	8' 03"
Hope (The)		PF	1975	D	87*	77' 00"	20' 00"	8' 03"
Miss Margy		PF	2015	D	70*	85' 00"	22' 00"	
Sacré Bleu		PK	1959	D	98*	94' 10"	31' 00"	9' 09"
Welcome (The)		PF	1969	D	66*	60' 06"	16' 08"	8' 02"
Wyandot		PF	1979	D	83*	77' 00"	20' 00"	8' 00"
SHORELINE CHARTERS, GILLS ROCK, WI *(shorelinecharters.net)*								
Shoreline (The)		ES	1973	D	12*	33' 00"	11' 4"	3' 00"
SHORELINE CONTRACTORS INC., WELLINGTON, OH *(shorelinecontractors.com)*								
Eagle		TB	1943	D	31*	57' 07"	35' 09"	6' 08"
Built: Defoe Shipbuilding Co., Bay City, MI (Jack Boyce '43-'78, Jan B. '78-'79, Sea Search II '79-'86)								
General		TB	1964	D	125*	63' 08"	15' 04"	6' 05"
SHORELINE SIGHTSEEING CO., CHICAGO, IL *(shorelinesightseeing.com)*								
Blue Dog		ES	1981	D	31*	47' 07"	18' 00"	5' 05"
Bright Star		ES	2003	D	93*	79' 03"	23' 00"	7' 01"
Cap Streeter		ES	1987	D	28*	63' 06"	24' 04"	7' 07"
Evening Star		ES	2001	D	93*	83' 00"	23' 00"	7' 00"
Lickety Split		ES	2010	D	43*	56' 00"	15' 03"	7' 00"
Marlyn		ES	1961	D	70*	65' 00"	25' 00"	7' 00"
Shoreline II		ES	1987	D	89*	75' 00"	26' 00"	7' 01"
Skyview		ES	2016	D	90*	94' 05"	35' 00"	7' 05"
Star of Chicago {2}		ES	1999	D	73*	64' 10"	22' 08"	7' 05"
Voyageur		ES	1983	D	98*	65' 00"	35' 00"	7' 00"

Heritage Marine's tug Helen H. tucks Arthur M. Anderson in for the winter at Duluth, Minn., on Jan. 15, 2017. (R.S. Hom)

SOCIÉTÉ DES TRAVERSIERS DU QUÉBEC, QUÉBEC, QC (traversiers.gouv.qc.ca)

Fleet Name / Vessel Name	Vessel IMO #	Vessel Type	Year Built	Engine Type	Cargo Cap. or Gross*	Overall Length	Vessel Breadth	Vessel Depth
Alphonse-Desjardins	7109233	PA/CF	1971	D	1,741*	214' 00"	71' 06"	20' 00"
Built: Davie Shipbuilding Co., Lauzon, QC								
Armand-Imbeau	7902269	PA/CF	1980	D	1,285*	203' 07"	72' 00"	18' 04"
Built: Marine Industries Ltd., Sorel, QC								
Camille-Marcoux	7343578	PA/CF	1974	D	6,122*	310' 09"	62' 09"	39' 00"
Built: Marine Industries Ltd., Sorel, QC								
Catherine-Legardeur	8409355	PA/CF	1985	D	1,348*	205' 09"	71' 10"	18' 10"
Built: Davie Shipbuilding Co., Lauzon, QC								
F.-A.-Gauthier	9669861	PA/CF	2015	DE	15,901*	436' 03"	73' 05"	26' 02"
Built: Fincantieri Castellammare di Stabia, Naples, Italy								
Felix-Antoine-Savard	9144706	PA/CF	1997	D	2,489*	272' 00"	70' 00"	21' 09"
Built: Davie Shipbuilding Co., Lauzon, QC (Fueled by liquid natural gas)								
Grue-des-Iles	8011732	PA/CF	1981	D	447*	155' 10"	41' 01"	12' 06"
Built: Bateaux Tur-Bec Ltd., Ste-Catherine, QC								
Ivan-Quinn	9554028	PA/CF	2008	D	241*	83' 07"	26' 09"	11' 03"
Built: Meridien Maritime Reparation Inc., Matane, QC								
Jos-Deschenes	391571	PA/CF	1980	D	1,287*	203' 07"	72' 00"	18' 04"
Built: Marine Industries Ltd., Sorel, QC								
Joseph-Savard	8409343	PA/CF	1985	D	1,445*	206' 00"	71' 10"	18' 10"
Built: Davie Shipbuilding Co., Lauzon, QC								
Lomer-Gouin	7109221	PA/CF	1971	D	1,741*	214' 00"	71' 06"	20' 00"
Built: Davie Shipbuilding Co., Lauzon, QC								
Lucien-L.	6721981	PA/CF	1967	D	867*	220' 10"	61' 06"	15' 05"
Built: Marine Industries Ltd., Sorel, QC								
Peter-Fraser		PA/CF	2012	DE	292*	110' 02"	39' 03"	7' 03"
Built: Chantier Naval Forillon, Gaspé, QC								
Radisson {1}		PA/CF	1954	D	1,037*	164' 03"	72' 00"	10' 06"
Built: Davie Shipbuilding Co., Lauzon, QC								

SOO LOCKS BOAT TOURS, SAULT STE. MARIE, MI (soolocks.com)

Fleet Name / Vessel Name	Vessel IMO #	Vessel Type	Year Built	Engine Type	Cargo Cap. or Gross*	Overall Length	Vessel Breadth	Vessel Depth
Bide-A-Wee {3}		ES	1955	D	99*	64' 07"	23' 00"	7' 11"
Hiawatha {2}		ES	1959	D	99*	64' 07"	23' 00"	7' 11"
Holiday		ES	1957	D	99*	64' 07"	23' 00"	7' 11"

Baie St. Paul meets Stewart J. Cort above Mission Point at Sault Ste. Marie. (Mike Sipper)

Fleet Name / Vessel Name	Vessel IMO #	Vessel Type	Year Built	Engine Type	Cargo Cap. or Gross*	Overall Length	Vessel Breadth	Vessel Depth
Le Voyageur		ES	1959	D	70*	65' 00"	25' 00"	7' 00"
Nokomis		ES	1959	D	70*	65' 00"	25' 00"	7' 00"

SOO MARINE SUPPLY INC., SAULT STE. MARIE, MI *(soomarine.com)*

Ojibway		SB	1945	D	53*	53' 00"	28' 00"	7' 00"

Built: Great Lakes Engineering Works, Ashtabula, OH

SPIRIT CRUISES LLC, CHICAGO, IL *(spiritcruises.com/chicago)*

Chicago Elite		ES	1988	D	96*	115' 00"	27' 00"	7' 06"
Mystic Blue		ES	1998	D	97*	138' 09"	36' 00"	10' 05"
Odyssey II		ES	1993	D	88*	162' 05"	40' 00"	13' 05"
Spirit of Chicago		ES	1988	D	92*	156' 00"	35' 00"	7' 01"

SPIRIT OF THE SOUND SCHOONER CO., PARRY SOUND, ON *(spiritofthesound.ca)*

Chippewa III		PA	1954	D	47*	65' 00"	16' 00"	6' 06"

Built: Russel-Hipwell Engines Ltd., Owen Sound, ON (Maid of the Mist III '54-'56, Maid of the Mist '56-'92)

ST. JAMES MARINE CO. & FOGG TOWING & MARINE, BEAVER ISLAND, MI *(stjamesmarine.com)*

American Girl		TB	1922	D	63*	62' 00"	14' 00"	6' 05"
Wendy Anne		TB	1955	D	89*	71' 00"	20' 00"	8' 05"

Built: Smith Basin Drydock, Port Everglades, FL (ST-2199)

ST. LAWRENCE CRUISE LINES INC., KINGSTON, ON *(stlawrencecruiselines.com)*

Canadian Empress		PA	1981	D	463*	108' 00"	30' 00"	8' 00"

Built: Algan Shipyards Ltd., Gananoque, ON

ST. LAWRENCE SEAWAY DEVELOPMENT CORP., MASSENA, NY *(www.seaway.dot.gov)*

Grasse River		GL	1958	GL		150 00"	65' 08"	5' 06"
Performance		TB	1997	D		50' 00"	16' 06"	7' 05"

Built: Marine Builders Inc., Utica, IN

Robinson Bay		TB	1958	DE	213*	103' 00"	26' 10"	14' 06"

Built: Christy Corp., Sturgeon Bay, WI

ST. LAWRENCE SEAWAY MANAGEMENT CORP., CORNWALL, ON *(greatlakes-seaway.com)*

VM/S Hercules		GL	1962	D	2,107*	200' 00"	75' 00"	18' 08"
VM/S St. Lambert		TB	1974	D	20*	30' 08"	13' 01"	6' 05"

Algoway passes fleetmate Algorail on the St. Clair River in 2016. (Jacob Northup)

ST. MARYS CEMENT INC. (CANADA), TORONTO, ON (stmaryscement.com)

Fleet Name / Vessel Name	Vessel IMO #	Vessel Type	Year Built	Engine Type	Cargo Cap. or Gross*	Overall Length	Vessel Breadth	Vessel Depth
Sea Eagle II	7631860	ATB	1979	D	560*	132' 00"	35' 00"	19' 00"

Built: Modern Marine Power Co., Houma, LA; paired with barge St. Marys Cement II (Sea Eagle '79-'81, Canmar Sea Eagle '81-'91)

St. Marys Cement	8972077	CC	1986	B	9,400	360' 00"	60' 00"	23' 03"

Built: Merce Industries East, Cleveland, OH

St. Marys Cement II	8879914	CC	1978	B	19,513	496' 06"	76' 00"	35' 00"

Built: Galveston Shipbuilding Co., Galveston, TX (Velasco '78-'81, Canmar Shuttle '81-'90)

THE FOLLOWING VESSEL CHARTERED BY ST. MARYS CEMENT GROUP FROM GREAT LAKES & INTERNATIONAL TOWING & SALVAGE CO., BURLINGTON, ON

Petite Forte	6826119	TB	1969	D	368*	127' 00"	32' 00"	14' 06"

Built: Cochrane and Sons Ltd., Selby, Yorkshire, England; paired with barge St. Marys Cement

STAR LINE MACKINAC ISLAND FERRY, ST. IGNACE, MI (mackinacferry.com)

Fleet Name / Vessel Name	Vessel IMO #	Vessel Type	Year Built	Engine Type	Cargo Cap. or Gross*	Overall Length	Vessel Breadth	Vessel Depth
Algomah		PF/PK	1961	D	81*	93' 00"	29' 08"	5' 02"
Anna May		ES	1947	D	94*	64' 10"	30' 00"	7' 03"

(West Shore '47-'12)

Cadillac {5}		PF	1990	D	73*	64' 07"	20' 00"	7' 07"
Chippewa {6}		PF/PK	1962	D	81*	93' 00"	29' 08"	5' 02"
Huron {5}		PF/PK	1955	D	99*	91' 06"	25' 00"	7' 00"
Joliet {3}		PF	1993	D	83*	64' 08"	22' 00"	8' 03"
LaSalle {4}		PF	1983	D	55*	65' 00"	20' 00"	7' 05"
Mackinac Islander		CF	1947	D	99*	84' 00"	30' 00"	8' 02"

(Drummond Islander '47-'02)

Marquette II {2}		PF	2005	D	65*	74' 00"	23' 06"	8' 00"
Ottawa {2}		PF/PK	1959	D	81*	93' 00"	29' 08"	5' 02"
Radisson {2}		PF	1988	D	97*	80' 00"	23' 06"	7' 00"
Straits Express		PF/CA	1995	D	99*	101' 00"	28' 08"	10' 00"
Straits of Mackinac II		PF/CA	1969	D	89*	90' 00"	27' 06"	8' 08"

STERLING FUELS (HAMILTON) LTD., HAMILTON, ON (mcasphalt.com)
A DIVISION OF McASPHALT INDUSTRIES LTD.

Fleet Name / Vessel Name	Vessel IMO #	Vessel Type	Year Built	Engine Type	Cargo Cap. or Gross*	Overall Length	Vessel Breadth	Vessel Depth
Hamilton Energy	6517328	RT	1965	D	1,282	201' 05"	34' 01"	14' 09"

Built: Grangemouth Dockyard Co., Grangemouth, Scotland; serves vessels in the vicinity of Hamilton and Toronto, ON, and the Welland Canal (Partington '65-'79, Shell Scientist '79-'81, Metro Sun '81-'85)

Provmar Terminal	5376521	TK	1959	B	7,300	403' 05"	55' 06"	28' 05"

Built: Sarpsborg Mekaniske, Verksted, Norway; last operated in 1984; in use as a fuel storage barge at Hamilton, ON (Varangnes '59-'70, Tommy Wiborg '70-'74, Ungava Transport '74-'85)

Sterling Energy	9277058	RT	2002	D	749*	226' 03"	32' 10"	14' 09"

Built: Selahattin Alsan Shipyard, Istanbul Turkey; serves vessels in the vicinity of Hamilton and Toronto, ON, and the Welland Canal (Melisa D '02-'13)

SVITZER CANADA LTD., HALIFAX, NS (svitzer.com)

Fleet Name / Vessel Name	Vessel IMO #	Vessel Type	Year Built	Engine Type	Cargo Cap. or Gross*	Overall Length	Vessel Breadth	Vessel Depth
Svitzer Cartier	8668248	TB	D	2007	350*	90' 05"	36' 07"	13' 08"

Built: Shanghai Harbor Foxing, Shanghai, China (Hai Gang 107 '07-'14, Svitzer Wombi '14-'15); tug is stationed at Montreal, QC

Svitzer Montreal	9295658	TB	D	2004	402*	101' 01"	36' 05"	16' 08"

Built: East Isle Shipyard, Georgetown, PEI (Caucedo '04-'15, Svitzer Caucedo '15-'16); tug is stationed at Montreal, QC

Svitzer Nerthus	9533048	TB	2009	D	381*	94' 60"	36' 50"	17' 10"

Built: East Isle Shipyard, Georgetown, PEI (Stevns Iceflower '09-'09); tug is stationed at Montreal, QC

Svitzer Njal	9533036	TB	2009	D	381*	94' 60"	36' 50"	17' 10"

Built: East Isle Shipyard, Georgetown, PEI; tug is stationed at Montreal, QC

T

TALL SHIP ADVENTURES OF CHICAGO, CHICAGO, IL (tallshipwindy.com)

Fleet Name / Vessel Name	Vessel IMO #	Vessel Type	Year Built	Engine Type	Cargo Cap. or Gross*	Overall Length	Vessel Breadth	Vessel Depth
Windy		ES/4S	1996	W	75*	148' 00"	25' 00"	8' 00"

Built: Detyens Shipyards Inc., North Charleston, SC

TALL SHIP RED WITCH LLC, KENOSHA, WI (redwitch.com)

Red Witch		ES/2S	1986	W	41*	77' 00"	17' 06"	6' 05"

Built: Nathaniel Zirlott, Bayou La Batre, AL

Fleet Name / Vessel Name	Vessel IMO #	Vessel Type	Year Built	Engine Type	Cargo Cap. or Gross*	Overall Length	Vessel Breadth	Vessel Depth
TGL MARINE HOLDINGS ULC, TORONTO, ON								
Jane Ann IV	7802809	ATB	1978	D	954*	150' 11"	42' 08"	21' 04"
Built: Mitsui Engineering & Shipbuilding Co., Tokyo, Japan; paired with barge Sarah Spencer; in long-term lay-up at Toledo, OH (Ouro Fino '78-'81, Bomare '81-'93, Tignish Sea '93-'98)								
Sarah Spencer	5002223	SU	1959	B	21,844	693' 10"	72' 00"	40' 00"
Built: Manitowoc Shipbuilding Co., Manitowoc, WI; engine removed, converted to a self-unloading barge by Halifax Dartmouth Industries, Halifax, NS, in '89; in long-term lay-up at Toledo, OH (Adam E. Cornelius {3} '59-'89, Capt. Edward V. Smith '89-'91, Sea Barge One '91-'96)								
THOUSAND ISLAND MARINE CONSTRUCTION LTD., GANANOQUE, ON *(timarineconstruction.com)*								
Steel Head		TB	1944	D	36*	56' 00"	20' 00"	5' 03"
THOUSAND ISLANDS & SEAWAY CRUISES, BROCKVILLE, ON *(1000islandscruises.com)*								
General Brock III		ES	1977	D	56*	56' 05"	15' 04"	5' 02"
Sea Fox II		ES	1988	D	55*	39' 08"	20' 00"	2' 00"
THUNDER BAY TUG SERVICES LTD., THUNDER BAY, ON *(thunderbaytugservices.ca)*								
Glenada		TB	1943	D	107*	80' 06"	25' 00"	10' 01"
Built: Russel Brothers Ltd., Owen Sound, ON (HMCS Glenada [W-30] '43-'45)								
Miseford		TB	1915	D	116*	85' 00"	20' 00"	9' 06"
Built: M. Beatty & Sons Ltd., Welland, ON								
Point Valour		TB	1958	D	246*	97' 08"	28' 02"	13' 10"
Built: Davie Shipbuilding Co., Lauzon, QC (Foundation Valour '58-'83)								
Robert W.		TB	1949	D	48*	60' 00"	16' 00"	8' 06"
Built: Russel Brothers Ltd., Owen Sound, ON								
Rosalee D.		TB	1943	D	22*	55' 00"	12' 07"	4' 11"
TORONTO BOAT CRUISES, TORONTO, ON *(torontoboatcruises.com)*								
Aurora Borealis		ES	1983	D	277*	108' 00"	24' 00"	6' 00"
TORONTO BRIGANTINE INC., TORONTO, ON *(torontobrigantine.org)*								
Pathfinder		W/TV	1963	D/W	32*	59' 08"	15' 00"	8' 00"
Playfair		W/TV	1973	D/W	33*	59' 08"	15' 00"	8' 00"
TORONTO DRYDOCK LTD., TORONTO, ON *(torontodrydock.com)*								
Coastal Titan	7700477	HL	1978	B	3,000*	300' 00"	55' 00"	27' 00"
Built: Peterson Builders, Sturgeon Bay, WI; converted to a barge in '09 at Port Colborne, ON (John Henry, Marinelink Explorer, Chaulk Lifter -'15)								
M.R. Kane		TB	1945	D	51*	60' 06"	16' 05"	6' 07"
Built: Central Bridge Co. Ltd., Trenton, ON (Tanac V-276 '45-'47)								
Menier Consol		FD	1962	B	2,575*	304' 05"	49' 06"	25' 06"
Built: Davie Shipbuilding Co., Lauzon, QC; former pulpwood carrier is now a floating dry dock at Toronto, ON								
Radium Yellowknife	5288956	TB	1948	D	235*	120' 00"	28' 00"	6' 06"
Built: Yarrows Ltd., Esquimalt, BC								
Salvage Monarch	5308275	TB	1959	D	219*	97' 09"	29' 00"	13' 06"
Built: P.K. Harris Ltd., Appledore, England								
TORONTO FIRE SERVICES, TORONTO, ON *(toronto.ca/fire)*								
William Thornton		FB	1982	D	55*	70' 10"	18' 00"	8' 09"
Built: Breton Industrial & Marine Ltd., Port Hawkesbury, NS (Cape Hurd '82-'14)								
Wm. Lyon Mackenzie	6400575	FB	1964	D	102*	81' 01"	20' 00"	10' 00"
Built: Russel Brothers Ltd., Owen Sound, ON								
TORONTO PADDLEWHEEL CRUISES LTD., NORTH YORK, ON *(pioneercruises.com)*								
Pioneer Princess		ES	1984	D	96*	56' 00"	17' 01"	3' 09"
Pioneer Queen		ES	1968	D	110*	85' 00"	30' 06"	7' 03"
TORONTO PORT AUTHORITY, TORONTO, ON *(torontoport.com)*								
Brutus I		TB	1992	D	10*	36' 01"	11' 09"	4' 04"
David Hornell VC		PA/CF	2006	D	219*	95' 10"	37' 07"	7' 05"
Built: Hike Metal Products, Wheatley, ON (TCCA 2 '09-'10)								
Iron Guppy		TB	2016	D	65*	66' 96"	21' 00"	10' 24"
Maple City		PA/CF	1951	D	135*	70' 06"	36' 04"	5' 11"
Marilyn Bell I		PA/CF	2009	D	270*	95' 10"	37' 07"	7' 05"
Built: Hike Metal Products, Wheatley, ON (TCCA 2 '09-'10)								
Windmill Point		PA/CF	1954	D	118*	65' 00"	36' 00"	10' 00"

Fleet Name / Vessel Name	Vessel IMO #	Vessel Type	Year Built	Engine Type	Cargo Cap. or Gross*	Overall Length	Vessel Breadth	Vessel Depth
TORONTO HARBOUR TOURS INC., TORONTO, ON *(harbourtourstoronto.ca)*								
Miss Kim Simpson		ES	1960	D	33*	90' 02"	13' 04"	3' 09"
New Beginnings		ES	1961	D	28*	41' 09"	13' 01"	4' 09"
Shipsands		ES	1972	D	23*	58' 03"	12' 01"	4' 07"
TRAVERSE RIVIERE-DU-LOUP ST-SIMEON LTEE, RIVIERE-DU-LOUP, QC *(traverserdl.com)*								
Trans-St-Laurent	5409586	CF/PA	1963	D	2,173*	249' 06"	60' 01"	15' 04"
Built: Geo. T. Davie & Sons Ltd., Lauzon, QC								
TRAVERSE TALL SHIP CO., TRAVERSE CITY, MI *(tallshipsailing.com)*								
Manitou {1}		ES/2S	1983	W	78*	114' 00"	21' 00"	9' 00"
30,000 ISLANDS CRUISE LINES INC., PARRY SOUND, ON *(islandqueencruise.com)*								
Island Queen V		ES	1990	D	526*	130' 00"	35' 00"	6' 06"
TRIDENT MARINE CORP., CLEVELAND, OH *(holidaycleveland.com)*								
Holiday		PA	1964	D	25*	60' 00"	16' 01"	5' 06"

U

Fleet Name / Vessel Name	Vessel IMO #	Vessel Type	Year Built	Engine Type	Cargo Cap. or Gross*	Overall Length	Vessel Breadth	Vessel Depth
UNCLE SAM BOAT TOURS, ALEXANDRIA, NY *(usboattours.com)*								
Alexandria Belle		ES	1988	D	92*	82' 00"	32' 00"	8' 00"
Island Duchess		ES	1988	D	73*	90' 03"	27' 08"	9' 00"
Island Wanderer		ES	1971	D	57*	62' 05"	22' 00"	7' 02"
Uncle Sam 7		ES	1976	D	55*	60' 04"	22' 00"	7' 01"
U.S. ARMY CORPS OF ENGINEERS – GREAT LAKES AND OHIO RIVER DIV., CINCINNATI, OH *(usace.army.mil)*								
U.S. ARMY CORPS OF ENGINEERS – BUFFALO DISTRICT								
Cheraw		TB	1970	D	356*	109' 00"	30' 06"	16' 03"
Built: Southern Shipbuilding Corp., Slidell, LA (USS Cheraw [YTB-802] '70-'96)								
McCauley		CS	1948	B		112' 00"	52' 00"	4' 25"
Mike Donlon		TB	1999	TB	64*	53' 00"	19' 02"	7' 07"
Simonsen		CS	1954	B		142' 00"	58' 00"	5' 00"
U.S. ARMY CORPS OF ENGINEERS – DETROIT DISTRICT, LAKE MICHIGAN AREA OFFICE, KEWAUNEE SUB-OFFICE								
Kenosha		TB	1954	D	82*	70' 00"	20' 00"	9' 08"
Built: Missouri Valley Bridge & Iron Works, Leavenworth, KS (U. S. Army ST-2011 '54-'65)								
Manitowoc		CS	1976	B		132' 00"	44' 00"	8' 00"
Racine		TB	1931	D	61*	66' 03"	18' 05"	7' 08"
U.S. ARMY CORPS OF ENGINEERS – DETROIT DISTRICT, DETROIT AREA OFFICE								
Demolen		TB	1974	D	356*	109' 00"	30' 06"	16' 03"
Built: Marinette Marine Corp., Marinette, WI (USS Metacom [YTB-829] '74-'01, Metacom '01-'02)								
Veler		CS	1991	B	613*	150' 00"	46' 00"	10' 06"
U.S. ARMY CORPS OF ENGINEERS – DETROIT DISTRICT, DULUTH AREA OFFICE								
D. L. Billmaier		TB	1968	D	356*	109' 00"	30' 06"	16' 03"
Built: Southern Shipbuilding Corp., Slidell, LA (USS Natchitoches [YTB-799] '68-'95)								
Hammond Bay		TB	1953	D	23*	45' 00"	13' 00"	7' 00"
H. J. Schwartz		DB	1995	B		150' 00"	48' 00"	11' 00"
U.S. ARMY CORPS OF ENGINEERS – DETROIT DISTRICT, SOO AREA OFFICE								
Harvey		DB	1961	B		120' 00"	40' 00"	8' 00"
Nicolet		DB	1971	B		120' 00"	40' 00"	8' 00"
Owen M. Frederick		TB	1942	D	56*	65' 00"	17' 00"	7' 06"
Paul Bunyan		GL	1945	B		150' 00"	65' 00"	12' 06"
Whitefish Bay		TB	1953	D	23*	45' 00"	13' 00"	7' 00"
U.S. COAST GUARD 9TH COAST GUARD DISTRICT, CLEVELAND, OH *(uscg.mil/d9)*								
Alder [WLB-216]	9271145	BT	2004	D	2,000*	225' 09"	46' 00"	19' 08"
Built: Marinette Marine Corp., Marinette, WI; stationed at Duluth, MN								
Biscayne Bay [WTGB-104]	8635148	IB	1979	D	662*	140' 00"	37' 06"	12' 00"
Built: Tacoma Boatbuilding Co., Tacoma, WA; stationed at St. Ignace, MI								
Bristol Bay [WTGB-102]	8635150	IB	1979	D	662*	140' 00"	37' 06"	12' 00"
Built: Tacoma Boatbuilding Co., Tacoma, WA; stationed at Detroit, MI								
Buckthorn [WLI-642]		BT	1963	D	200*	100' 00"	24' 00"	4' 08"
Built: Mobile Ship Repair Inc., Mobile, AL; stationed at Sault Ste. Marie, MI								

Tug Calusa Coast of Dann Marine Towing. (Alain Gindroz)

CSL Assiniboine on the lower St. Marys River. (Steve Hogler)

Fleet Name Vessel Name	Vessel IMO #	Vessel Type	Year Built	Engine Type	Cargo Cap. or Gross*	Overall Length	Vessel Breadth	Vessel Depth
CGB-12001		BT	1991	B	700*	120' 00"	50' 00"	6' 00"
CGB-12002		BT	1992	B	700*	120' 00"	50' 00"	6' 00"
Hollyhock [WLB-214]	9271133	BT	2003	D	2,000*	225' 09"	46' 00"	19' 08"
Built: Marinette Marine Corp., Marinette, WI; stationed at Port Huron, MI								
Katmai Bay [WTGB-101]		IB	1978	D	662*	140' 00"	37' 06"	12' 00"
Built: Tacoma Boatbuilding Co., Tacoma, WA; stationed at Sault Ste. Marie, MI								
Mackinaw [WLBB-30]	9271054	IB	2005	D	3,407*	240' 00"	58' 00"	15' 05"
Built: Marinette Marine Corp., Marinette, WI; stationed at Cheboygan, MI								
Mobile Bay [WTGB-103]	8635162	IB	1979	D	662*	140' 00"	37' 06"	12' 00"
Built: Tacoma Boatbuilding Co., Tacoma, WA; stationed at Sturgeon Bay, WI								
Morro Bay [WTGB-106]	8635215	IB	1979	D	662*	140' 00"	37' 06"	12' 00"
Built: Tacoma Boatbuilding Co., Tacoma, WA; stationed at Cleveland, OH								
Neah Bay [WTGB-105]	8635174	IB	1980	D	662*	140' 00"	37' 06"	12' 00"
Built: Tacoma Boatbuilding Co., Tacoma, WA; stationed at Cleveland, OH								

U.S. ENVIRONMENTAL PROTECTION AGENCY, DULUTH, MN & CHICAGO, IL *(epa.gov)*

Lake Explorer II		RV	1966	D	150*	86' 09"	22' 00"	7' 02"
Built: Jackobson Shipyard, Oyster Bay, NY (NOAA Rude '66-'08)								
Lake Guardian	8030609	RV	1981	D	959*	180' 00"	40' 00"	14' 00"
Built: Halter Marine Inc., Moss Point MS (Marsea Fourteen '81-'90)								

U.S. FISH & WILDLIFE SERVICE, JORDAN RIVER NATIONAL FISH HATCHERY, ELMIRA, MI

Spencer F. Baird	9404326	RV	2006	D	256*	95' 00"	30' 00"	9' 05"

U.S. NATIONAL PARK SERVICE - ISLE ROYALE NATIONAL PARK, HOUGHTON, MI *(nps.gov)*

Greenstone II		TK	2003	B	114*	70' 01"	24' 01"	8' 00"
Ranger III	7618234	PK	1958	D	648*	152' 08"	34' 00"	13' 00"

U.S. NAVAL SEA CADET CORPS *(seacadets.org)*

Grayfox [TWR-825]		TV	1985	D	213*	120' 00"	25' 00"	12' 00"
Built: Marinette Marine Corp., Marinette, WI; based at Port Huron, MI (USS TWR-825 '85-'97)								
Manatra [YP-671]		TV	1974	D	67*	80' 05"	17' 09"	5' 04"
Based at Chicago, IL; name stands for MArine NAvigation and TRaining Association (USS YP-671 '74-'89)								
Pride of Michigan [YP-673]		TV	1977	D	70*	80' 06"	17' 08"	5' 03"
Built: Peterson Builders Inc., Sturgeon Bay, WI; based at Mount Clemens, MI (USS YP-673 '77-'89)								

U.S. OIL, A DIVISION OF U.S. VENTURE INC., APPLETON, WI *(usoil.com)*
MANAGED BY BETTER WAY LOGISTICS LLC, MUSKEGON, MI

Great Lakes {2}		TK	1982	B	5,024*	414' 00"	60' 00"	30' 00"
Built: Bay Shipbuilding Co., Sturgeon Bay, WI (Amoco Great Lakes '82-'85)								
Michigan {10}	8121795	AT	1982	D	292*	107' 08"	34' 00"	16' 00"
Built: Bay Shipbuilding Co., Sturgeon Bay, WI (Amoco Michigan '82-'85)								

A rainbow backdrop for Capt. Henry Jackman. (Ted Wilush)

Fleet Name Vessel Name	Vessel IMO #	Vessel Type	Year Built	Engine Type	Cargo Cap. or Gross*	Overall Length	Vessel Breadth	Vessel Depth
UNIVERSITY OF MINNESOTA-DULUTH, DULUTH, MN *(d.umn.edu)*								
Blue Heron		RV	1985	D	175*	87' 00"	23' 00"	11' 00"*
Built: Goudy and Stevens, East Boothbay, ME (Fairtry '85-'97)								
UNIVERSITY OF WISCONSIN, GREAT LAKES WATER INSTITUTE, MILWAUKEE, WI *(glwi.uwm.edu)*								
Neeskay		RV	1952	D	75*	71' 00"	17' 06"	7' 06"
URGENCE MARINE INC., MONTREAL, QC *(urgencemarine.com)*								
Simon Cote		TB	1953	D	14*	38' 02"	11' 05"	4' 00"
USS GREAT LAKES LLC, NEW YORK, NY								
Robert F. Deegan		TK	1968	B	2,424*	225' 08"	60' 00"	18' 00"
Built: Wyatt Industries, Houston, TX; usually paired with tug Zeus								

V-W

VANENKEVORT TUG & BARGE INC., ESCANABA MI *(vtbarge.com)*								
Great Lakes Trader	8635966	SU	2000	B	39,600	740' 00"	78' 00"	45' 00"
Built: Halter Marine, Pearlington, MS; paired with tug Joyce L. VanEnkevort								
Joseph H. Thompson		SU	1944	B	21,200	706' 06"	71' 06"	38' 06"
Built: Sun Shipbuilding & Drydock Co., Chester, PA; converted from a saltwater vessel to a Great Lakes bulk carrier by Maryland Dry Dock, Baltimore, MD, and American Shipbuilding Co., South Chicago, IL, in '52; converted to a self-unloading barge by the owners in '91 (USNS Marine Robin '44-'52)								
Joseph H. Thompson Jr.	5175745	ATB	1990	D	841*	146' 06"	38' 00"	30' 00"
Built at Marinette, WI, from steel left over from the conversion of Joseph H. Thompson (above)								
Joyce L. VanEnkevort	8973033	AT	1998	D	1,179*	135' 04"	50' 00"	26' 00"
Built: Bay Shipbuilding Co., Sturgeon Bay, WI; paired with barge Great Lakes Trader								
OWNED BY SEAJON LLC, FORT LAUDERDALE, FL; OPERATED BY VANENKEVORT TUG & BARGE INC.								
Clyde S. VanEnkevort		ATB	2011	D	1,179*	135' 04"	50' 00"	26' 00"
Built: Donjon Shipbuilding & Repair, Erie, PA; paired with the barge Lakes Contender (Ken Boothe Sr. '11-'17)								
Erie Trader		SU	2012	B	37,600	740' 04"	78' 00"	30' 00"
Built: Donjon Shipbuilding & Repair, Erie, PA (Lakes Contender '12-'17)								
VICTORIAN PRINCESS CRUISE LINES INC., ERIE, PA *(victorianprincess.com)*								
Victorian Princess		ES	1985	D	46*	67' 00"	24' 00"	4' 05"
VISTA FLEET, DULUTH, MN *(vistafleet.com)*								
Vista Queen		ES	1987	D	97*	64' 00"	16' 00"	6' 02"
Built: Mid-City Steel Fabricating Inc., La Crosse, WI (Queen of Excelsior)								

Inflatable rubber duck was a hit at tall ship events in 2016. (Glenn Blaszkiewicz)

Fleet Name Vessel Name	Vessel IMO #	Vessel Type	Year Built	Engine Type	Cargo Cap. or Gross*	Overall Length	Vessel Breadth	Vessel Depth
Vista Star		ES	1987	D	95*	91' 00"	24' 09"	5' 02"

Built: Freeport Shipbuilding Inc., Freeport, FL (Island Empress '87-'88)

VOIGHT'S MARINE SERVICES LTD., ELLISON BAY AND GILLS ROCK, WI *(islandclipper.com)*

Island Clipper {2}		ES	1987	D	71*	65' 00"	20' 00"	8' 00"
Yankee Clipper		ES	1971	D	41*	46' 06"	17' 00"	6' 00"

WALPOLE-ALGONAC FERRY LINE, PORT LAMBTON, ON *(walpolealgonacferry.com)*

City of Algonac		CF	1990	D	82*	62' 06"	27' 09"	5' 09"
Walpole Islander		CF	1986	D	72*	54' 05"	27' 09"	6' 03"

WALSTROM MARINE, HARBOR SPRINGS, MI *(walstrom.com)*

Elizabeth		TB	1945	D	21*	42' 02"	12' 01"	5' 05"

Built: Burger Boat Co., Manitowoc, WI (ST-912 '45-'48, Ashland '48-'72, Charles F. Liscomb '72-'94, 'Jason 94-'01, Lydie Rae '01-'03)

WARNER PETROLEUM CORP., CLARE, MI *(warnerpetroleum.com)*

Coloma L. Warner	7337892	TB	1955	D	134*	86' 00"	24' 00"	10' 00"

Built: Sturgeon Bay Shipbuilding, Sturgeon Bay, WI; paired with the barge Warner Provider (Harbor Ace '55-'61, Gopher State '61-'71, Betty Gale '71-'93, Hannah D. Hannah '93-'10)

Warner Provider	8641185	RT	1962	B	1,698*	264' 00"	52' 05"	12' 00"

Built: Port Houston Iron Works, Houston, TX (Hannah 2903); in use as a fueling barge at south Lake Michigan ports

William L. Warner	7322055	RT	1973	D	492*	120' 00"	40' 00"	14' 00"

Built: Halter Marine, New Orleans, LA; (Jos. F. Bigane '73-'04); in use as a vessel fueling barge at Detroit, MI

WASHINGTON ISLAND FERRY LINE INC., WASHINGTON ISLAND, WI *(wisferry.com)*

Arni J. Richter		PA/CF	2003	D	92*	104' 00"	38' 06"	10' 11"
Eyrarbakki		PA/CF	1970	D	95*	87' 00"	36' 00"	7' 06"
Karfi		PA/CF	1967	D	23*	36' 00"	16' 00"	4' 08"
Robert Noble		PA/CF	1979	D	97*	90' 04"	36' 00"	8' 03"
Washington {2}		PA/CF	1989	D	97*	100' 00"	37' 00"	9' 00"

WENDELLA BOAT TOURS, CHICAGO, IL *(wendellaboats.com)*

Linnea		ES	2010	D	77*	85' 05"	30' 00"	7' 01"
Lucia		ES	2015	D	80*	85' 05"	30' 00"	7' 01"
Ouilmette		ES	2001	D	43*	65' 00"	22' 04"	4' 05"
Wendella		ES	2007	D	77*	85' 05"	30' 00"	7' 01"
Wendella LTD		ES	1992	D	66*	68' 00"	20' 00"	4' 09"

WHITE LAKE DOCK & DREDGE INC., MONTAGUE, MI *(wlddi.com)*

Captain George		TB	1929	D	61*	60' 09"	16' 07"	7' 07"

Built: Charles Ward Engine Works, Charleston, WV (Captain George '29-'73, Kurt R. Luedtke '73-'91)

J-Krab		TW	2010	D	14*	25' 05"	14' 00"	5' 070"
Lauren A		TB	1980	D	68*	51' 05"	21' 00"	6' 00"

WILLY'S CONTRACTING CO., SOUTHAMPTON, ON *(willyscontracting.com)*

Pride		TB	1957	D	47*	52' 06"	29' 08"	5' 01"

WINDSOR RIVER CRUISES LTD., WINDSOR, ON *(windsorrivercruises.com)*

Macassa Bay	8624709	ES	1986	D	210*	93' 07"	29' 07"	10' 04"

WOHLLEB-SOCIE CO., TOLEDO, OH

Bessie B		TB	1947	D	30*	52' 03"	13' 09"	5' 05"

WISCONSIN DEPARTMENT OF NATURAL RESOURCES, BAYFIELD AND STURGEON BAY, WI *(dnr.wi.gov)*

Coregonus		RV	2011	D	37*	60' 00"	16' 00"	5' 09"
Gaylord Nelson		RV	1992	D	12*	45' 09"	16' 00"	5' 05"
Hack Noyes		RV	1947	D	50*	56' 00"	14' 05"	4' 00"

1089856 ONTARIO LTD., THUNDER BAY, ON

W. N. Twolan	5384360	TB	1962	D	299*	106' 00"	29' 05"	15' 00"

Built: George T. Davie & Sons, Lauzon, QC

BoatNerd.com
News ☞ Photos ☞ Information

Alpena arriving at the Lafarge dock in Superior, Wis, to unload cement into the storage vessel J.A.W. Iglehart. (Chris Mazzella)

Tall ship-watching was popular on the lakes in 2016. Here, passengers on the Lady Michigan view the Viking ship Draken Harald Hårfagre near Alpena, Mich. (Ben McClain)

ALPENASHIPWRECKTOURS.COM

LAKER LONGEVITY

1906: St. Marys Challenger *(re: '67, '14)* **1936**: J.A.W. Iglehart *(re:'65)***1937**: St. Marys Conquest *(re:'87)*

1941: Pere Marquette 41 *(re: '97)* **1942**: Alpena *(re:'91)*, American Victory *(re:'61,'82)*** Lee A. Tregurtha *(re:'61)* **1943**: Cuyahoga *(re:'74)*, Manistee *(re:'64)***, Mississagi *(re:'67)* **1944**: Joseph H. Thompson *(re '52, '91)*, McKee Sons *(re: '53, '91**)* **1945**: Paul H. Townsend *(re:'52)*** **1949**: Wilfred Sykes

1952: Arthur M. Anderson *(re: '75,'82)*, Kaye E. Barker *(re: '76, '81)*, Cason J. Callaway *(re: '74,'82)*, Philip R. Clarke *(re: '74,'82)*, Lewis J. Kuber *(re:'06)*, Michipicoten *(re: '57, '80)*, Ojibway, John G. Munson **1953**: American Valor *(re: '74,'82)***, Badger, James L. Kuber *(re:'07)*, Pathfinder *(re:'98)*, Saginaw **1958**: John Sherwin**

1959: Cedarglen *(re:'77)*, Hon. James L. Oberstar *(re:'72, '81)*, Herbert C. Jackson *(re:'75)*, Sarah Spencer *(re:'89)***

1960: Edward L. Ryerson** **1961**: English River *(re:'74)* **1965**: Stephen B. Roman *(re:'83)* **1966**: Algosteel *(re: '89)* **1967**: Tim S. Dool *(re:'96)*, John D. Leitch *(re:'02)*, Manitoba **1968**: Algorail, Frontenac *(re:'73)* **1969**: CSL Tadoussac *(re:'01)*

1972: Algoway, Roger Blough, CSL Niagara *(re:'99)*, Stewart J. Cort **1973**: Adam E. Cornelius, Calumet, Manitowoc, John J. Boland, Rt. Hon. Paul J. Martin *(re: '00)*, Presque Isle, Tecumseh **1974**: H. Lee White, Robert S. Pierson **1975**: Sam Laud **1976**: James R. Barker, Joseph L. Block, Algoma Olympic, Amelia Desgagnés, St. Clair **1977**: Algolake, CSL Assiniboine *(re:'05)*, CSL

Laurentien *(re:'01)*, Walter J. McCarthy Jr., Mesabi Miner **1978**: Radcliffe R. Latimer *(re:'09)*, American Integrity, American Spirit, Buffalo **1979**: American Courage, Algoma Enterprise, Algoma Transport, Edwin H. Gott, Indiana Harbor

1980: American Mariner, Burns Harbor, Salarium, Edgar B. Speer, Oakglen **1981**: Algowood *(re:'00)*, American Century, Great Republic, Capt. Henry Jackman *(re:'96)*, Paul R. Tregurtha **1982**: Camilla Desgagnés, Michigan, Ashtabula **1983**: John B. Aird, Spruceglen, Kaministiqua **1984**: Atlantic Huron *(re:'89,'03)* **1985**: Pineglen **1986**: Anna Desgagnés, Algoma Spirit **1987**: Algoma Discovery, Algoma Guardian

1991: Manitoulin *(re:'15)* **1992**: Dara Desgagnés, Esta Desgagnés **1993**: Jana Desgagnés **1996**: Integrity **1998**: Algosea **1999**: Maria Desgagnés

2000: Great Lakes Trader **2001**: Norman McLeod **2004**: Algoscotia, Lake Express **2006**: Innovation **2007**: Rosaire A. Desgagnés, Evans Spirit **2008**: Algocanada, Algonova, John J. Carrick, Zélada Desgagnés **2009**: Sedna Desgagnés

2011: Algoma Mariner, Claude A. Desgagnés **2012**: Erie Trader, Bella Desgagnés, Baie St. Paul **2013**: Algoma Equinox, Thunder Bay, Whitefish Bay, Baie Comeau **2014**: Algoma Harvester, G3Marquis, CSL Welland, CSL St-Laurent **2016**: Mia Desgagnés, Damia Desgagnés **2017**: Algoma Innovator

*(re = major rebuild; * storage barge; ** long-term lay-up)*

Happy 50th birthday to the Tim S. Dool and John D. Leitch in 2017.

John C. Knecht (right) and Jim Hoffman

ENGINES – Great Lakes & Seaway Vessels

Vessel Name	Engine Manufacturer & Model #	Engine Type	Total Engines	Total Cylinders	Rated HP	Total Props	Speed MPH
Adam E. Cornelius	GM EMD - 20-645-E7B	Diesel	2	20	7,200 bhp	1 cpp	16.1
Alder (USCG)	Caterpillar - 3608TA	Diesel	2	6	3,100 bhp	1 cpp	
Algocanada	MaK - 9M32C	Diesel	1	9	6,118 bhp	1 cpp	16.1
Algolake	Pielstick - 10PC2-2V-400	Diesel	2	10	9,000 bhp	1 cpp	17.3
Algoma Dartmouth	MAN-B&W - 6L23/30A	Diesel	2	6	2,310 bhp	2 cpp	13.3
Algoma Discovery	Sulzer - 6RTA62	Diesel	1	6	15,499 bhp	1 cpp	16.4
Algoma Enterprise	MAN - 7L40/45	Diesel	2	7	8,804 bhp	1 cpp	13.8
Algoma Equinox	Wartsila 5RT-flex50-D	Diesel	1	5	11,863 bhp	1 cpp	16.1
Algoma Guardian	Sulzer - 6RTA62	Diesel	1	6	15,499 bhp	1 cpp	16.4
Algoma Hansa	Wartsila - 6L46A	Diesel	1	6	6,525 bhp	1 cpp	15.8
Algoma Harvester	Wartsila 5RT-flex50-D	Diesel	1	5	11,863 bhp	1 cpp	16.1
Algoma Integrity	Sulzer - 6RT-FLEX-58T-B	Diesel	1	6	14,895 bhp	1	
Algoma Mariner	MAN-B&W - 6L48/60CR	Diesel	1	6	9,792 bhp	1 cpp	
Algoma Olympic	MAN - 8L40/54A	Diesel	2	8	10,000 bhp	1 cpp	15.0
Algoma Spirit	Sulzer - 6RTA62	Diesel	1	6	11,284 bhp	1 cpp	16.4
Algoma Transport	MAN - 8L40/45	Diesel	2	8	10,000 bhp	1 cpp	13.8
Algomarine	Sulzer - 6RND76	Diesel	1	6	9,600 bhp	1 cpp	17.0
Algonova	MaK - 9M32C	Diesel	1	9	6,118 bhp	1 cpp	16.1
Algorail	Fairbanks Morse - 10-38D8-1/8	Diesel	4	10	6,662 bhp	1 cpp	13.8
Algoscotia	Wartsila - 6L46C	Diesel	1	6	8,445 bhp	1 cpp	16.0
Algosea	Wartsila - 6L46A	Diesel	1	6	6,434 bhp	1 cpp	15.0
Algosteel	Sulzer - 6RND76	Diesel	1	6	9,599 bhp	1	17.0
Algoway	Fairbanks Morse - 10-38D8-1/8	Diesel	4	10	6,662 bhp	1 cpp	13.8
Algowood	MaK - 6M552AK	Diesel	2	6	10,200 bhp	1 cpp	13.8
Alpena	De Laval Steam Turbine Co.	Turbine	1	**	4,400 shp	1	14.1
Amelia Desgagnés	Allen - 12PVBCS12-F	Diesel	2	12	4,000 bhp	1 cpp	16.1
American Century	GM - EMD - 20-645-E7B	Diesel	4	20	14,400 bhp	2 cpp	17.3
American Courage	GM - EMD - 20-645-E7	Diesel	2	20	7,200 bhp	1 cpp	16.1
American Integrity	GM EMD - 20-645-E7	Diesel	4	20	14,400 bhp	2 cpp	18.4
American Mariner	GM EMD - 20-645-E7	Diesel	2	20	7,200 bhp	1 cpp	15.0
American Spirit	Pielstick - 16PC2-2V-400	Diesel	2	16	16,000 bhp	2 cpp	17.3
American Valor	Westinghouse Elec. Corp.	Turbine	1	**	7,700 shp	1	16.1
American Victory	Bethlehem Steel Corp.	Turbine	1	**	7,700 shp	1	19.0
Amundsen (CCG)	Alco - 16V251F	Diesel	6	16	17,700 bhp	2	18.6
Anglian Lady *	Deutz - SBA12M528	Diesel	2	12	3,480 bhp	2 cpp	15.5
Anna Desgagnés	MAN - K5SZ70/125B	Diesel	1	5	10,332 bhp	1	17.8
Arctic	MAN - 14V52/55A	Diesel	1	14	14,769 bhp	1	17.8
Ardita	Wartsila-C	Diesel	1	6	5,831 bhp	1 cpp	16.1
Arthur M. Anderson	Westinghouse Elec. Corp.	Turbine	1	**	7,700 shp	1	16.1
Atlantic Huron	Sulzer - 6RLB66	Diesel	1	6	11,094 bhp	1 cpp	17.3
Avenger IV *	British Polar	Diesel	1	9	2,700 bhp	1 cpp	12.0
Badger **	Skinner Engine Co. - Steeple Compound Uniflow	Steam	2	4	8,000 ihp	2	18.4
Baie Comeau	MAN B&W - 6S50ME-B9	Diesel	1	6	11,897 bhp	1	15.5
Baie St. Paul	MAN B&W - 6S50ME-B9	Diesel	1	6	11,897 bhp	1	15.5
Barbara Andrie *	GM EMD 16-645-EF	Diesel	1	16	2,000 bhp	1	
Bella Desgagnés	Wartsila - 9L20CR	Diesel	4	9	8,320 bhp	2 azimuth	17.3
Beverly M 1 *	Niigata - 6L28HX	Diesel	2	6	1,971 bhp	2	16.0
Biscayne Bay (USCG)	Fairbanks Morse - 10-38D8-1/8	Diesel	2	10	2,500 bhp	1	13.8
Bradshaw McKee *	GM EMD - 12-645-E5	Diesel	2	12	4,320 bhp	2	11.5
Bristol Bay (USCG)	Fairbanks Morse - 10-38D8-1/8	Diesel	2	10	2,500 bhp	1	13.8
Buffalo	GM EMD - 20-645-E7	Diesel	2	20	7,200 bhp	1 cpp	16.1
Burns Harbor	GM EMD - 20-645-E7	Diesel	4	20	14,400 bhp	2 cpp	18.4

* = tug   ** = ferry

bhp: brake horsepower, a measure of diesel engine output measured at the crankshaft before entering gearbox or any other power take-out device

ihp: indicated horsepower, based on an internal measurement of mean cylinder pressure, piston area, piston stroke and engine speed; used for reciprocating engines

shp: shaft horsepower, a measure of engine output at the propeller shaft at the output of the reduction gearbox; used for steam and diesel-electric engines

cpp: controllable pitch propeller

Vessel Name	Engine Manufacturer & Model #	Engine Type	Total Engines	Total Cylinders	Rated HP	Total Props	Speed MPH
Calumet	Alco - 16V251E	Diesel	2	16	5,600 bhp	1	16.1
Calusa Coast*	GM EMD 12-645-E2	Diesel	2	12	3,400 bhp	2	
Camilla Desgagnés	Werkspoor - 12TM410	Diesel	1	12	7,797 bhp	1 cpp	
Capt. Henry Jackman	MaK - 6M552AK	Diesel	2	6	9,465 bhp	1 cpp	17.3
Cason J. Callaway	Westinghouse Elec. Corp.	Turbine	1	**	7,700 shp	1	16.1
Cedarglen	B&W - 7-74VTBF-160	Diesel	1	7	8,750 bhp	1 cpp	15.5
Chi-Cheemaun **	Caterpillar - C280-6	Diesel	4	6	9,280 bhp	2	
Claude A. Desgagnés	MaK/Caterpillar - 6M43C	Diesel	1	6	7,342 bhp	1 cpp	17.8
Clyde S. VanEnkevort *	Cat-MaK - 8M32C	Diesel	2	8	10,876 bhp	2 cpp	18.4
CSL Assiniboine	MaK/Caterpillar - 6M32C	Diesel	2	6	8,060 bhp	1 cpp	
CSL Laurentien	MaK/Caterpillar - 6M32C	Diesel	2	6	8,060 bhp	1 cpp	
CSL Niagara	MaK/Caterpillar - 6M32C	Diesel	2	6	8,060 bhp	1 cpp	
CSL St-Laurent	MAN B&W 6S50ME-B	Diesel	1	6	11,897 bhp	1 cpp	15.5
CSL Tadoussac	Sulzer - 6RND76	Diesel	1	6	9,600 bhp	1	17.0
CSL Welland	MAN B&W 6S50ME-B	Diesel	1	6	11,897 bhp	1 cpp	15.5
Cuyahoga	Caterpillar - 3608	Diesel	1	8	3,000 bhp	1 cpp	12.6
Damia Desgagnés	Wärtsilä 5RT-flex 50DF	Diesel/LNG	1	5	7,305 bhp	1 cpp	15
Dara Desgagnés	B&W - 6L35MC	Diesel	1	6	5,030 bhp	1 cpp	14.4
Defiance *	GM EMD - 20-645-E7	Diesel	2	20	7,200 bhp	2	15.0
Des Groseilliers (CCG)	Alco - 16V251F	Diesel	6	16	17,700 bhp	2	18.6
Donny S *	GM -12-278A	Diesel	2	12	1,850 bhp	2	
Dorothy Ann *	GM EMD - 20-645-E7B	Diesel	2	20	7,200 bhp	2 Z-drive cpp	16.1
Ecosse *	GM Detroit - 16V92 N	Diesel	2	16	1,800 bhp	2	13.8
Edgar B. Speer	Pielstick - 18PC2-3V-400	Diesel	2	18	19,260 bhp	2 cpp	17.0
Edward L. Ryerson	General Electric Co.	Turbine	1	**	9,900 shp	1	19.0
Edwin H. Gott	MaK - 8M43C	Diesel	2	8	19,578 bhp	2 ccp	16.7
English River	Werkspoor - TMAB-390	Diesel	1	8	1,850 bhp	1 cpp	13.8
Espada Desgagnés	B&W - 6S60MC-C	Diesel	1	5	18,605 bhp	1 cpp	18.4
Esta Desgagnés	B&W - 6L35MC	Diesel	1	6	5,030 bhp	1 cpp	14.4
Evans McKeil *	GM EMD - 16-645C	Diesel	1	16	2,150 bhp	1	11.5
Evans Spirit	Wartsila - 6L38B	Diesel	1	6	5,831 bhp	1 cpp	16.1
Everlast *	Daihatsu - 8DSM-32	Diesel	2	8	6,000 bhp	2	16.5
Federal Asahi	B&W - 6S46MC-C	Diesel	1	6	10,710 bhp	1	16.1
Federal Baltic	B&W - 6S46MC-C	Diesel	1	5	10,710 bhp	1	16.1
Federal Barents	B&W - 6S46MC-C	Diesel	1	6	10,710 bhp	1	16.1
Federal Beaufort	B&W - 6S46MC-C	Diesel	1	6	10,710 bhp	1	16.1
Federal Bering	B&W - 6S46MC-C	Diesel	1	6	10,710 bhp	1	16.1
Federal Biscay	B&W - 6S46MC-C	Diesel	1	6	10,710 bhp	1	16.1
Federal Bristol	B&W - 6S46MC-C	Diesel	1	6	10,710 bhp	1	16.1
Federal Caribou	B&W - 6S46MC-C	Diesel	1	6	10,710 bhp	1	16.1
Federal Cedar	B&W - 6S46MC-C	Diesel	1	6	10,710 bhp	1	16.1
Federal Champlain	B&W - 6S46MC-C	Diesel	1	6	10,710 bhp	1	16.1
Federal Churchill	B&W - 6S46MC-C	Diesel	1	6	10,710 bhp	1	16.1
Federal Clyde	B&W - 6S46MC-C	Diesel	1	6	10,710 bhp	1	16.1
Federal Columbia	B&W - 6S46MC-C	Diesel	1	6	10,710 bhp	1	16.1
Federal Danube	B&W - 6S46MC-C	Diesel	1	6	10,686 bhp	1	16.1
Federal Elbe	B&W - 6S46MC-C	Diesel	1	6	10,686 bhp	1	16.1
Federal Ems	B&W - 6S46MC-C	Diesel	1	6	10,686 bhp	1	16.1
Federal Hudson	B&W - 6S46MC-C	Diesel	1	6	10,710 bhp	1	15.5
Federal Hunter	B&W - 6S46MC-C	Diesel	1	6	10,710 bhp	1	15.5
Federal Katsura	Mitsubishi (Tokyo) - 6UEC52LA	Diesel	1	6	9,490 bhp	1	19.2
Federal Kivalina	B&W - 6S46MC-C	Diesel	1	6	10,710 bhp	1	16.1
Federal Kumano	B&W - 6S46MC-C	Diesel	1	6	10,710 bhp	1	16.1
Federal Kushiro	Mitsubishi - 6UEC52LA	Diesel	1	6	9,626 bhp	1	16.6
Federal Leda	B&W - 6S46MC-C	Diesel	1	6	10,686 bhp	1	16.1
Federal Maas	B&W - 6S50MC	Diesel	1	6	11,640 bhp	1	16.1
Federal Mackinac	B&W - 6S46MC-C	Diesel	1	6	10,540 bhp	1	16.1
Federal Margaree	B&W - 6S46MC-C	Diesel	1	6	10,686 bhp	1	16.1
Federal Mayumi	MAN B&W - 6S46MC-C	Diesel	1	6	10,686 bhp	1	16.1
Federal Nakagawa	B&W - 6S46MC-C	Diesel	1	6	10,710 bhp	1	16.1
Federal Oshima	B&W - 6S46MC-C	Diesel	1	6	10,710 bhp	1	16.1
Federal Rhine	B&W - 6S50MC	Diesel	1	6	11,640 bhp	1	16.1

Vessel Name	Engine Manufacturer & Model #	Engine Type	Total Engines	Total Cylinders	Rated HP	Total Props	Speed MPH
Federal Rideau	B&W - 6S46MC-C	Diesel	1	6	10,710 bhp	1	16.1
Federal Saguenay	B&W - 6S50MC	Diesel	1	6	11,665 bhp	1	16.1
Federal Satsuki	MAN B&W - 6S46MC-C	Diesel	1	6	8,960 bhp	1	16.1
Federal Satsuki	B&W - 6S46MC-C	Diesel	1	6	8.833 bhp	1	16.1
Federal Schelde	B&W - 6S50MC	Diesel	1	6	11,640 bhp	1	16.1
Federal Seto	MAN B&W - 6S46MC-C	Diesel	1	6	10,711 bhp	1	16.7
Federal Shimanto	Mitsubishi - 6UEC52LA	Diesel	1	6	9,600 bhp	1	16.6
Federal Welland	B&W - 6S46MC-C	Diesel	1	6	10,710 bhp	1	16.1
Federal Weser	B&W - 6S46MC-C	Diesel	1	6	10,686 bhp	1	18.0
Federal Yoshino	Mitsubishi - 6UEC52LA	Diesel	1	6	9,600 bhp	1	16.6
Federal Yukon	B&W - 6S46MC-C	Diesel	1	6	10,710 bhp	1	15.5
Florence M. *	Fairbanks Morse - 8-28D8-1/4	Diesel	2	8	1,450 bhp	2	
Florence Spirit	Wartsila C - 6L38B	Diesel	1	6	5,831 bhp	1	15.5
Frontenac	Sulzer - 6RND76	Diesel	1	6	9,600 bhp	1 cpp	17.0
G3 Marquis	Wartsila 5RT-flex50-D	Diesel	1	5	11,863 bhp	1 cpp	16.1
G.L. Ostrander *	Caterpillar - 3608-DITA	Diesel	2	8	6,008 bhp	2	17.3
Great Republic	GM EMD - 20-645-E7	Diesel	2	20	7,200 bhp	2 cpp	15.0
Grayfox (USNCS)	Caterpillar - 3512 TAC	Diesel	2	12	2,350 bhp.	2	20.7
Griffon (CCG)	Fairbanks Morse - 8-38D8-1/8	Diesel	4	8	5,332 bhp	2	13.0
H. Lee White	GM EMD - 20-645-E7B	Diesel	2	20	7,200 bhp	1 cpp	15.0
Herbert C. Jackson	MaK - 6M32E	Diesel	2	6	6,250 bhp	1 cpp	
Hollyhock (USCG)	Caterpillar - 3608TA	Diesel	2	6	3,100 bhp	1 cpp	
Hon. James L. Oberstar	Rolls-Royce Bergen - B32:40L6P	Diesel	2	6	8,160 shp	1 ccp	17.0
Indiana Harbor	GM EMD - 20-645-E7	Diesel	4	20	14,400 bhp	2 cpp	16.1
Invincible *	GM EMD - 16-645-E7B	Diesel	2	16	5,750 bhp	2	13.8
J. A. W. Iglehart	De Laval Steam Turbine Co.	Turbine	1	**	4,400 shp	1	15.0
J. S. St. John	GM EMD - 8-567	Diesel	1	8	850 bhp	1	
James R. Barker	Pielstick - 16PC2-2V-400	Diesel	2	16	16,000 bhp	2 cpp	15.5
Jana Desgagnés	B&W - 6L35MC	Diesel	1	6	5,030 bhp	1 cpp	14.4
Jane Ann IV *	Pielstick - 8PC2-2L-400	Diesel	2	8	8,000 bhp	2	15.8
Jiimaan **	Ruston Paxman Diesels Ltd. - 6RK215	Diesel	2	6	2,839 bhp	2 cpp	15.0
John B. Aird	MaK - 6M552AK	Diesel	2	6	9,460 bhp	1 cpp	13.8
John D. Leitch	B&W - 5-74VT2BF-160	Diesel	1	5	7,500 bhp	1 cpp	16.1
John G. Munson	MaK - 6M46C	Diesel	1	6	7,000 bhp	1 cpp	16.1
John J. Boland	GM EMD - 20-645-E7B	Diesel	2	20	7,200 bhp	1 cpp	15.0
Joseph H. Thompson Jr. *	Caterpillar	Diesel	2			1	
Joseph L. Block	GM EMD - 20-645-E7	Diesel	2	20	7,200 bhp	1 cpp	17.3
Joyce L. VanEnkevort *	Caterpillar - 3612	Diesel	2	12	10,200 bhp	2 cpp	
Kaministiqua	Sulzer - 4RLB76	Diesel	4	4	10,880 bhp	1cpp	15.5
Karen Andrie *	GM EMD - 8-710G7C	Diesel	2	8	4,000 bhp	2	19.0
Katmai Bay (USCG)	Fairbanks Morse - 10-38D8-1/8	Diesel	2	10	2,500 bhp	1	13.8
Kaye E. Barker	Rolls-Royce Bergen - B32:40L6P	Diesel	2	6	8,160 shp	1 ccp	17.0
Lake Express **	MTU 16V4000M70	Diesel	4	16	12,616 bhp	4 water jet	40.0
Laurentia Desgagnés	B&W - 6S60MC-C	Diesel	1	5	18,605 bhp	1 cpp	18.4
Lee A. Tregurtha	Rolls-Royce Bergen B32:40L6P	Diesel	2	6	8,160 shp	1 ccp	17.0
Leo A. McArthur *	MaK - 6M25	Diesel	2	6	5,384 bhp	2 cpp	12.1
Leonard M	Ruston P - 6RK270M	Diesel	2	6	2,097 bhp	2	13.8
Mackinaw (USCG)	Caterpillar - 3612	Diesel	3	12	9,119 bhp	2 Azipod	17.3
Manistee	GM EMD - 20-645-E6	Diesel	1	20	2,950 bhp	1	
Manitoba	Fairbanks Morse - 8-38D8-1/8	Diesel	4	8	5,332 bhp	1 cpp	16.1
Manitoulin	B&W - 5L50MC	Diesel	1	5	8,113 bhp	1 cpp	16.5
Manitowoc	Alco - 16V251E	Diesel	2	16	5,600 bhp	1	16.1
Maria Desgagnés	B&W - 6S42MC	Diesel	1	6	8,361 bhp	1 cpp	16.1
Martha L. Black (CCG)	GM EMD - 16V251F	Diesel	3	16	8,973 bhp	2	13.8
Mary E. Hannah *	GM EMD - 16-567C	Diesel	2	16	3,200 bhp	2	15.0
Mesabi Miner	Pielstick - 16PC2-2V-400	Diesel	2	16	16,000 bhp	2 cpp	15.5
Mia Desgagnés	Wärtsilä 5RT-flex 50DF	Diesel/LNG	1	5	7,305 bhp	1 cpp	15.0
Michigan *	GM EMD - 20-645-E6	Diesel	2	16	3,900 bhp	2	13.2
Michipicoten	MaK - 6M32C	Diesel	2	6	8,160 bhp	1 cpp	14.0
Mississagi	Caterpillar - 3612-TA	Diesel	1	12	4,500 bhp	1 cpp	13.8
Mobile Bay (USCG)	Fairbanks Morse - 10-38D8-1/8	Diesel	2	10	2,500 bhp	1	13.8
Morro Bay (USCG)	Fairbanks Morse - 10-38D8-1/8	Diesel	2	10	2,500 bhp	1	13.8

Vessel Name	Engine Manufacturer & Model #	Engine Type	Total Engines	Total Cylinders	Rated HP	Total Props	Speed MPH
Neah Bay (USCG)	Fairbanks Morse - 10-38D8-1/8	Diesel	2	10	2,500 bhp	1	13.8
Nordik Express	GM EMD - 20-645-E7	Diesel	2	20	7,200 bhp	2 ccp	16.0
Nunavik	MAN-B&W 7S70ME-C	Diesel	1	7	29,623 bhp	1 cpp	15.5
Oakglen	B&W - 6K67GF	Diesel	1	6	11,600 bhp	1	15.5
Ojibway	GE - 7FDM EFI	Diesel	1	16	4,100 bhp	1 cpp	
Olive L. Moore *	Alco - 16V251	Diesel	2	16	5,830 bhp	1	
Paul H. Townsend	Nordberg - TSM-216	Diesel	1	6	2,150 bhp	1	12.1
Paul R. Tregurtha	MaK - 6M43C	Diesel	2	6	17,120 bhp	2 cpp	15.5
Pearl Mist	Caterpillar - 3516C-DITA	Diesel	2	16	3,386 bhp	2	
Pelee Islander **	Caterpillar - 3408	Diesel	2	8	910 bhp	2	
Petite Forte *	Ruston - 8ATC	Diesel	2	8	4,200 bhp	2	15.5
Philip R. Clarke	Westinghouse Elec. Corp.	Turbine	1	**	7,700 shp	1	16.1
Pierre Radisson (CCG)	Alco - 16V251F	Diesel	6	16	17,700 bhp	2	18.4
Pineglen	MaK - 6M601AK	Diesel	1	6	8,158 bhp	1 cpp	15.5
Prentiss Brown *	GM EMD - 12-645-E2	Diesel	2	12	3,900 bhp	1	
Presque Isle *	Mirrlees Blackstone Ltd. - KVMR-16	Diesel	2	16	14,840 bhp	2 cpp	
Quinte Loyalist **	Caterpillar - 3196	Diesel	2	6	770 bhp		
Radcliffe R. Latimer	MaK - 8M32C	Diesel	2	8	10,442 bhp	1 cpp	
Rebecca Lynn *	GM EMD - 16-567-BC	Diesel	2	16	3,600 bhp	2	
Reliance *	A.B. Nohab - SVI 16VS-F	Diesel	2	16	5,600 bhp	1 cpp	17.6
Robert S. Pierson	Alco - 16V251E	Diesel	2	16	5,600 bhp	1	17.8
Roger Blough	Pielstick - 16PC2V-400	Diesel	2	16	14,200 bhp	1 cpp	16.7
Rosaire A. Desgagnés	MaK/Caterpillar - 6M43	Diesel	1	6	7,344 bhp	1 cpp	17.8
Rt. Hon. Paul J. Martin	MaK/Caterpillar - 6M32**C**	Diesel	2	6	8,060 bhp (est)	1 cpp	
Saginaw	MaK - 6M43C	Diesel	1	6	8,160 bhp	1 cpp	16.1
Salarium	Pielstick - 10PC2-2V-400	Diesel	2	10	10,700 bhp	1 cpp	13.8
Salvor *	GM EMD - 16-645-E7	Diesel	2	16	5,750 bhp	2	13.8
Sam Laud	GM EMD - 20-645-E7	Diesel	2	20	7,200 bhp	1 cpp	16.1
Samuel de Champlain *	GM EMD - 20-645-E5	Diesel	2	20	7,200 bhp	2 cpp	17.3
Samuel Risley (CCG)	Wartsila - VASA 12V22HF	Diesel	4	12	8,836 bhp	2 cpp	17.3
Sarah Desgagnés	MaK - 7M43	Diesel	1	7	9,517 bhp	1 cpp	15.0
Sea Eagle II *	GM EMD - 20-645-E7	Diesel	2	20	7,200 bhp	2	13.8
Sedna Desgagnés	MaK/Caterpillar - 6M43	Diesel	1	6	7,344 bhp	1 cpp	17.8
Sharon M 1 *	Niigata - 6L38HX	Diesel	2	6	1,934 bhp	2	16.0
Spruceglen	Sulzer - 4RLB76	Diesel	1	4	10,880 bhp	1 cpp	13.8
St. Clair	GM EMD - 20-645-E7	Diesel	3	20	10,800 bhp	1 cpp	16.7
Stephen B. Roman	Total	Diesel			5,996 bhp	1 cpp	18.4
(Center)	Fairbanks Morse - 10-38D8-1/8	Diesel	2	10	3,331 bhp		
(Wing)	Fairbanks Morse - 8-38D8-1/8	Diesel	2	8	2,665 bhp		
Sterling Energy	GUASCOR - F360TA-SP	Diesel	1	12	900 bhp	1	
Stewart J. Cort	GM EMD - 20-645-E7	Diesel	4	20	14,400 bhp	2 cpp	18.4
Sugar Islander II **	Caterpillar - 3412	Diesel	2	12	1,280 bhp		
Tecumseh	Pielstick - 12PC-2V-400	Diesel	2	12	12,000 bhp	1 cpp	16.1
Tim McKeil*	Niigata 6L38HX	Diesel	2	6	2,400 bhp	2	15.3
Tim S. Dool	MaK - 8M43C	Diesel	1	8	10,750 bhp	1 cpp	17.3
Tony MacKay *	Ruston - 12C-5VM	Diesel	1	12	2,800 bhp	1 cpp	15.0
Thunder Bay	MAN-B&W - 6S50ME-B9	Diesel	1	6	11,897 bhp	1	15.5
Umiak I	M.A.N.-B&W - 7S70ME-C	Diesel	1	7	29,598 bhp	1 cpp	16.5
Umiavut	Hanshin - 6LF58	Diesel	1	6	6,000 bhp	1 cpp	16.2
Undaunted *	Cummins K38-M	Diesel	2	12	2,000 bhp	2	
Vectis Castle	Yanmar D.E.C. - 6M32C	Diesel	1	6	4,021 bhp	1	15
Victory *	MaK - 6MU551AK	Diesel	2	6	7,880 bhp	2	16.1
Victory 1	Caterpillar 3516TA-B	Diesel	2	16	4,000 bhp	2	11.5
Walter J. McCarthy Jr.	GM EMD - 20-645-E7B	Diesel	4	20	14,400 bhp	2 cpp	16.1
Whitefish Bay	MAN-B&W - 6S50ME-B9	Diesel	1	6	11,897 bhp	1	15.5
Wilfred Sykes	Westinghouse Elec. Corp.	Turbine	1	**	7,700 shp	1	16.1
Wilf Seymour *	GM EMD - 16-645-E7	Diesel	2	16	5,750 bhp	2	13.8
Wolfe Islander III **	Caterpillar - 3412E	Diesel	4	12	2,284 bhp	2 x 2	13.8
Zélada Desgagnés	MaK/Caterpillar - 6M43	Diesel	1	6	7,344 bhp	1 cpp	17.8
Zeus *	Caterpillar - D399	Diesel	2	8	2,250 bhp	2	

SOO LOCKS BOAT TOURS

Sault Ste. Marie, Michigan

SOO LOCKS SIGHTSEEING CRUISES Ride with the freighters & experience this engineering marvel. Your narrator explains the history and operation of the Soo Locks & historical sights along the waterfront. Many departure times, no reservations necessary.

SOO LOCKS LUNCHEON & DINNER CRUISES Enjoy a relaxing cruise on the St. Mary's River, sightseeing in Sugar Island's North Channel & a tour through the Soo Locks. A delicious buffet style dinner is served aboard. Your narrator explains all the interesting sights along the waterfronts of Michigan & Canada. Reservations recommended.

SOO LOCKS LIGHTHOUSE CRUISES Journey through the Soo Locks & navigate into Whitefish Bay, exploring the lighthouses & navigational markers leading ships into the Locks from Lake Superior. Continental breakfast served. Reservations recommended.

800-432-6301
www.soolocks.com

515 & 1157 E. Portage Ave. Sault Ste. Marie, MI 49783

Saltwater Fleets

Saltie Floretegracht inbound on Saginaw Bay. *(Logan Vasicek)*

A

ABC MARITIME, NYON, SWITZERLAND *(abcmaritime.ch)*

Fleet Name / Vessel Name	Vessel IMO #	Vessel Type	Year Built	Engine Type	Cargo Cap. or Gross*	Overall Length	Vessel Breadth	Vessel Depth
Adfines Sea	9580962	TK	2011	D	19,118	530' 05"	75' 06"	40' 08"
(Osttank Norway '11-'12)								
Adfines Star	9580974	TK	2011	D	19,118	530' 05"	75' 06"	40' 08"
(Osttank Denmark '11-'11, Osttank Sweden '11-'11)								

ACE TANKERS CV, AMSTERDAM, NETHERLANDS *(ace-tankers.com)*

Fleet Name / Vessel Name	Vessel IMO #	Vessel Type	Year Built	Engine Type	Cargo Cap. or Gross*	Overall Length	Vessel Breadth	Vessel Depth
Chem Hydra	9486180	TK	2009	D	17,055	475' 01"	75' 06"	40' 08"
Chem Norma	9486192	TK	2009	D	17,055	475' 01"	75' 06"	40' 08"
Chem Polaris	9416044	TK	2008	D	19,859	481' 00"	77' 09"	42' 00"
*(Braken '08-'10, **Maemi** '10-'15)*								

ALLIANCE TANKERS, HAMILTON, BERMUDA *(alliance-tankers.com)*

Fleet Name / Vessel Name	Vessel IMO #	Vessel Type	Year Built	Engine Type	Cargo Cap. or Gross*	Overall Length	Vessel Breadth	Vessel Depth
Askholmen	9436381	TK	2009	D	16,850	472' 05"	74' 02"	42' 00"
*(**Hellespont Charger** '09-'14)*								
Brentholmen	9436393	TK	2010	D	16,850	472' 05"	74' 02"	42' 00"
*(**Hellespont Chieftan** '10-'14)*								
Furuholmen	9553397	TK	2010	D	16,500	473' 02"	75' 06"	40' 08"
Kirkeholmen	9553402	TK	2010	D	16,730	473' 02"	75' 06"	40' 08"
(CF Sophia '10-'12)								
Larsholmen	9436410	TK	2009	D	16,850	472' 05"	74' 02"	42' 00"
*(**Hellespont Centurion** '10-'14)*								
Lokholmen	9433303	TK	2010	D	16,850	472' 05"	74' 02"	42' 00"
*(**Hellespont Crusader** '10-'14)*								
Morholmen	9553414	TK	2011	D	16,500	472' 05"	75' 06"	40' 08"
*(**C.F. Max** '11-'11)*								

ALVTANK REDERI AB, DONSO, SWEDEN *(alvtank.se)*

Fleet Name / Vessel Name	Vessel IMO #	Vessel Type	Year Built	Engine Type	Cargo Cap. or Gross*	Overall Length	Vessel Breadth	Vessel Depth
Ramira	9362152	TK	2008	D	12,164	472' 07"	75' 07"	40' 08"

ARA GROUP, WERKENDAM, NETHERLANDS *(aragroup.nl)*

Fleet Name / Vessel Name	Vessel IMO #	Vessel Type	Year Built	Engine Type	Cargo Cap. or Gross*	Overall Length	Vessel Breadth	Vessel Depth
ARA Rotterdam	9240471	BC	2002	D	10,500	468' 02"	59' 10"	33' 04"
*(Sabrina '02-'02, MSC Rades '02-'04, Sabrina '04-'04, SCM Olympic '04-'05, **Sabrina** '05-'14)*								

ARMADOR GEMI ISLETMECILIGI TICARET LTD., ISTANBUL, TURKEY *(armadorshipping.com)*

Fleet Name / Vessel Name	Vessel IMO #	Vessel Type	Year Built	Engine Type	Cargo Cap. or Gross*	Overall Length	Vessel Breadth	Vessel Depth
Cornelia	9216597	BC	2001	D	16,807	574' 02"	75' 09"	44' 09"
(Pine '01-'04)								
Pochard S	9262534	BC	2003	D	37,384	655' 10"	77' 09"	50' 02"
*(**Pochard** '03-'14)*								

ARNE BLYSTAD AS, OSLO, NORWAY *(blystad.no)*
FOLLOWING VESSELS UNDER CHARTER TO SONGA SHIPMANAGEMENT

Fleet Name / Vessel Name	Vessel IMO #	Vessel Type	Year Built	Engine Type	Cargo Cap. or Gross*	Overall Length	Vessel Breadth	Vessel Depth
Songa Challenge	9409510	TK	2009	D	17,596	472' 05"	74' 02"	41' 00"
Songa Diamond	9460459	TK	2009	D	17,596	472' 05"	74' 02"	41' 00"
Songa Emerald	9473937	TK	2009	D	17,596	472' 05"	74' 02"	41' 00"
Songa Jade	9473925	TK	2009	D	17,596	472' 05"	74' 02"	41' 00"
Songa Opal	9473913	TK	2009	D	17,596	472' 05"	74' 02"	41' 00"
Songa Peace	9409522	TK	2009	D	17,596	472' 05"	74' 02"	41' 00"
(Global Peace '09-'13)								
Songa Sapphire	9444467	TK	2008	D	17,596	472' 05"	74' 02"	41' 00"
Songa Topaz	9460461	TK	2009	D	17,596	472' 05"	74' 02"	41' 00"

ATLANTSKA PLOVIDBA D.D., DUBROVNIK, REPUBLIC OF CROATIA *(atlant.hr)*

Fleet Name / Vessel Name	Vessel IMO #	Vessel Type	Year Built	Engine Type	Cargo Cap. or Gross*	Overall Length	Vessel Breadth	Vessel Depth
Orsula	9110901	BC	1996	D	34,372	656' 02"	77' 01"	48' 10"
*(**Federal Calumet** {2} '96-'97)*								

B

BD-SHIPSNAVO GMBH & CO., HAREN-EMS, GERMANY *(shipsnavo.de)*

Fleet Name / Vessel Name	Vessel IMO #	Vessel Type	Year Built	Engine Type	Cargo Cap. or Gross*	Overall Length	Vessel Breadth	Vessel Depth
Active	9343821	BC	2008	D	12,523	378' 03"	64' 04"	37' 05"
(Antilles VII '08-'14)								

Fleet Name / Vessel Name	Vessel IMO #	Vessel Type	Year Built	Engine Type	Cargo Cap. or Gross*	Overall Length	Vessel Breadth	Vessel Depth
BERNHARD SCHULTE GROUP OF COMPANIES, HAMBURG, GERMANY *(schultegroup.com)*								
Edzard Schulte	9439852	TK	2011	D	16,658	476' 02"	75' 06"	41' 00"
Elisabeth Schulte	9439840	TK	2010	D	16,658	476' 02"	75' 06"	41' 00"
Elisalex Schulte	9439876	TK	2011	D	16,658	476' 02"	76' 05"	41' 00"
Eva Schulte	9439826	TK	2010	D	16,658	476' 02"	75' 06"	41' 00"
Everhard Schulte	9439838	TK	2010	D	16,658	476' 02"	75' 06"	41' 00"
BESIKTAS LIKID TASIMACILIK DENIZCILIK TICARET, ISTANBUL, TURKEY *(besiktasgroup.com)*								
Mainland	9431056	TK	2008	D	7,724	402' 05"	56' 05"	28' 10"
Purple Gem	9403827	TK	2009	D	6,824	390' 09"	55' 05"	27' 07"
BIGLIFT SHIPPING BV, AMSTERDAM, NETHERLANDS *(bigliftshipping.com)*								
Happy Ranger	9139311	HL	1998	D	15,593	452' 09".	74' 10"	42' 06"
Happy River	9139294	HL	1997	D	15,593	452' 09"	74' 10"	42' 06"
Happy Rover	9139309	HL	1997	D	15,593	452' 09"	74' 10"	42' 06"
Tracer	9204702	HL	2000	D	8,874	329' 09"	73' 06"	26' 11"
Transporter	9204714	HL	1999	D	8,469	329' 09"	80' 01"	36' 05"
BRIESE SCHIFFAHRTS GMBH & CO. KG, LEER, GERMANY *(briese.de)*								
BBC Austria	9433327	GC	2009	D	7,530	393' 00"	66' 03"	32' 02"
BBC Balboa	9501667	GC	2012	D	8,129	423' 01"	54' 02"	32' 10"
BBC Elbe	9347059	GC	2006	D	17,348	469' 07"	75' 11"	42' 08"
(*Horumersiel '06-'06*)								
BBC Europe	9266308	GC	2003	D	7,409	391' 09"	66' 03"	32' 02"
BBC Fuji	9508419	GC	2011	D	9,310	412' 09"	72' 02"	35' 05"
BBC Hudson	9435868	GC	2009	D	17,349	469' 07"	75' 11"	43' 08"
BBC Jade	9421116	BC	2007	D	12,000	469' 00"	62' 00"	35' 11"
BBC Kibo	9508421	GC	2011	D	9,310	412' 09"	72' 02"	35' 05"
BBC Kwiatkowski	9436953	GC	2008	D	7,733	401' 09"	59' 09"	31' 02"
(*Eugeniusz Kwiatkowski '08-'08*)								
BBC Mont Blanc	9508433	GC	2011	D	9,310	412' 09"	72' 02"	35' 05"
BBC Olympus	9508457	GC	2012	D	9,310	412' 09"	72' 02"	35' 05"
BBC Rushmore	9508469	GC	2012	D	9,310	412' 09"	72' 02"	35' 05"
BBC Sweden	9278600	GC	2003	D	4,325	324' 06"	45' 03"	24' 03"
BBC Switzerland	9433315	GC	2008	D	7,530	393' 00"	66' 03"	32' 02"
BBC Xingang	9508483	GC	2013	D	9,310	412' 09"	72' 02"	35' 05"
Kurt Paul	9435856	GC	2009	D	17,300	469' 07"	74' 10"	43' 08"
Peter Ronna	9198628	BC	2002	D	4,303	324' 03"	49' 10"	24' 03"
(*Peter Ronna '02-'03, Svend '03-'05*)								
Sjard	9303314	GC	2007	D	17,348	469' 07"	75' 11"	42' 08"
BROSTROM AB, COPENHAGEN, DENMARK *(brostrom.com)*								
Bro Agnes	9348302	TK	2008	D	16,796	472' 07"	75' 07"	40' 09"

C

Fleet Name / Vessel Name	Vessel IMO #	Vessel Type	Year Built	Engine Type	Cargo Cap. or Gross*	Overall Length	Vessel Breadth	Vessel Depth
CANADA FEEDER LINES BV, GRONINGEN, NETHERLANDS *(cfl.nl)*								
Industrial More	9534482	GC	2013	D	10,049	381' 05"	58' 05"	34' 05"

A Note About Saltwater Listings

Observers will likely spot saltwater vessels that are not included in this book. These may be newcomers to the Great Lakes/Seaway system, recent renames or new construction. This is not meant to be an exhaustive listing of every saltwater vessel that could potentially visit the Great Lakes and St. Lawrence Seaway. To attempt to do so, given the sheer number of world merchant ships, would be space and cost prohibitive.

This list reflects vessels whose primary trade routes are on saltwater but which also regularly visit Great Lakes and St. Lawrence Seaway ports above Montreal. Fleets listed may operate other vessels worldwide than those included herein; additional vessels may be found on fleet websites, which have been included where available. **Former names listed in boldface type indicate the vessel visited the Seaway system under that name.**

CANADIAN FOREST NAVIGATION CO. LTD., MONTREAL, QUEBEC, CANADA *(canfornav.com)*

At press time, Canadian Forest Navigation Co. Ltd. had the following vessels under long or short-term charter. Please consult their respective fleets for details: **Andean, Barnacle, Blacky, Bluebill, Bluewing, Brant, Cape, Chestnut, Cinnamon, Eider, Gadwall, Garganey, Greenwing, Labrador, Maccoa, Mandarin, Mottler, Puffin, Redhead, Ruddy, Shoveler, Sunda, Torrent, Tufty, Tundra, Whistler, Wigeon.**

CARISBROOKE SHIPPING LTD., COWES, UNITED KINGDOM *(carisbrookeshipping.co)*

Vessel Name	IMO #	Type	Built	Eng	Cargo	Length	Breadth	Depth
Charlotte C	9528706	BC	2009	D	13,517	447' 06"	69' 07"	37' 01"
Greta C	9528720	BC	2009	D	13,517	447' 06"	69' 07"	37' 01"
Heleen C	9331490	BC	2006	D	13,517	447' 06"	69' 07"	37' 01"
Jasmine C	9463542	BC	2010	D	12,948	453' 01"	68' 11"	36' 01"
Johanna C	9430131	BC	2009	D	12,948	453' 01"	68' 11"	36' 01"
Michelle C	9452218	BC	2010	D	12,948	453' 01"	68' 11"	36' 01"

(Michelle-C '10-'10, Nirint Pioneer '10-'11)

Nomadic Hjellestad	9452220	BC	2010	D	12,948	453' 01"	68' 11"	36' 01"

CANDLER SCHIFFAHRT GMBH, BREMEN, GERMANY *(candler-schiffahrt.de)*

Pioneer	9488633	BC	2008	D	8,091	381' 04"	59' 01"	34' 01"

(FCC Pioneer '08-'08, BBC Tasmania '08-'10, Thorco Bronco '10-'15)

CHEMFLEET SHIPPING LTD., ISTANBUL, TURKEY *(chemfleet.org)*

Mehmet A	9418822	TK	2011	D	20,000	530' 04"	73' 06"	34' 01"

(Aldemar '11-'11)

CHEMIKALIEN SEETRANSPORT GMBH, HAMBURG, GERMANY *(cst-hamburg.de)*

Chemtrans Elbe	9439345	TK	2008	D	13,073	421' 11"	66' 11"	37' 09"
Chemtrans Havel	9439333	TK	2009	D	13,073	421' 11"	66' 11"	37' 09"

CLIPPER CRUISES LIMITED, NASSAU, BAHAMAS
OPERATED BY VICTORY CRUISE LINES, MIAMI, FL *(victorycruiselines.com)*

Victory I	9213129	PA	2001	D	4,954*	298' 07"	49' 10"	20' 00"

Built: Atlantic Marine Inc., Jacksonville, FL (**Cape May Light** '01-'09, Sea Voyager '09 -'14, **Saint Laurent** '14 -'16)

Heavy-lift vessel Happy Ranger is from the Netherlands. *(Jeff Cameron)*

Fleet Name / Vessel Name	Vessel IMO #	Vessel Type	Year Built	Engine Type	Cargo Cap. or Gross*	Overall Length	Vessel Breadth	Vessel Depth
COASTAL SHIPPING LTD., GOOSE BAY, NEWFOUNDLAND, CANADA (woodwards.nf.ca)								
Alsterstern	9053220	TK	1994	D	17,078	528' 03"	75' 06"	38' 05"
Havelstern	9053218	TK	1994	D	17,078	528' 03"	75' 06"	38' 05"
C.O.E. SHIPPING GMBH & CO., BUXTEHUDE, GERMANY (coeshipping.com)								
COE Leni	9453793	HL	2010	D	12,767	454' 05"	68' 11"	36' 01"
*(Marselisborg '10-'12, Clipper Anne '12-'14, **Marselisborg** '14-'16)*								
COLUMBIA SHIPMANAGEMENT, HAMBURG, GERMANY (csm-d.com)								
Cape Egmont	9262819	TK	2003	D	12,950	417' 04"	67' 00"	37' 09"
Rio Dauphin	9449417	TK	2009	D	12,835	399' 07"	67' 00"	39' 00"
(Ida Theresa '09-'13)								
COSCO SOUTHERN ASPHALT SHIPPING CO. LTD, GUANGZHOU, CHINA (www.coscogz.com.cn/en)								
Zhuang Yuan Ao	9650339	TK	2012	D	12,000	479' 00"	72' 02"	35' 05"

D-E

DANSER VAN GENT, DELFZIJL, NETHERLANDS (danservangent.nl)								
FOLLOWING VESSELS UNDER CHARTER TO WAGENBORG SHIPPING								
Marietje Deborah	9481594	GC	2011	D	8,200	413' 10"	50' 06"	30' 02"
Marietje Marsilla	9458248	GC	2010	D	8,200	413' 10"	50' 06"	30' 02"
DUZGIT GEMI INSA SANAYI, ISTANBUL, TURKEY (duzgit.com)								
Duzgit Dignity	9581019	TK	2014	D	8,488	390' 09"	56' 05"	30' 02"
Duzgit Endeavour	9581007	TK	2013	D	16,004	509' 09"	71' 02"	36' 05"
EASTERN PACIFIC SHIPPING, SINGAPORE								
Ebony Ray	9363857	TK	2008	D	19,998	477' 05"	77' 09"	43' 10"
(Millennium Park '08-'14)								
ELBE SHIPPING GMBH, DROCHTERSEN, GERMANY (reederei-elbe-shipping.de)								
BBC Alberta	9468102	HL	2010	D	12,744	452' 11"	68' 11"	36' 01"
*(Beluga Maturity '10-'10, Beluga Firmament '10-'11, **BBC Celina** '11-'15)*								

Federal Alster, chartered to the Fednav fleet. (Alain Gindroz)

Fleet Name Vessel Name	Vessel IMO #	Vessel Type	Year Built	Engine Type	Cargo Cap. or Gross*	Overall Length	Vessel Breadth	Vessel Depth
BBC Rhine	9368338	HL	2008	D	12,782	468'06"	70'06"	43'08"
(Beluga Gratification '08-'08)								
BBC Steinhoeft	9358046	HL	2006	D	12,744	452'11"	68'11"	36'01"
(Beluga Fusion '06-'11)								
BBC Steinwall	9358058	HL	2007	D	12,744	452'11"	68'11"	36'01"
(Beluga Function '07-'11)								
BBC Thames	9368340	HL	2008	D	17,110	469'02"	70'06"	43'08"
(Beluga Graduation '08-'09)								

EMPIRE CHEMICAL TANKER HOLDINGS INC., PIRAEUS, GREECE *(empiretankers.com)*

Malmo	9373242	TK	2008	D	19,992	491'11"	76'01"	42'10"

ENZIAN SHIP MANAGEMENT, ZÜRICH, SWITZERLAND *(www.enzian-shipping.com)*

SCL Bern	9304461	GC	2005	D	12,680	459'03"	70'06"	38'03"

F-G

FAIRFIELD CHEMICAL CARRIERS, WILTON, CONNECTICUT, USA *(fairfieldchemical.com)*

Fairchem Charger	9367401	TK	2009	D	19,998	477'04"	77'10"	43'10"
Fairchem Colt	9304344	TK	2005	D	19,998	477'04"	77'10"	43'10"
Fairchem Steed	9311256	TK	2005	D	19,998	477'04"	77'10"	43'10"
Fairchem Yuka	9477505	TK	2010	D	19,998	477'04"	77'10"	43'10"

Fleet Name Vessel Name	Vessel IMO #	Vessel Type	Year Built	Engine Type	Cargo Cap. or Gross*	Overall Length	Vessel Breadth	Vessel Depth
FEDNAV LTD., MONTREAL, QUEBEC, CANADA *(fednav.com)*								
CANARCTIC SHIPPING CO. LTD. – DIVISION OF FEDNAV LTD.								
Arctic	7517507	GC	1978	D	26,440	692'04"	75'05"	49'05"
Built: Port Weller Dry Docks, Port Weller, ON								
Nunavik	9673850	GC	2013	D	24,997	619'05"	87'03"	51'06"
Umiak I	9334715	BC	2006	D	31,992	619'04"	87'02"	51'50"
FEDNAV INTERNATIONAL LTD. - DIVISION OF FEDNAV LTD.								
Federal Asahi {2}	9200419	BC	2000	D	36,563	656'02"	77'11"	48'09"
Federal Baltic	9697806	BC	2015	D	34,564	656'01"	77'11"	48'09"
Federal Barents	9697820	BC	2015	D	34,564	656'01"	77'11"	48'09"
Federal Beaufort	9697818	BC	2015	D	34,564	656'01"	77'11"	48'09"
Federal Bering	9697832	BC	2015	D	34,564	656'01"	77'11"	48'09"
Federal Biscay	9697856	BC	2015	D	34,564	656'01"	77'11"	48'09"
Federal Bristol	9697844	BC	2015	D	34,564	656'01"	77'11"	48'09"
Federal Caribou	9671096	BC	2016	D	34,500	656'01"	77'11"	48'09"
Federal Cedar	9671101	BC	2016	D	34,500	656'01"	77'11"	48'09"
Federal Champlain	9671058	BC	2016	D	34,500	656'01"	77'11"	48'09"
Federal Churchill	9671060	BC	2016	D	34,500	656'01"	77'11"	48'09"
Federal Clyde	9671072	BC	2016	D	34,500	656'01"	77'11"	48'09"
Federal Columbia	9671084	BC	2016	D	34,500	656'01"	77'11"	48'09"
Federal Danube	9271511	BC	2003	D	37,372	652'11"	78'05"	50'02"
Federal Elbe	9230000	BC	2003	D	37,372	652'11"	78'05"	50'02"

Netherlands-flagged Beauforce on Lake Ontario. (Jeff Cameron)

Fleet Name Vessel Name	Vessel IMO #	Vessel Type	Year Built	Engine Type	Cargo Cap. or Gross*	Overall Length	Vessel Breadth	Vessel Depth
Federal Ems	9229984	BC	2002	D	37,372	652' 11"	78' 05"	50' 02"
Federal Hudson {3}	9205902	BC	2000	D	36,563	656' 02"	77' 11"	48' 09"
Federal Hunter {2}	9205938	BC	2001	D	36,563	656' 02"	77' 11"	48' 09"
Federal Kivalina	9205885	BC	2000	D	36,563	656' 02"	77' 11"	48' 09"
Federal Kumano	9244257	BC	2001	D	32,787	624' 08"	77' 05"	49' 10"
Federal Kushiro	9284702	BC	2003	D	32,787	624' 08"	77' 05"	49' 10"
Federal Leda	9229996	BC	2003	D	37,372	652' 11"	78' 05"	50' 02"
Federal Maas {2}	9118135	BC	1997	D	34,372	656' 02"	77' 01"	48' 10"
Federal Mackinac	9299460	BC	2004	D	27,000	606' 11"	77' 09"	46' 25"
Federal Margaree	9299472	BC	2005	D	27,000	606' 11"	77' 09"	46' 25"
Federal Mayumi	9529578	BC	2012	D	35,300	655' 06"	78' 09"	48' 09"
Federal Nakagawa	9278791	BC	2005	D	36,563	656' 02"	77' 11"	48' 09"
Federal Oshima	9200330	BC	1999	D	36,563	656' 02"	77' 11"	48' 09"
Federal Rhine {2}	9110925	BC	1997	D	34,372	656' 02"	77' 01"	48' 10"
Federal Rideau	9200445	BC	2000	D	36,563	656' 02"	77' 11"	48' 09"
Federal Saguenay {2}	9110913	BC	1996	D	34,372	656' 02"	77' 01"	48' 10"
Federal Satsuki	9529578	BC	2012	D	35,300	655' 06"	78' 09"	48' 09"
Federal Schelde {3}	9118147	BC	1997	D	34,372	656' 02"	77' 01"	48' 10"
Federal Seto	9267209	BC	2004	D	36,563	656' 02"	77' 11"	48' 09"
Federal Shimanto	9218404	BC	2001	D	32,787	624' 08"	77' 05"	49' 10"
Federal Welland	9205926	BC	2000	D	36,563	656' 02"	77' 11"	48' 09"
Federal Weser	9229972	BC	2002	D	37,372	652' 11"	78' 05"	50' 02"
Federal Yoshino	9218416	BC	2001	D	32,787	624' 08"	77' 05"	49' 10"
Federal Yukon	9205897	BC	2000	D	36,563	656' 02"	77' 11"	48' 09"

At press time, FedNav Ltd. also had the following vessels under charter. Please consult their respective fleets for details: **Federal Alster, Federal Katsura, Federal Sakura, Federal Yukina**

FINBETA, SAVONA, ITALY *(finbeta.com)*

Sapphire	9114969	TK	1997	D	14,015	467' 06"	72' 02"	36' 01"

FORESTWAVE NAVIGATION, HEERENVEEN, NETHERLANDS *(forestwave.nl)*

FWN Bonafide	9321108	BC	2006	D	10,683	477' 09"	59' 10"	33' 10"
(UAL Antwerp '06-'12, UAL Nigeria '12-'15, Anna C '15-'15)								

FREESE SHIPPING, STADE, GERMANY *(freeseship.com)*

BBC Kansas	9349291	HL	2006	D	12,711	453' 00"	68' 11"	36' 01"
*(Beluga Foundation '06-'11, **Opal Gallant** '11-'11, Freya Scan '11-'13, Thorco Denmark '13-'15, **Amber** '15-'16)*								
BBC Rio Grande	9368326	HL	2008	D	17,294	468' 06"	70' 05"	43' 08"
*(Beluga Gravitation '08-'08, **BBC Rio Grande** '08-'11, Gabrielle Scan '11-'12, **Clipper Macau** '12-'16)*								
Lisanna	9283954	HL	2004	D	12,700	453' 00"	68' 11"	36' 01"
*(Beluga Efficiency '04-'06, BBC Carolina '06-'07, **Beluga Efficiency** '07-'11, Lilia '11-'11, Freese Scan '11-'12 BBC Washington '12-'15)*								
Pacific Huron	9546796	BC	2010	D	30,000	623' 04"	77' 11"	47' 11"
(Seven Islands '10-'10)								
Three Rivers	9546784	BC	2010	D	30,000	623' 04"	77' 11"	47' 11"

H

HAMMONIA REEDEREI GMBH & CO., HAMBURG, GERMANY *(www.hammonia-reederei.de)*

HR Constitution	9273791	GC	2006	D	12,477	514' 04"	70' 06"	30' 06"
*(**Beluga Constitution** '06-'11)*								
HR Maria	9164017	GC	1998	D	17,539	465' 10"	70' 06"	43' 08"
*(**Maria Green** '98-'04, **BBC India** '04-'08, **Maria Green** '08-'10, SE Viridian '08-'12)*								
Industrial Royal	9267754	GC	2005	D	10,536	441' 04"	70' 06"	30' 06"
*(Beluga Resolution '05-'11, **HR Resolution** '11-'15)*								

HANSA HEAVY LIFT GMBH, BREMEN, GERMANY *(hansaheavylift.com)*

HHL Amur	9435753	HL	2007	D	12,744	452' 11"	68' 11"	36' 01"
*(**Beluga Fidelity** '07-'11)*								
HHL Congo	9467005	HL	2011	D	12,700	453' 00"	68' 11"	36' 01"
(Beluga Fealty '11-'11)								

Fleet Name Vessel Name	Vessel IMO #	Vessel Type	Year Built	Engine Type	Cargo Cap. or Gross*	Overall Length	Vessel Breadth	Vessel Depth
HHL Elbe	9433262	HL	2008	D	12,840	454' 05"	68' 11"	36' 01"
(BBC Alaska '08-'13, Elbe '13-'14)								
HHL Mississippi	9435765	HL	2009	D	12,744	452' 11"	68' 11"	36' 01"
(Beluga Fantasy '09-'11, OXL Fantasy '11-'11)								
HHL Rhine	9467017	HL	2011	D	12,837	453' 00"	68' 11"	36' 01"
(Beluga Feasibility '11-'11)								
HHL Tyne	9433274	HL	2009	D	12,782	454' 05"	68' 11"	36' 01"
(BBC Montana '09-'13, Tyne '13-'14)								
HHL Volga	9381392	HL	2007	D	12,744	452' 11"	68' 11"	36' 01"
*(**Beluga Fidelity** '07-'11)*								

HARREN & PARTNER SCHIFFAHRTS GMBH, BREMEN, GERMANY *(harren-partner.de)*

Patras	9348297	TK	2007	D	16,979	472' 07"	75' 06"	40' 08"
(Gan-Sword '07-'10)								
FOLLOWING VESSELS UNDER CHARTER TO COMBI LIFT								
Palabora	9501875	HL	2010	D	10,052	436' 04"	75' 06"	37' 05"
Palau	9501899	HL	2010	D	10,052	436' 04"	75' 06"	37' 05"
Palmerton	9501863	HL	2009	D	10,052	436' 04"	75' 06"	37' 05"
Panagia	9305295	HL	2004	D	7,837	393' 00"	66' 03"	32' 02"
Pantanal	9316579	HL	2004	D	7,837	393' 00"	66' 03"	32' 02"
FOLLOWING VESSELS UNDER CHARTER TO CANADIAN FOREST NAVIGATION LTD.								
Puffin	9262522	BC	2003	D	37,384	655' 10"	77' 09"	50' 02"

HARTMAN SEATRADE, URK, NETHERLANDS *(hartmanseatrade.com)*

Deo Volente	9391658	BC	2006	D	3,750	343' 10"	52' 06"	24' 03"
Pacific Dawn	9558464	BC	2010	D	3,750	343' 10"	52' 06"	24' 03"

HERMANN BUSS GMBH, LEER, GERMANY *(gbshipping.de)*

BBC Carolina	9402043	HL	2007	D	12,744	452' 11"	68' 11"	36' 01"
(Beluga Fantastic '07-'11)								
BBC Manitoba	9384320	HL	2007	D	12,837	453' 00"	68' 11"	36' 01"
*(**Beluga Formation** '07-'12, Formation '12-'14, Thorco Diamond '14-'15)*								
BBC Quebec	9402031	HL	2007	D	12,700	453' 00"	68' 11"	36' 01"
(Beluga Fiction '07-'11, Fiction '11-'11)								

HERNING SHIPPING AS, HERNING, DENMARK *(herning-shipping.com)*

Charlotte Theresa	9400708	TK	2008	D	11,383	424' 10"	63' 00"	36' 01"
Jette Theresa	9406582	TK	2009	D	11,383	424' 10"	63' 00"	36' 01"
Tina Theresa	9478298	TK	2009	D	7,902	332' 08"	62' 06"	34' 05"

HS SCHIFFAHRTS GMBH & CO, HAREN-EMS, GERMANY *(hs-schiffahrt.de)*

BBC Haren	9511636	GC	2010	D	11,121	477' 09"	59' 10"	33' 10"
(Beluga Loyalty '10-'12, BBC Haren '12-'15, Haren '15-'15)								
Onego Rotterdam	9631345	GC	2013	D	8,096	387' 07"	52' 02"	28' 10"

HUARONG HUIYIN LTD., HONG KONG, CHINA

Chemical Aquarius	9576820	TK	2012	D	18,044	467' 06"	75' 06"	41' 04"

I-J-K

INTERMARINE, HOUSTON, TEXAS, USA *(intermarineusa.com)*

Industrial Charger	9213959	GC	2000	D	8,040	393' 01"	65' 07"	37' 01"
(Virgo J '00-'00, Industrial Charger '00-'09, Ocean Charger '09-'15)								
Industrial Chief	9213947	GC	2000	D	8,040	393' 01"	65' 07"	37' 01"
(Industrial Chief '00-'05, Ocean Titan '05-'14)								
Industrial Eagle	9407574	GC	2008	D	10,340	456' 00"	65' 07"	27' 03"
Ocean Crescent	9258193	GC	2002	D	8,097	393' 01"	65' 07"	37' 01"
(Pollux J. '02-'02, Industrial Crescent '02-'10)								

INTERSHIP NAVIGATION CO. LTD., LIMASSOL, CYPRUS *(intership-cyprus.com)*

Atlantic Patriot	9223904	BC	2003	D	17,471	469' 08"	74' 10"	43' 08"
*(Atlantic Progress '03-'03, **BBC Russia** '03-'08, **Federal Patriot** '08-'10, Hal Patriot '10-'13)*								
FOLLOWING VESSELS UNDER CHARTER TO FEDNAV LTD.								
Federal Alster	9766164	BC	2016	D	22,947	655' 05"	77' 11"	50' 03"

Fleet Name Vessel Name	Vessel IMO #	Vessel Type	Year Built	Engine Type	Cargo Cap. or Gross*	Overall Length	Vessel Breadth	Vessel Depth
Federal Katsura	9293923	BC	2005	D	32,787	624' 08"	77' 05"	49' 10"
Federal Sakura	9288291	BC	2005	D	32,787	624' 08"	77' 05"	49' 10"

INTREPID SHIPPING LLC., STAMFORD, CONNECTICUT, USA *(intrepidshipping.com)*

Intrepid Canada	9466740	TK	2011	D	16,427	476' 02"	75' 06"	41' 00"
Intrepid Republic	9466752	TK	2011	D	16,427	476' 02"	75' 06"	41' 00"

JO TANKERS BV, SPIJKENISSE, NETHERLANDS

Jo Spirit	9140841	TK	1998	D	6,248	352' 02"	52' 02"	30' 02"

JOHANN M. K. BLUMENTHAL GMBH & CO., HAMBURG, GERMANY *(bluships.com)*

Ida	9109536	BC	1995	D	18,796	486' 03"	74' 10"	40' 00"
Lita	9117416	BC	1995	D	18,796	486' 03"	74' 10"	40' 00"

JOHS THODE GMBH & CO., HAMBURG, GERMANY *(johs-thode.de)*

Hanse Gate	9283540	BC	2004	D	27,780	606' 11"	77' 09"	46' 03"
*(**Federal Matane** '04-'11, **CL Hanse Gate** '11-'15)*								

JUMBO SHIPPING CO. SA, ROTTERDAM, NETHERLANDS *(jumbomaritime.nl)*

Fairlane	9153654	HL	2000	D	7,123	362' 06"	67' 03"	44' 03"
Fairlift	8806905	HL	1990	D	7,780	330' 08"	68' 10"	43' 08"
Jumbo Vision	9153642	HL	2000	D	7,123	362' 06"	67' 03"	44' 03"
Stellaprima	8912326	HL	1991	D	7,780	330' 08"	68' 10"	43' 08"

JUNGERHANS MARITIME SERVICES GMBH & CO., HAREN EMS, GERMANY *(juengerhans.de)*

BBC Kimberley	9407586	HL	2009	D	10,340	456' 00"	65' 07"	37' 01"
*(**Bellatrix J** '09-'09, **Industrial Egret** '09-'12)*								
BBC Lena	9147693	HL	1998	D	9,928	497' 05"	66' 11"	34' 05"
*(**Lena** '98-'15, **Lena J** '15-'15)*								

KALLIANIS BROS SHIPPING, ATHENS, GREECE *(kallianisbros.gr)*

Dimitrios K	9216602	BC	2001	D	24,765	574' 02"	75' 09"	44' 09"
*(**Cedar** '01-'03, **Atlantic Castle** '03-'07, **Ladytramp** '07-'13)*								

KNUTSEN O.A.S. SHIPPING AS, HAUGESUND, NORWAY *(knutsenoas.com)*

Kristin Knutsen	9141405	TK	1998	D	19,152	477' 05"	75' 06"	42' 06"

Federal Biscay at Oshawa, Ont., assisted by Omni Richelieu. (Brian Way)

L-M

LAURANNE SHIPPING BV, GHENT, NETHERLANDS *(lauranne-shipping.com)*

LS Evanne	9519614	TK	2010	D	7,003	390' 09"	55' 05"	27' 07"
(Kormel '10-'12)								

LUBECA MARINE GERMANY GMBH & CO., LUBECK, GERMANY *(lubeca-marine.de)*

Gotland	9480136	BC	2011	D	17,409	471' 11"	74' 10"	43' 10"
(Rickmers Tianjin '11-'15)								

MASSOEL LTD., GENEVA, SWITZERLAND *(massoel.com)*

Lugano	9244087	BC	2002	D	20,035	509' 00"	77' 09"	42' 08"
(DS Regent '02-'06)								
Martigny	9229867	BC	2002	D	20,035	509' 00"	77' 09"	42' 08"
(VOC Regal '02-'03, Clipper Regal '03-'06)								

MASTERMIND SHIPMANAGEMENT LTD., LIMASSOL, CYPRUS *(mastermind-cyprus.com)*

MSM Douro	9519028	BC	2012	D	6,500	357' 08"	49' 10"	25' 11"
(Dourodiep '12-'12)								
Onego Bora	9613604	BC	2011	D	7,658	383' 10"	64' 08"	27' 11"

MED MARITIME LTD., LONDON, ENGLAND

Med Arctic	9410545	TK	2009	D	8,239	403' 10"	56' 05"	30' 02"
(Nordic Harmony '09-'09, Med Arctic '09-'15, Sea Dolphin '15-'15)								

MINERALIEN SCHIFFAHRT, SCHNAITTENBACH, GERMANY *(minship.com)*

Lady Doris	9459955	BC	2011	D	30,930	606' 11"	77' 09"	47' 11"
(Merganser '11-'11)								
Trudy	9415246	BC	2009	D	30,930	606' 11"	77' 09"	47' 11"
(Cresty '09-'09)								
Yulia	9459967	BC	2011	D	30,930	606' 11"	77' 09"	47' 11"
(Harlequin '11-'11)								

MTM SHIP MANAGEMENT LTD., SINGAPORE *(mtmshipmanagement.com)*

MTM Southport	9416032	TK	2008	D	20,216	481' 00"	77' 09"	42' 08"
(Golten '08-'10)								

Bluebill unloads at Duluth, with Great Lakes Towing tugs in the foreground. *(Ben McClain)*

N-O

NAVARONE SA MARINE ENTERPRISES, LIMASSOL, CYPRUS
FOLLOWING VESSELS UNDER CHARTER TO CANADIAN FOREST NAVIGATION LTD.

Fleet Name / Vessel Name	Vessel IMO #	Vessel Type	Year Built	Engine Type	Cargo Cap. or Gross*	Overall Length	Vessel Breadth	Vessel Depth
Andean	9413925	BC	2009	D	30,930	606'11"	77'09"	47'11"
Barnacle	9409742	BC	2009	D	30,807	606'11"	77'09"	47'11"
Blacky	9393149	BC	2008	D	30,801	607'04"	77'09"	47'11"
Bluebill	9263306	BC	2004	D	37,200	632'10"	77'09"	50'10"
Brant	9393151	BC	2008	D	30,807	606'11"	77'09"	47'11"
Chestnut	9477866	BC	2009	D	30,807	606'11"	77'09"	47'11"
Labrador	9415222	BC	2010	D	30,899	606'11"	77'09"	47'11"
Maccoa	9413913	BC	2009	D	30,930	606'11"	77'09"	47'11"
Mottler	9477828	BC	2009	D	30,807	606'11"	77'09"	47'11"
Ruddy	9459981	BC	2009	D	30,930	606'11"	77'09"	47'11"
Shoveler	9459979	BC	2009	D	30,930	606'11"	77'09"	47'11"
Torrent	9415210	BC	2010	D	30,930	606'11"	77'09"	47'11"
Tufty	9393163	BC	2009	D	30,807	606'11"	77'09"	47'11"
Tundra	9415208	BC	2009	D	30,930	606'11"	77'09"	47'11"

NAVIGATION MARITIME BULGARE LTD., VARNA, BULGARIA *(navbul.com)*

Fleet Name / Vessel Name	Vessel IMO #	Vessel Type	Year Built	Engine Type	Cargo Cap. or Gross*	Overall Length	Vessel Breadth	Vessel Depth
Belasitza	9498262	BC	2011	D	30,688	610'03"	77'09"	48'01"
Bogdan	9132492	BC	1997	D	13,960	466'04"	72'10"	36'07"
Kom	9132480	BC	1997	D	13,960	466'04"	72'10"	36'07"
Ludogorets	9415155	BC	2010	D	29,635	622'04"	77'05"	47'11"
(Fritz '10-'15, MarBacan '15-'16)								
Lyulin	9498248	BC	2011	D	30,688	610'03"	77'09"	48'01"
Oborishte	9415167	BC	2010	D	29,635	622'04"	77'05"	47'11"
(Luebbert '10-'15, MarBioko '15-'16)								
Osogovo	9498250	BC	2010	D	30,688	610'03"	77'11"	47'11"
Perelik	9132507	BC	1998	D	13,960	466'04"	72'10"	36'07"
Rodopi	9498274	BC	2012	D	30,688	610'03"	77'09"	48'01"
Strandja	9564140	BC	2010	D	30,688	610'03"	77'11"	47'11"
(Eastwind York '10-'10, Federal Yangtze '10-'10)								
Vitosha	9564138	BC	2010	D	30,688	610'03"	77'11"	47'11"
(Eastwind Yates '10-'10, Federal Pearl '10-'10)								

NGM ENERGY S.A., PIRAEUS, GREECE

Fleet Name / Vessel Name	Vessel IMO #	Vessel Type	Year Built	Engine Type	Cargo Cap. or Gross*	Overall Length	Vessel Breadth	Vessel Depth
El Zorro	9344801	TK	2007	D	13,073	451'11"	66'11"	37'09"

NORBULK SHIPPING CO. LTD., HAMILTON, BERMUDA *(www.norbulkshipping.com)*

Fleet Name / Vessel Name	Vessel IMO #	Vessel Type	Year Built	Engine Type	Cargo Cap. or Gross*	Overall Length	Vessel Breadth	Vessel Depth
Anuket Ruby	9393668	TK	2008	D	7,315	332'08"	62'06"	34'05"

NORDIC TANKERS MARINE A/S, COPENHAGEN, DENMARK *(nordictankers.com)*

Fleet Name / Vessel Name	Vessel IMO #	Vessel Type	Year Built	Engine Type	Cargo Cap. or Gross*	Overall Length	Vessel Breadth	Vessel Depth
Njord Clear	9230012	TK	2001	D	16,875	453'01"	75'06"	40'02"
(Jo Chiara D '01-'04, Chiara '04-'06, Nora '06-'09, Harbour Clear '09-'15)								
Njord Cloud	9291066	TK	2004	D	16,875	453'01"	75'06"	40'02"
(Phase D '04-'04, Phase '04-'09, Harbour Cloud '09-'15)								
Nordic Mari	9422677	TK	2009	D	19,822	481'00"	77'10"	42'08"
(Clipper Mari '09-'14)								

NOVAALGOMA CEMENT CARRIERS, LUGANO, SWITZERLAND *(novaalgomacc.com)*
PARTNERSHIP BETWEEN ALGOMA CENTRAL CORP. & NOVA MARINE HOLDING SA of LUXEMBOURG

Fleet Name / Vessel Name	Vessel IMO #	Vessel Type	Year Built	Engine Type	Cargo Cap. or Gross*	Overall Length	Vessel Breadth	Vessel Depth
NACC Toronto	9287302	CC	2003	D	8,938	447'05"	69'05"	37'07
(Arklow Wave '03-'16); converted to a cement carrier in '16								
NACC Quebec	9546057	CC	2011	D	N/A	459'01"	68'09"	34'08
(Tenace '11-'16); converted to a cement carrier in '16								

OCEAN CHALLENGE LTD., NICOSIA, CYPRUS
FOLLOWING VESSELS UNDER CHARTER TO CANADIAN FOREST NAVIGATION LTD.

Fleet Name / Vessel Name	Vessel IMO #	Vessel Type	Year Built	Engine Type	Cargo Cap. or Gross*	Overall Length	Vessel Breadth	Vessel Depth
Bluewing	9230919	BC	2002	D	26,747	611'00"	77'09"	46'07"
Cinnamon	9239800	BC	2002	D	26,747	611'00"	77'09"	46'07"
Greenwing	9230921	BC	2002	D	26,737	611'08"	77'09"	46'07"
Mandarin	9239812	BC	2003	D	26,747	611'00"	77'09"	46'07"

Fleet Name / Vessel Name	Vessel IMO #	Vessel Type	Year Built	Engine Type	Cargo Cap. or Gross*	Overall Length	Vessel Breadth	Vessel Depth
OCEANEX INC., MONTREAL, QUEBEC, CANADA *(oceanex.com)*								
Oceanex Avalon	9315044	CO	2005	D	14,747	481' 11"	85' 00"	45' 11"
Oceanex Connaigra	9649718	CO	2013	D	19,460	689' 00"	97' 01"	56' 01"
Oceanex Sanderling	7603502	RR	1977	D	15,195	364' 01"	88' 05"	57' 07
(Rauenfels '77-'80, Essen '80-'81, Kongsfjord '81-'83, Onno '83-'87, ASL Sanderling '87-'08)								
OSLO BULK SHIPPING AS, OSLO, NORWAY *(oslobulk.com)*								
Oslo Bulk 6	9589968	D	2011	D	8,053	355' 00"	59' 09"	29' 06"
OSM GROUP AS, KRISTIANSAND, NORWAY *(osm.no)*								
Tromso	9435791	BC	2008	D	12,697	393' 08"	67' 00"	39' 00"
(Gemi '08-'08, M. Y. Arctic '08-'11)								

P

Fleet Name / Vessel Name	Vessel IMO #	Vessel Type	Year Built	Engine Type	Cargo Cap. or Gross*	Overall Length	Vessel Breadth	Vessel Depth
PARAKOU SHIPPING LTD., HONG KONG, CHINA *(parakougroup.com)*								
FOLLOWING VESSELS UNDER CHARTER TO CANADIAN FOREST NAVIGATION LTD.								
Eider	9285938	BC	2004	D	37,249	655' 10"	77' 09"	50' 02"
Gadwall	9358369	BC	2007	D	37,249	655' 10"	77' 09"	50' 02"
Garganey	9358383	BC	2007	D	37,249	655' 10"	77' 09"	50' 02"
Redhead	9285940	BC	2005	D	37,249	655' 10"	77' 09"	50' 02"
Whistler	9358371	BC	2007	D	37,249	655' 10"	77' 09"	50' 02"
Wigeon	9358395	BC	2007	D	37,249	655' 10"	77' 09"	50' 02"
PEARL SEAS CRUISES LLC., GUILFORD, CT *(pearlseascruises.com)*								
Pearl Mist	9412701	PA	2009	D	5,109*	335' 00"	56' 00"	12' 00"
PETER DOHLE SCHIFFAHRTS, HAMBURG, GERMANY *(doehle.de)*								
Diana	9370082	BC	2007	D	13,450	453' 00"	68' 11"	36' 01"
Foresight	9388912	HL	2008	D	12,782	453' 00"	70' 01"	36' 01"
(Beluga Foresight '08-'11)								
Fortune	9402067	HL	2008	D	12,782	453' 00"	70' 01"	36' 01"
(Beluga Fortune '08-'11)								
PHOENIX SHIPPING & TRADING SA, PIRAEAUS, GREECE *(phoenix-shipping.ro)*								
Fearless	9228265	BC	2001	D	30,778	606' 11"	77' 05"	48' 11"
(Bright Laker '01-'13)								
POLISH STEAMSHIP CO., SZCZECIN, POLAND *(polsteam.com)*								
Drawsko	9393450	BC	2010	D	30,206	623' 04"	77' 11"	47' 11"
Gardno	9767704	BC	2017	D	36,500	656' 02"	77' 09"	50' 02"
Ina	9521875	BC	2012	D	17,096	492' 00"	77' 05"	41' 00"
Irma	9180396	BC	2000	D	34,946	655' 10"	77' 05"	50' 02"
Iryda	9180384	BC	1999	D	34,946	655' 10"	77' 05"	50' 02"
Isa	9180358	BC	1999	D	34,946	655' 10"	77' 05"	50' 02"
Isadora	9180372	BC	1999	D	34,946	655' 10"	77' 05"	50' 02"
Isolda	9180360	BC	1999	D	34,946	655' 10"	77' 05"	50' 02"
Juno	9422378	BC	2011	D	30,206	623' 04"	77' 11"	47' 11"
Lubie	9441984	BC	2011	D	30,206	623' 04"	77' 11"	47' 11"
Mamry	9496264	BC	2012	D	30,206	623' 04"	77' 11"	47' 11"
Miedwie	9393448	BC	2010	D	30,206	623' 04"	77' 11"	47' 11"
Narew	9521813	BC	2012	D	17,096	492' 00"	77' 05"	41' 00"
Olza	9521837	BC	2012	D	17,096	492' 00"	77' 05"	41' 00"
Prosna	9521849	BC	2012	D	17,096	492' 00"	77' 05"	41' 00"
Raba	9521825	BC	2012	D	17,096	492' 00"	77' 05"	41' 00"
Regalica	9521758	BC	2011	D	17,096	492' 00"	77' 05"	41' 00"
Resko	9393462	BC	2010	D	30,206	623' 04"	77' 11"	47' 11"
San	9521851	BC	2012	D	17,096	492' 00"	77' 05"	41' 00"
Skawa	9521863	BC	2012	D	17,096	492' 00"	77' 05"	41' 00"
Solina	9496252	BC	2012	D	30,206	623' 04"	77' 11"	47' 11"
Wicko	9393474	BC	2010	D	30,206	623' 04"	77' 11"	47' 11"

Fleet Name / Vessel Name	Vessel IMO #	Vessel Type	Year Built	Engine Type	Cargo Cap. or Gross*	Overall Length	Vessel Breadth	Vessel Depth

POT SCHEEPVAART BV, DELFZIJL, NETHERLANDS *(pot-scheepvaart.nl)*

  FOLLOWING VESSELS UNDER CHARTER TO WAGENBORG SHIPPING

Fleet Name / Vessel Name	Vessel IMO #	Vessel Type	Year Built	Engine Type	Cargo Cap. or Gross*	Overall Length	Vessel Breadth	Vessel Depth
Kwintebank	9234288	GC	2002	D	8,664	433' 10"	52' 01"	31' 08"
Varnebank	9213739	GC	2000	D	8,664	433' 10"	52' 01"	31' 08"
Vikingbank	9604184	GC	2012	D	11,850	468' 00"	51' 09"	35' 04"

PRINCIPAL MARITIME MANAGEMENT LLC, SOUTHPORT, CONNECTICUT, USA *(princimar.com)*

Fleet Name / Vessel Name	Vessel IMO #	Vessel Type	Year Built	Engine Type	Cargo Cap. or Gross*	Overall Length	Vessel Breadth	Vessel Depth
Princimar Equinox	9486245	TK	2012	D	19,900	530' 10"	75' 06"	40' 08"

  (Chem Vela '12-'12, Xinle No 25 '12-'12, Angel No. 12 '12-'14)

R

REDERIET STENERSEN AS, BERGEN, NORWAY *(stenersen.com)*

Fleet Name / Vessel Name	Vessel IMO #	Vessel Type	Year Built	Engine Type	Cargo Cap. or Gross*	Overall Length	Vessel Breadth	Vessel Depth
Sten Aurora	9318565	TK	2008	D	16,613	472' 07"	75' 06"	40' 08"
Sten Baltic	9307671	TK	2005	D	16,613	472' 07"	75' 06"	40' 08"
Sten Bergen	9407988	TK	2009	D	16,611	472' 11"	76' 01"	40' 08"
Sten Suomi	9378723	TK	2008	D	16,611	472' 11"	76' 01"	40' 08"

REEDEREI HEINO WINTER, HAMBURG, GERMANY *(reederei-winter.de)*

Fleet Name / Vessel Name	Vessel IMO #	Vessel Type	Year Built	Engine Type	Cargo Cap. or Gross*	Overall Length	Vessel Breadth	Vessel Depth
BBC Iowa	9261085	HL	2005	D	12,828	452' 09"	68' 11"	36' 01"

  (Beluga Energy '05-'11, Linde '11-'13, Rickmers Chittagong '13-'14, Nordana Emma '14-'16, Linde '16-'16)

Fleet Name / Vessel Name	Vessel IMO #	Vessel Type	Year Built	Engine Type	Cargo Cap. or Gross*	Overall Length	Vessel Breadth	Vessel Depth
BBC Nebraska	9312169	HL	2005	D	12,645	454' 04"	68' 11"	36' 01"

  (Beluga Endurance '05-'11, Martin '11-'13, Rickmers Mumbai '13-'14, Nordana Emilie '14-'16, Martin '16-'16)

Fleet Name / Vessel Name	Vessel IMO #	Vessel Type	Year Built	Engine Type	Cargo Cap. or Gross*	Overall Length	Vessel Breadth	Vessel Depth
Jule	9357999	HL	2005	D	12,711	453' 00"	68' 11"	36' 01"

  (Beluga Expectation '05-'11, Jule '11-'13, OXL Avatar '13-'13, Clipper Anita '13-'15, Thorco Dolphin '15-'15)

REEDEREI HEINZ CORLEIS KG, STADE, GERMANY

Fleet Name / Vessel Name	Vessel IMO #	Vessel Type	Year Built	Engine Type	Cargo Cap. or Gross*	Overall Length	Vessel Breadth	Vessel Depth
Stade	9535620	BC	2011	D	10,872	477' 10"	59' 10"	33' 10"

REEDEREI KARL SCHLUTER GMBH & CO., RENDSBURG, GERMANY

  FOLLOWING VESSEL UNDER CHARTER TO FEDNAV LTD.

Fleet Name / Vessel Name	Vessel IMO #	Vessel Type	Year Built	Engine Type	Cargo Cap. or Gross*	Overall Length	Vessel Breadth	Vessel Depth
Ocean Castle	9315537	BC	2005	D	18,825	606' 11"	77' 09"	46' 03"

  (Federal Mattawa '05-'15)

REEDEREI NORD GMBH, HAMBURG, GERMANY *(reederei-nord.com)*

Fleet Name / Vessel Name	Vessel IMO #	Vessel Type	Year Built	Engine Type	Cargo Cap. or Gross*	Overall Length	Vessel Breadth	Vessel Depth
Nordisle	9457828	TK	2009	D	12,810	393' 08"	66' 11"	39' 00")

  (Rio Daintree '09-'09)

Fleet Name / Vessel Name	Vessel IMO #	Vessel Type	Year Built	Engine Type	Cargo Cap. or Gross*	Overall Length	Vessel Breadth	Vessel Depth
Nordport	9404144	TK	2008	D	13,132	421' 11"	67' 00"	37' 09")

  (E R Elbe '08-'08)

Flevogracht downbound into the St. Clair River. (Marc Dease)

Fleet Name Vessel Name	Vessel IMO #	Vessel Type	Year Built	Engine Type	Cargo Cap. or Gross*	Overall Length	Vessel Breadth	Vessel Depth
RIGEL SCHIFFAHRTS GMBH, BREMEN, GERMANY *(rigel-hb.com)*								
Amur Star	9480368	TK	2010	D	13,073	421' 11"	66' 11"	37' 09"
Colorado Star	9527609	TK	2010	D	13,073	421' 11"	66' 11"	37' 09"
Ganges Star	9496692	TK	2010	D	13,073	421' 11"	66' 11"	37' 09"
Isarstern	9105140	TK	1995	D	17,078	528' 03"	75' 06"	38' 05"
Kongo Star	9508823	TK	2010	D	13,073	421' 11"	66' 11"	37' 09"
Shannon Star	9503926	TK	2010	D	13,073	421' 11"	66' 11"	37' 09"

S

Fleet Name Vessel Name	Vessel IMO #	Vessel Type	Year Built	Engine Type	Cargo Cap. or Gross*	Overall Length	Vessel Breadth	Vessel Depth
SCHULTE & BURNS GMBH & CO., PAPENBURG, GERMANY								
Tiwala	9376775	GC	2008	D	5,484	350' 04"	49' 10"	21' 08"
SE SHIPPING, SINGAPORE, SINGAPORE *(seshipping.com)*								
SE Potentia	9431472	BC	2009	D	12,840	454' 05"	68' 11"	36' 01"
(Brattingsborg '09-'09)								
SEAFARERS SHIPPING INC., MANILA, PHILIPPINES								
AS Omaria	9363819	TK	2008	D	19,992	447' 05"	77' 09"	43' 10"
(Bow Omaria '08-'11)								
SEASTAR SHIPMANAGEMENT LTD., ATHENS, GREECE								
Sunda	9498236	BC	2010	D	29,800	610' 03"	77' 11"	47' 11"
(Emilie '10-'15)								
Cape	9498224	BC	2010	D	29,800	610' 03"	77' 11"	47' 11"
(Heloise '10-'15)								
SERROMAH SHIPPING BV, ROTTERDAM, NETHERLANDS *(serromahshipping.com)*								
Shamrock Jupiter	9416082	TK	2009	D	19,998	481' 00"	77' 09"	42' 08"
SHANGHAI DIHENG SHIPPING CO., SHANGHAI, CHINA								
Han Xin	9125889	BC	1996	D	7,713	352' 02"	62' 04"	34' 09"
(Svenja '96-'06, Atlant Svenja '06-'12)								
SLOMAN NEPTUN SHIFFAHRTS, BREMEN, GERMANY *(sloman-neptun.com)*								
Sloman Hera	9466714	TK	2012	D	16,427	476' 02"	75' 06"	41' 00"
Sloman Herakles	9466726	TK	2012	D	16,427	476' 02"	75' 06"	41' 00"
Sloman Hermes	9466738	TK	2012	D	16,427	476' 02"	75' 06"	41' 00"
Sun Dispatcher	9620657	HL	2012	D	12,634	453' 01"	68' 11"	36' 01"
(Sloman Dispatcher '12-'16)								

Gadwall and Federal Yukina anchored off Thunder Bay, Ont. (Chris Mazzella)

Fleet Name Vessel Name	IMO #	Vessel Type	Year Built	Engine Type	Cargo Cap. or Gross*	Overall Length	Breadth	Depth
SPLIETHOFF'S BEVRACHTINGSKANTOOR B.V., AMSTERDAM, NETHERLANDS *(spliethoff.com)*								
Elandsgracht	9081332	HL	1995	D	12,754	447' 04"	62' 00"	38' 03"
Fagelgracht	9428425	HL	2011	D	12,178	447' 10"	62' 00"	38' 03"
Flevogracht	9509956	HL	2011	D	12,178	447' 10"	62' 00"	38' 03"
Floragracht	9509968	HL	2011	D	12,178	447' 10"	62' 00"	38' 03"
Floretgracht	9507611	HL	2012	D	12,178	447' 10"	62' 00"	38' 03"
Florijngracht	9428413	HL	2010	D	12,178	447' 10"	62' 00"	38' 03"
Fortunagracht	9507609	HL	2012	D	12,178	447' 10"	62' 00"	38' 03"
Heemskerkgracht	9443669	HL	2009	D	12,700	453' 00"	68' 11"	36' 01"
*(Beluga Faculty '09-'11, **HHL Nile** '11-'16)*								
Hemgracht	9466996	HL	2009	D	12,700	453' 00"	68' 11"	36' 01"
*(Beluga Fairy '09-'11, **HHL Amazon** '11-'16)*								
Marsgracht	9571507	HL	2007	D	11,759	464' 11"	62' 00"	38' 03"
Merwedegracht	9571519	HL	2011	D	11,759	464' 11"	62' 00"	38' 03"
Minervagracht	9571521	HL	2011	D	11,759	464' 11"	62' 00"	38' 03"
Muntgracht	9571545	HL	2012	D	11,759	464' 11"	62' 00"	38' 03"
SUNSHIP SCHIFFAHRTSKONTOR KG, EMDEN, GERMANY *(sunship.de)*								
Copenhagen	9457115	BC	2011	D	5,627	354' 11"	54' 06"	28' 03"
Lake Ontario	9283538	BC	2004	D	27,000	606' 11"	77' 09"	46' 03"
(Federal Manitou '04-'11)								
Lake St. Clair	9315549	BC	2004	D	27,000	606' 11"	77' 09"	46' 03"
(Federal Miramichi '04-'16)								
SWISS CHEM TANKERS AG, ZURICH, SWITZERLAND *(mega-chemicals.ch)*								
SCT Breithorn	9298375	TK	2007	D	19,950	539' 02"	76' 01"	42' 00"
(MCT Breithorn '07-'15)								
SCT Matterhorn	9298351	TK	2006	D	19,950	539' 02"	76' 01"	42' 00"
*(HLL Arctic '06-'06, **MCT Matterhorn** '06-'15)*								
SCT Monte Rosa	9298363	TK	2007	D	19,950	539' 02"	76' 01"	42' 00"
(MCT Monte Rosa '07-'15)								

HHL Rhine unloading pig iron at Marinette, Wis. *(Scott Best)*

Fleet Name Vessel Name	Vessel IMO #	Vessel Type	Year Built	Engine Type	Cargo Cap. or Gross*	Overall Length	Vessel Breadth	Vessel Depth
SCT Stockhorn	9298387	TK	2006	D	19,950	539' 02"	76' 01"	42' 00"
(MCT Stockhorn '06-'15)								

SYMPHONY SHIPPING BV, ETTEN-LEUR, NETHERLANDS (symphonyshipping.com)

Nordana Sky	9721633	HL	2015	D	10,600	401' 11"	55' 09"	35' 01
(Symphony Sky '14-'15)								

T-V

TARBIT TANKERS B.V., DORDRECHT, NETHERLANDS (tarbittankers.nl)

Stella Polaris	9187057	TK	1999	D	8,000	387' 02"	55' 09"	34' 05"

TB MARINE SHIPMANAGEMENT GMBH & CO., HAMBURG GERMANY (tbmarine.de)

Harbour Fashion	9473080	TK	2011	D	16,909	473' 02"	75' 06"	40' 08"
Harbour Feature	9473092	TK	2011	D	16,909	473' 02"	75' 06"	40' 08"
(Nordtank Lerner '11-'11)								
Harbour First	9473119	TK	2011	D	16,909	473' 02"	75' 06"	40' 08"
Harbour Fountain	9473107	TK	2011	D	16,909	473' 02"	75' 06"	40' 08"
Harbour Pioneer	9572757	TK	2010	D	19,122	530' 05"	75' 06"	40' 08"
(Harbour Pioneer '10-'10, Nordtank Franklin '10-'10)								
Harbour Progress	9572745	TK	2010	D	19,122	530' 05"	75' 06"	40' 08"

TEAM TANKERS MANAGEMENT AS, HELLERUP, DENMARK (teamtankers.com)

Sichem Beijing	9397042	TK	2007	D	13,073	421' 11"	66' 11"	37' 09"
Sichem Challenge	9196448	TK	1998	D	17,485	382' 06"	62' 04"	33' 02"
(Queen of Montreaux '98-'99, **North Challenge** *'99-'06, Songa Challenge '06-'07)*								
Sichem Defiance	9244374	TK	2001	D	17,369	442' 11"	74' 10"	41' 00"
*(***North Defiance** *'01-'06,* **Songa Defiance** *'06-'07)*								
Sichem Dubai	9376933	TK	2007	D	12,956	417' 04"	67' 00"	37' 09"
Sichem Hong Kong	9397054	TK	2007	D	13,073	421' 11"	66' 11"	37' 09"

Polish-flagged Prosna upbound past Port Huron, Mich. (Marc Dease)

Fleet Name / Vessel Name	Vessel IMO #	Vessel Type	Year Built	Engine Type	Cargo Cap. or Gross*	Overall Length	Vessel Breadth	Vessel Depth
Sichem Melbourne	9376921	TK	2007	D	12,936	417' 04"	67' 00"	37' 09"
Sichem Montreal	9404900	TK	2008	D	13,073	421' 11"	66' 11"	37' 09"
Sichem Mumbai	9322085	TK	2006	D	13,141	421' 11"	66' 11"	37' 09"
Sichem New York	9337834	TK	2007	D	12,956	417' 04"	67' 00"	37' 09"

TERAS BBC OCEAN NAVIGATION ENTERPRISES, HOUSTON, TEXAS (terasamerica.com)

Houston	9331593	GC	2005	D	7,530	393' 00"	66' 03"	32' 02"

(BBC Australia '05-'05, Wesier Hiede '05-'05, BBC Australia '05-'10, BBC Houston '10-'14)

THORCO PROJECTS, COPENHAGEN, DENMARK (thorcoprojects.com)

Thorco Alliance	9559884	GC	2011	D	9,755	433' 09"	52' 01"	31' 08"

(Sinus Iridium '11-'12, Velocity Scan '12-'12)

Thorco Arctic	9484209	GC	2009	D	8,500	433' 09"	52' 01"	31' 08"

(Beluga Notion '09-'09, BBC Newcastle '09-'11)

Thorco Marjanne	9232462	GC	2001	D	17,539	465' 10"	70' 06"	43' 08"

(Magdalena Green '01-'12, Clipper Magdalena '12-'16)

TRADEWIND TANKERS, BARCELONA, SPAIN (tradewindtankers.com)

Tradewind Adventure	9485590	TK	2008	D	13,000	467' 06"	72' 02"	39' 04"

TRANSAL DENIZCILIK TICARET, ISTANBUL, TURKEY (www.transal.com.tr)

Ruby-T	9457878	TK	2010	D	21,224	541' 01"	75' 02"	42' 00"

UNI-TANKERS A/S, MIDDELFART, DENMARK (unitankers.com)

Erria Swan	9347748	TK	2006	D	11,336	425' 08"	65' 07"	34' 01"

(Alaattin Bey '06-'07, Erria Helen '07-'12)

Wagenborg Shipping's Volgaborg on the St. Lawrence Seaway. *(Josh Roth)*

Fleet Name Vessel Name	Vessel IMO #	Vessel Type	Year Built	Engine Type	Cargo Cap. or Gross*	Overall Length	Vessel Breadth	Vessel Depth
Fionia Swan	9328974	TK	2005	D	15,602	485' 07"	70' 10"	37' 01"
Mona Swan	9371804	TK	2006	D	11,336	425' 08"	65' 07"	34' 01"
(M Can Bey '06–'08, Erria Ida '08–'12)								
Selandia Swan	9371787	TK	2008	D	17,998	438' 11"	73' 06"	41' 04"
Swan Baltic	9386249	TK	2007	D	11,530	426' 11"	64' 04"	35' 09"
(Ozay-5 '07–'14)								
Swan Biscay	9438444	TK	2008	D	11,530	426' 11"	64' 04"	35' 09"
(Ozay-6 '08–'14)								

UNICORN TANKERS INTERNATIONAL LTD., LONDON, UNITED KINGDOM

Kowie	9382504	TK	2010	D	16,885	472' 05"	75' 06"	41' 00"
Umgeni	9382499	TK	2011	D	16,500	472' 05"	75' 06"	41' 00"
(Siyanda '11–'11, Umzimvubu '11–'11)								

UNISEA SHIPPING B.V., SNEEK, NETHERLANDS

Beauforce	9526095	BC	2010	D	8,284	387' 07"	52' 02"	28' 10"

UTKILEN AS, BERGEN, NORWAY *(utkilen.no)*

Susana S	9406714	TK	2009	D	12,862	539' 02"	76' 01"	42' 00"

VBG DENIZCILIK SANAYI VE TICARET AS, ISTANBUL, TURKEY *(vbgshipping.com)*

Halit Bey	9410143	TK	2009	D	19,999	530' 04"	73' 06"	42' 00"
Nilufer Sultan	9410131	TK	2008	D	19,999	530' 04"	73' 06"	42' 00"

W-Z

W. BOCKSTIEGEL REEDEREI KG, EMDEN, GERMANY *(reederei-bockstiegel.de)*

Fleet Name Vessel Name	Vessel IMO #	Vessel Type	Year Built	Engine Type	Cargo Cap. or Gross*	Overall Length	Vessel Breadth	Vessel Depth
BBC Alabama	9384318	HL	2007	D	12,837	453' 00"	68' 11"	36' 01"
BBC Arizona	9501253	HL	2010	D	12,837	453' 00"	68' 11"	36' 01"
*(BBC Barbuda '10-'10, **BBC Arizona** '10-'14, Industrial Sailor '14-'15, Arizona '15-'15)*								
BBC Campana	9291963	HL	2003	D	12,837	453' 00"	68' 11"	36' 01"
BBC Colorado	9435117	HL	2004	D	12,837	453' 00"	68' 11"	36' 01"
BBC Delaware	9357212	HL	2004	D	12,767	454' 05"	68' 11"	36' 01"
BBC Florida	9433286	HL	2009	D	12,767	454' 05"	68' 11"	36' 01"
BBC Louisiana	9435105	HL	2008	D	12,837	453' 00"	68' 11"	36' 01"
BBC Maine	9357200	HL	2007	D	12,767	454' 05"	68' 11"	36' 01"
BBC Ohio	9435129	HL	2009	D	12,837	453' 00"	68' 11"	36' 01"
BBC Oregon	9501265	HL	2010	D	12,837	453' 00"	68' 11"	36' 01"
BBC Plata	9291975	HL	2005	D	12,837	453' 00"	68' 11"	36' 01"
(Asian Voyager '05-'05)								
BBC Zarate	9337236	HL	2007	D	12,767	454' 05"	68' 11"	36' 01"

WAGENBORG SHIPPING BV, DELFZIJL, NETHERLANDS *(wagenborg.com)*

Fleet Name Vessel Name	Vessel IMO #	Vessel Type	Year Built	Engine Type	Cargo Cap. or Gross*	Overall Length	Vessel Breadth	Vessel Depth
Adriaticborg	9546497	GC	2011	D	17,110	469' 02"	70' 06"	43' 08"
Africaborg	9365661	GC	2007	D	17,110	469' 02"	70' 06"	43' 08"
(Africaborg '07-'08, Tianshan '08-'09)								
Alamosborg	9466348	GC	2011	D	17,110	469' 02"	70' 06"	43' 08"
Alaskaborg	9466374	GC	2012	D	17,110	469' 02"	70' 06"	43' 08"
Albanyborg	9466300	GC	2010	D	17,110	469' 02"	70' 06"	43' 08"
Amazoneborg	9333541	GC	2007	D	17,110	469' 02"	70' 06"	43' 08"
Americaborg	9365659	GC	2007	D	17,110	469' 02"	70' 06"	43' 08"
Amstelborg	9333527	GC	2006	D	17,110	469' 02"	70' 06"	43' 08"
Amurborg	9466336	GC	2011	D	17,110	469' 02"	70' 06"	43' 08"
Andesborg	9466324	GC	2011	D	17,110	469' 02"	70' 06"	43' 08"
Aragonborg	9466312	GC	2011	D	17,110	469' 02"	70' 06"	43' 08"
Arneborg	9333539	GC	2006	D	17,110	469' 02"	70' 06"	43' 08"
Arubaborg	9466295	GC	2010	D	17,110	469' 02"	70' 06"	43' 08"
Atlanticborg	9466350	GC	2012	D	17,110	469' 02"	70' 06"	43' 08"

German tanker Harbour Pioneer. (Sean Vary)

Fleet Name Vessel Name	Vessel IMO #	Vessel Type	Year Built	Engine Type	Cargo Cap. or Gross*	Overall Length	Vessel Breadth	Vessel Depth
Avonborg	9466362	GC	2012	D	17,110	469' 02"	70' 06"	43' 08"
Beatrix	9419280	GC	2009	D	14,603	507' 03"	56' 05"	37' 11"
(Fivelborg '09-'09)								
Dintelborg	9163685	GC	1999	D	8,867	437' 07"	52' 00"	32' 02"
(Dintelborg '00-'01, MSC Dardanelles '01-'04)								
Ebroborg	9463451	GC	2010	D	10,750	452' 03"	52' 01"	36' 01"
Edenborg	9463449	GC	2010	D	10,750	452' 03"	52' 01"	36' 01"
Eeborg	9568328	GC	2012	D	12,004	474' 03"	52' 01"	36' 07"
Eemsborg	9225586	GC	2009	D	10,750	452' 03"	52' 01"	36' 01"
Elbeborg	9568249	GC	2011	D	12,004	474' 03"	52' 01"	36' 07"
Erieborg	9463437	GC	2009	D	10,750	452' 03"	52' 01"	36' 01"
Exeborg	9650482	GC	2011	D	12,004	474' 03"	52' 01"	36' 07"
Finnborg	9419321	GC	2011	D	14,603	507' 03"	56' 05"	37' 11"
Fivelborg	9419307	GC	2010	D	14,603	507' 03"	56' 05"	37' 11"
Flevoborg	9419292	GC	2010	D	14,603	507' 03"	56' 05"	37' 11"
Fraserborg	9419319	GC	2011	D	14,603	507' 03"	56' 05"	37' 11"
Fuldaborg	9559092	GC	2012	D	14,603	507' 03"	56' 05"	37' 11"
Jan van Gent	9456721	GC	2010	D	12,000	469' 00"	62' 00"	35' 11"
(Jan van Gent '10-'14, Nordana Madeleine '14-'16)								
Kasteelborg	9155937	GC	1998	D	9,150	427' 01"	52' 01"	33' 06"
Koningsborg	9155925	GC	1999	D	9,150	427' 01"	52' 01"	33' 06"
Medemborg	9142514	GC	1997	D	9,141	441' 05"	54' 02"	32' 02"
(Arion '97-'03)								
Mississippiborg	9207508	GC	2000	D	9,141	441' 05"	54' 02"	32' 02"
Moezelborg	9180839	GC	1999	D	9,141	441' 05"	54' 02"	32' 02"
Nassauborg	9248564	GC	2006	D	16,740	467' 03"	72' 06"	42' 00"
Reestborg	9592563	GC	2013	D	23,249	556' 11"	66' 11"	37' 11"
Reggeborg	9592575	GC	2014	D	23,249	556' 11"	66' 11"	37' 11"
Roerborg	9592599	GC	2014	D	23,249	556' 11"	66' 11"	37' 11"
Taagborg	9546461	GC	2013	D	21,338	565' 03"	70' 06"	43' 08"
Trinityborg	9546485	GC	2013	D	21,338	565' 03"	70' 06"	43' 08"
Vaasaborg	9196242	GC	1999	D	8,664	433' 10"	52' 01"	31' 08"
(Vaasaborg '00-'03, Normed Hamburg '03-'04)								
Vancouverborg	9213741	GC	2001	D	9,857	433' 10"	52' 01"	31' 08"
Victoriaborg	9234276	GC	2001	D	9,857	433' 10"	52' 01"	31' 08"

Heavy-lift vessel Jule downbound in the Soo Locks. (Roger LeLievre)

Fleet Name Vessel Name	Vessel IMO #	Vessel Type	Year Built	Engine Type	Cargo Cap. or Gross*	Overall Length	Vessel Breadth	Vessel Depth
Virginiaborg	9234290	GC	2001	D	9,857	433' 10"	52' 01"	31' 08"
Vlieborg	9554781	GC	2012	D	11,850	468' 00"	52' 01"	35' 04"
Volgaborg	9631072	GC	2013	D	11,850	468' 00"	51' 09"	35' 04"
Voorneborg	9179373	GC	1999	D	8,664	433' 10"	52' 01"	31' 08"

At press time, Wagenborg Shipping also had the following vessels under charter. Please consult their respective fleets for details: **Kwintebank, Marietje Deborah, Marietje Marsilla, Morgenstond I, Morgenstond II, Varnebank, Vikingbank**

WECO SHIPPING, RUNDSTED, DENMARK *(wecobulk.com)*

Billesborg	9488047	HL	2011	D	12,767	454' 05"	68' 11"	36' 01"

(Billesborg '11-'11, Clipper Angela '11-'12)

WIJNNE BARENDS, DELFZIJL, NETHERLANDS *(wijnnebarends.com)*

Morgenstond I	9320506	BC	2006	D	12,000	469' 00"	62' 00"	35' 11"

(Morgenstond I '06-'06, Beluga Locomotion '06-'08, Kent Locomotion '08-'08, Beluga Locomotion '08-'09, Morgenstond I '09-'10, **Kent Sunrise** *'10-'12, Morgenstond I '12-'12, Clipper Athena '12-'14)*

Morgenstond II	9367073	BC	2007	D	12,000	469' 00"	62' 00"	35' 11"

*(**Morgenstond II** '07-'07, Beluga Legislation '07-'07, Kent Legislation '07-'09,* **Beluga Legislation** *'09-'10,* **Kent Sunset** *'10-'13,* **Morgenstond II** *'13-'13, Clipper Aurora '13-'15)*

Federal Biscay unloading at Nicholson's Dock in Detroit, Mich. (Neil Schultheiss)

Fleet Name Vessel Name	Vessel IMO #	Vessel Type	Year Built	Engine Type	Cargo Cap. or Gross*	Overall Length	Vessel Breadth	Vessel Depth
YARDIMCI SHIPPING GROUP, ISTANBUL, TURKEY *(www.yardimci.gen.tr)*								
Ayane	9395991	TK	2010	D	16,745	472' 07"	75' 06"	40' 08"
CT Dublin	9395989	TK	2008	D	16,745	472' 07"	75' 06"	40' 08"
Elevit	9466609	TK	2012	D	16,745	472' 07"	75' 06"	40' 08"
YAWATAHAMA KISEN Y. K., YAWATAHAMA, JAPAN								
FOLLOWING VESSEL UNDER CHARTER TO FEDNAV LTD.								
Federal Yukina	9476977	BC	2010	D	35,868	656' 01"	78' 01"	48' 09"
YILMAR SHIPPING & TRADING LTD., ISTANBUL, TURKEY *(yilmar.com)*								
YM Jupiter	9291597	TK	2007	D	16,000	485' 07"	70' 10"	37' 01"
YM Saturn	9362138	TK	2007	D	16,000	485' 07"	70' 10"	37' 01"
ZEALAND SHIPPING BV, ALMERE, NETHERLANDS *(zealand-shipping.nl)*								
Zealand Beatrix	9507087	BC	2010	D	13,089	441' 11"	67' 03"	36' 01"
Zealand Delilah	9507075	BC	2011	D	13,089	441' 11"	67' 03"	36' 01"

Bridge ahead on the Welland Canal. *(Alain Gindroz)*

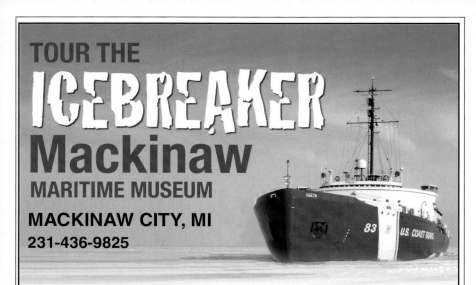
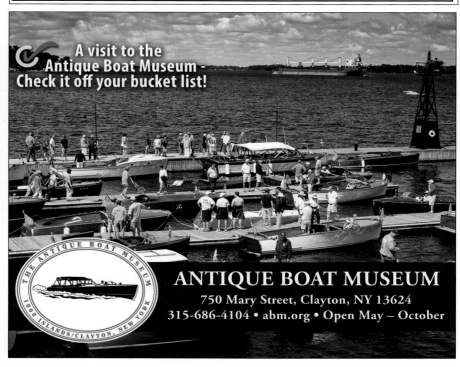

Marine Museums

Former destroyer USS Edson is a museum ship at Bay City, Mich. Here, the laker Calumet passes her on the Saginaw River. *(Gordy Garris)*

MUSEUMS AFLOAT

Museum Name Vessel Name	Vessel Type	Year Built	Engine Type	Cargo Cap. or Gross*	Overall Length	Breadth	Depth
BUFFALO AND ERIE COUNTY NAVAL & MILITARY PARK, BUFFALO, NY *(buffalonavalpark.org)*							
Croaker	MU	1944	D	1,526*	311'07"	27'02"	33'09"
Former U. S. Navy Gato class submarine IXSS-246; open to the public at Buffalo, NY							
Little Rock	MU	1945	T	10,670*	610'01"	66'04"	25'00"
Former U. S. Navy Cleveland / Little Rock class guided missile cruiser; open to the public at Buffalo, NY							
The Sullivans	MU	1943	T	2,500*	376'06"	39'08"	22'08"
Former U. S. Navy Fletcher class destroyer; open to the public at Buffalo, NY (Launched as USS Putnam)							
CITY OF KEWAUNEE, KEWAUNEE, WI							
Ludington	MU	1943	D	249*	115'00"	26'00"	13'08"
Built: Jakobson Shipyard, Oyster Bay, NY; former U.S. Army Corps of Engineers tug is open to the public as a marine museum at Kewaunee, WI (Major Wilbur F. Browder [LT-4] '43–'47)							
DOOR COUNTY MARITIME MUSEUM & LIGHTHOUSE PRESERVATION SOCIETY INC., **STURGEON BAY, WI** *(dcmm.org)*							
John Purves	TB/MU	1919	D	436*	150'00"	27'06"	16'08"
Built: Bethlehem Steel Co., Elizabeth, NJ; former Roen/Andrie Inc. tug has been refurbished as a museum display at Sturgeon Bay, WI (Butterfield '19–'42, LT-145 '42–'57)							
DULUTH ENTERTAINMENT CONVENTION CENTER, DULUTH, MN *(decc.org/william-a-irvin)*							
William A. Irvin	MU	1938	T	14,050	610'09"	60'00"	32'06"
Built: American Shipbuilding Co., Lorain, OH; former United States Steel Corp. bulk carrier last operated Dec. 16, 1978; open to the public at Duluth, MN							
ERIE MARITIME MUSEUM, ERIE, PA *(flagshipniagara.org)*							
Niagara	MU/2B	1988	W	295*	198'00"	32'00"	10'06"
Reconstruction of Oliver Hazard Perry's U. S. Navy brigantine from the War of 1812							
GREAT LAKES NAVAL MEMORIAL & MUSEUM, MUSKEGON, MI *(glnmm.org)*							
McLane	MU	1927	D	289*	125'00"	24'00"	12'06"
Built: American Brown Boveri Electric Co.,Camden, NJ; former U.S. Coast Guard Buck & A Quarter class medium endurance cutter; on display at Muskegon, MI (USCGC McLane '27–'70, Manatra II '70–'93)							
Silversides	MU	1941	D/V	1,526*	311'08"	27'03"	33'09"
Built: Mare Island Naval Yard, Vallejo, CA; former U.S. Navy Albacore (Gato) class submarine AGSS-236; open to the public at Muskegon, MI							
GREAT LAKES SCIENCE CENTER, CLEVELAND, OH *(greatscience.com)*							
William G. Mather {2}	MU	1925	T	13,950	618'00"	62'00"	32'00"
Built: Great Lakes Engineering Works, Ecorse, MI; former Cleveland-Cliffs Steamship Co. bulk carrier last operated Dec. 21, 1980; open to the public at Cleveland, OH							
HMCS HAIDA NATIONAL HISTORICAL SITE, HAMILTON, ON *(hmcshaida.com)*							
Haida	MU	1943	T	2,744*	377'00"	37'06"	15'02"
Former Royal Canadian Navy Tribal class destroyer G-63 / DDE-215; open to the public at Hamilton, ON							
ICEBREAKER MACKINAW MARITIME MUSEUM INC., MACKINAW CITY, MI *(themackinaw.org)*							
Mackinaw [WAGB-83]	MU	1944	D	5,252*	290'00"	74'00"	29'00"
Built: Toledo Shipbuilding Co., Toledo, OH; former U.S. Coast Guard icebreaker was decommissioned in 2006; open to the public at Mackinaw City, MI (Launched as USCGC Manitowoc [WAG-83])							
LAKE COUNTY HISTORICAL SOCIETY, TWO HARBORS, MN *(lakecountyhistoricalsociety.org)*							
Edna G.	MU	1896	R	154*	102'00"	23'00"	14'06"
Built: Cleveland Shipbuilding Co., Cleveland, OH; former Duluth, Missabe & Iron Range Railroad tug last operated in 1981; open to the public at Two Harbors, MN							
LE SAULT DE SAINTE MARIE HISTORIC SITES INC., SAULT STE. MARIE, MI *(saulthistoricsites.com)*							
Valley Camp {2}	MU	1917	R	12,000	550'00"	58'00"	31'00"
Built: American Shipbuilding Co., Lorain, OH; former Hanna Mining Co./Wilson Marine Transit Co./Republic Steel Corp. bulk carrier last operated in 1966; open to the public at Sault Ste. Marie, MI (Louis W. Hill '17–'55)							
MUSÉE MARITIME DU QUÉBEC, L' ISLET, QC *(mmq.qc.ca)*							
Ernest Lapointe	MU	1941	R	1,179*	185'00"	36'00"	22'06"
Built: Davie Shipbuilding Co., Lauzon, QC; former Canadian Coast Guard icebreaker; open to the public at L'Islet, QC							
MUSEUM SHIP COL. JAMES M. SCHOONMAKER, TOLEDO, OH *(inlandseas.org)*							
Col. James M. Schoonmaker	MU	1911	T	15,000	617'00"	64'00"	33'01"
Built: Great Lakes Engineering Works, Ecorse, MI; former Shenango Furnace Co./Republic Steel Co./Cleveland-							

Our Great Lakes contain 84% of the continent's fresh water and there's a different story in every drop.

NATIONAL MUSEUM *of the* GREAT LAKES

More than 500 breathtaking photographs, 250 incredible artifacts, 45 interactive exhibits and a 617' iron ore freighter tell the awe-inspiring history of the Great Lakes and provide a unique destination for family fun!

Rated #4 of 74 "Things to Do in Toledo" from tripadvisor.com

Photo courtesy of The Blade

1701 Front St., Toledo, OH 43605
419.214.5000 • inlandseas.org

118

Cliffs Steamship Co. bulk carrier last operated in 1980; open to the public at Toledo, OH, under the auspices of the National Museum of the Great Lakes (Col. James M. Schoonmaker 1911-'69, Willis B. Boyer '69-'11)

PORT HURON MUSEUM, PORT HURON, MI (phmuseum.org)

| Huron | MU | 1920 | D | 392* | 96' 05" | 24' 00" | 10' 00" |

Built: Charles L. Seabury Co., Morris Heights, NY; former U.S. Coast Guard lightship WLV-526 was retired Aug. 20, 1970; open to the public at Port Huron, MI (Lightship 103 – Relief [WAL-526] '20-'36)

SAGINAW VALLEY NAVAL SHIP MUSEUM, BAY CITY, MI (ussedson.org)

| Edson [DD-946] | MU | 1958 | D | | 418' 03" | 45' 03" | |

Built: Bath Iron Works, Bath, ME; Forrest Sherman class destroyer was decommissioned in '88; from '89-'04 on display at the Intrepid Air and Sea Museum, New York, N.Y. Declared a U.S. National Historic Landmark in '90; returned to U.S. Navy in '04; open to the public at Bay City, MI

S.S. CITY OF MILWAUKEE – NATIONAL HISTORIC LANDMARK, MANISTEE, MI (carferry.com)

| Acacia | MU | 1944 | DE | 1,025* | 180' 00" | 37' 00" | 17' 04" |

Built: Marine Iron and Shipbuilding Corp., Duluth, MN; former U.S. Coast Guard bouy tender/icebreaker was decommissioned in '06 (Launched as USCGC Thistle [WAGL-406])

| City of Milwaukee | MU | 1931 | R | 26 cars | 360' 00" | 56' 03" | 21' 06" |

Built: Manitowoc Shipbuilding Co., Manitowoc, WI; train ferry sailed for the Grand Trunk Railroad '31-'78 and the Ann Arbor Railroad '78-'81; open to the public at Manistee, MI

S.S. COLUMBIA PROJECT, NEW YORK, NY (sscolumbia.org)

| Columbia {2} | 5077333 | PA | 1902 | R | 968* | 216' 00" | 60' 00" | 13' 06" |

Built: Detroit Dry Dock Co, Wyandotte, MI; former Detroit to Bob-Lo Island passenger steamer last operated Sept. 2, 1991; moved to Buffalo, N.Y., Sept. 2, 2015, for further restoration and possible return to service

SS KEEWATIN MARINE MUSEUM, PORT McNICOLL, ON (sskeewatin.com)

| Keewatin {2} | MU | 1907 | Q | 3,856* | 346' 00" | 43' 08" | 26' 06" |

Built: Fairfield Shipbuilding and Engineering Co. Ltd., Govan, Scotland; former Canadian Pacific Railway Co. passenger vessel last operated Nov. 29, 1965; served as a marine museum since 1967 in Douglas, MI, and now Port McNicoll, ON; operated by the non-profit group Friends of the Keewatin

S.S. METEOR WHALEBACK SHIP MUSEUM, SUPERIOR, WI (superiorpublicmuseums.org/s-s-meteor-2)

| Meteor {2} | MU | 1896 | R | 40,100 | 380' 00" | 45' 00" | 26' 00" |

Built: American Steel Barge Co., Superior, WI; former ore carrier/auto carrier/tanker is the last vessel of whaleback design surviving on the Great Lakes; Cleveland Tankers vessel last operated in 1969; open to the public at Superior, WI (Frank Rockefeller 1896-'28, South Park '1928-'43)

S.S. MILWAUKEE CLIPPER PRESERVATION INC., MUSKEGON, MI (milwaukeeclipper.com)

| Milwaukee Clipper | MU | 1904 | Q | 4,272 | 361' 00" | 45' 00" | 28' 00" |

Built: American Shipbuilding Co., Cleveland, OH; rebuilt in '40 at Manitowoc Shipbuilding Co., Manitowoc, WI; former Wisconsin & Michigan Steamship Co. passenger/auto carrier last operated in 1970; undergoing restoration and open to the public at Muskegon, MI (Juniata '04-'41)

ST. MARYS RIVER MARINE CENTRE, SAULT STE. MARIE, ON (norgoma.org)

| Norgoma | MU | 1950 | D | 1,477* | 188' 00" | 37' 06" | 22' 06" |

Built: Collingwood Shipyards, Collingwood, ON; former Ontario Northland Transportation Commission passenger vessel last operated in 1974; museum is no longer open and its future is unknown

USCG BRAMBLE, PORT HURON, MI (uscgcbramble.com)

| Bramble | MU | 1944 | DE | 1,025* | 180' 00" | 37' 00" | 17' 04" |

Built: Zenith Dredge Co., Duluth, MN; former U.S. Coast Guard bouy tender/icebreaker was retired in 2003; open as an operational marine museum at Port Huron, MI (USCGC Bramble [WLB-392] '44-'03)

USS COD SUBMARINE MEMORIAL, CLEVELAND, OH (usscod.org)

| Cod | MU | 1943 | D/V | 1,525* | 311' 08" | 27' 02" | 33' 09" |

Built: Electric Boat Co., Groton, CT; former U.S. Navy Albacore (Gato) class submarine IXSS-224 open to the public at Cleveland, OH

USS LST 393 PRESERVATION ASSOCIATION, MUSKEGON, MI (lst393.org)

| LST-393 | MU | 1942 | D | 2,100 | 328' 00" | 50' 00" | 25' 00" |

Built: Newport News Shipbuilding and Dry Dock Co., Newport News, VA; former U.S. Navy/Wisconsin & Michigan Steamship Co. vessel last operated July 31, 1973; open to the public at Muskegon, MI (USS LST-393 '42-'47, Highway 16 '47-'99)

WISCONSIN MARITIME MUSEUM, MANITOWOC, WI (wisconsinmaritime.org)

| Cobia | MU | 1944 | D/V | 1,500* | 311' 09" | 27' 03" | 33' 09" |

Built: Electric Boat Co., Groton, CT; former U. S. Navy Gato class submarine AGSS-245 is open to the public at Manitowoc, WI

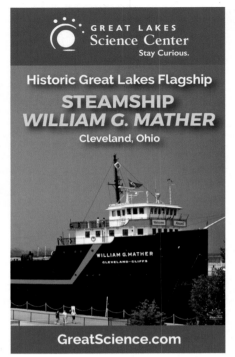
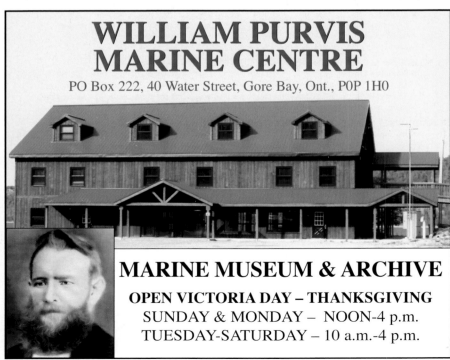

MUSEUMS ASHORE

Information can change without notice. Call ahead to verify location and hours.

ANTIQUE BOAT MUSEUM, 750 MARY ST., CLAYTON, NY – (315) 686-4104: A large collection of freshwater boats and engines. Annual show is the first weekend of August. Seasonal. *(abm.org)*

ASHTABULA MARINE & U.S. COAST GUARD MEMORIAL MUSEUM, 1071 WALNUT BLVD., ASHTABULA, OH – (440) 964-6847: Housed in the 1898-built former lighthouse keeper's residence, the museum includes models, paintings, artifacts, photos, the world's only working scale model of a Hullett ore unloading machine and the pilothouse from the steamer *Thomas Walters*. Seasonal.

BUFFALO HARBOR MUSEUM, 66 ERIE ST., BUFFALO, NY – (716) 849-0914: Exhibits explore local maritime history. Open all year, Thursday and Sunday only. *(llmhs.org)*

CANAL PARK MARINE MUSEUM, ALONGSIDE THE SHIP CANAL, DULUTH, MN – (218) 727-2497: Museum provides displays, historic artifacts and programs that explain the roles of Duluth and Superior in Great Lakes shipping, as well as the job of the U.S. Army Corps of Engineers in maintaining the nation's waterways. Many excellent models and other artifacts are on display. Open all year. *(lsmma.com)*

Continued on Page 123

Museum Ship Stack Markings

Museum Ship City of Milwaukee
Manistee, MI

Museum Ship Col. James M. Schoonmaker
Toledo, OH

Museum Ship Keewatin
Port McNicoll, ON

Museum Ship Alexander Henry
Relocating in 2017

Museum Ship HMCS Haida
Hamilton, ON

Museum Ships USS Little Rock USS The Sullivans
Buffalo, N.Y.

Museum Ship Meteor
Superior, WI

Museum Ship Milwaukee Clipper
Muskegon, MI

Museum Ship Norgoma
Sault Ste. Marie, ON

Museum Ship Valley Camp
Sault Ste. Marie, MI

Museum Ship William A. Irvin
Duluth, MN

Museum Ship William G. Mather
Cleveland, OH

Museum Ship USCG Mackinaw
Mackinaw City, MI

Museum Tug John Purves
Sturgeon Bay, WI

Museum Tug Edna G.
Two Harbors, MN

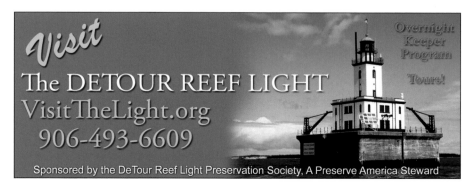

DOOR COUNTY MARITIME MUSEUM & LIGHTHOUSE PRESERVATION SOCIETY INC., 120 N. MADISON AVE., STURGEON BAY, WI – (920) 743-5958: Many excellent models help portray the role shipbuilding has played in the Door Peninsula. Open all year. *(dcmm.org)*

DOSSIN GREAT LAKES MUSEUM, 100 THE STRAND, BELLE ISLE, DETROIT, MI – (313) 852-4051: Models, interpretive displays, the smoking room from the 1912 passenger steamer *City of Detroit III*, an anchor from the *Edmund Fitzgerald* and the pilothouse from the steamer *William Clay Ford* are on display. *(detroithistorical.org/main/dossin)*

ELGIN MILITARY MUSEUM, ST. THOMAS, ON – (519) 633-7641: *HMCS Ojibwa*, a Cold War Oberon-class submarine, is open to the public at Port Burwell, Ont. *(projectojibwa.ca)*

ERIE MARITIME MUSEUM, 150 E. FRONT ST., ERIE, PA – (814) 452-2744: Displays depict the Battle of Lake Erie and more. Check ahead to see if the U.S. brig *Niagara* is in port. Open all year. *(eriemaritimemuseum.org)*

FAIRPORT HARBOR MUSEUM, 129 SECOND ST., FAIRPORT, OH – (440) 354-4825: Located in the Fairport Lighthouse, displays include the pilothouse from the *Frontenac* and the mainmast of the first *USS Michigan*. Seasonal. *(fairportharborlighthouse.org)*

GREAT LAKES LORE MARITIME MUSEUM, 367 N. THIRD ST., ROGERS CITY, MI – (989) 734-0706: The generations of men and women who risked their lives to sail and make their livings on the Great Lakes are enshrined and remembered here, as are their uniforms, personal possessions and navigational and other maritime tools. *(gllmm.com)*

GREAT LAKES SHIPWRECK MUSEUM, WHITEFISH POINT, MI – (906) 635-1742 or (800)-635-1742: Museum includes lighthouse and shipwreck artifacts, a shipwreck video theater, the restored lighthouse keeper's quarters and an *Edmund Fitzgerald* display that features the ship's bell. Seasonal. *(shipwreckmuseum.com)*

LE SAULT DE SAINTE MARIE HISTORICAL SITES INC., 501 E. WATER ST., SAULT STE. MARIE, MI – (906) 632-3658: The 1917-built steamer *Valley Camp* is the centerpiece of this museum. The ship's three cargo holds house artifacts, models, aquariums, photos and other memorabilia, as well as a tribute to the *Edmund Fitzgerald* that includes the ill-fated vessel's lifeboats. Seasonal. *(saulthistoricsites.com)*

MARITIME MUSEUM OF SANDUSKY, 125 MEIGS ST., SANDUSKY, OHIO – (419) 624-0274: Exhibits explore local maritime history. Open all year. *(sanduskymaritime.org)*

MARQUETTE MARITIME MUSEUM, EAST RIDGE & LAKESHORE BLVD., MARQUETTE, MI – (906) 226-2006: Museum re-creates the offices of the first commercial fishing and passenger freight companies. Displays also include charts, photos, models and maritime artifacts. Seasonal. *(mqtmaritimemuseum.com)*

MICHIGAN MARITIME MUSEUM, 260 DYCKMAN AVE., SOUTH HAVEN, MI – (269) 637-8078: Exhibits are dedicated to the U.S. Lifesaving Service and Coast Guard. The tall ship *Friends Good Will* operates during the summer. Open all year. *(michiganmaritimemuseum.org)*

Continued on Page 124

100 YEARS

Sault Ste. Marie's Museum Ship Valley Camp was launched in 1917, making her 100 this year. She's operated by Sault Historic Sites, which turns 50 in 2017. A steamy 3L2S salute to both!

Valley Camp on Lake Superior in 1963. (John Vournakis)

MUSKOKA BOAT AND HERITAGE CENTRE, GRAVENHURST, ON – (705) 687-2115: Visiting this museum, which includes many models of the early steamships to serve the area, is the perfect complement to a trip on the vintage *RMS Segwun*, moored adjacent. *(realmuskoka.com/muskoka-boat-and-heritage-centre)*

PORT COLBORNE HISTORICAL AND MARINE MUSEUM, 280 KING ST., PORT COLBORNE, ON – (905) 834-7604: Wheelhouse from the steam tug *Yvonne Dupre Jr.*, an anchor from the *Raleigh* and a lifeboat from the steamer *Hochelaga* are among the museum's displays. Seasonal.

STRAITS OF MACKINAC SHIPWRECK MUSEUM, OLD MACKINAC POINT LIGHT, MACKINAC CITY, MI – (231) 436-4100: Houses artifacts recovered from the sunken *Cedarville* as well as other artifacts that tell the story of the many shipwrecks that dot the Straits of Mackinac. Seasonal. *(mackinacparks.com)*

U.S. ARMY CORPS OF ENGINEERS MUSEUM, SOO LOCKS VISITOR CENTER, SAULT STE. MARIE, MI – (906) 632-7020: Exhibits include a working model of the Soo Locks, historic photos and a 25-minute film. Free; open Mother's Day weekend through mid-October. Check at the Visitor Center information desk for a list of vessels expected at the locks.

WELLAND CANAL VISITOR CENTRE, AT LOCK 3, THOROLD, ON – (905) 984-8880: Museum traces the development of the Welland Canal. Museum and adjacent gift shop open year-round. Observation deck open during the navigation season. Check at the information desk for vessels expected at Lock 3. *(infoniagara.com)*

WILLIAM PURVIS MARINE CENTRE, 40 WATER ST., GORE BAY, ON: This marine museum and archive is open Victoria Day-Thanksgiving Day (Canadian).

WISCONSIN MARITIME MUSEUM, 75 MARITIME DRIVE, MANITOWOC, WI – (866) 724-2356: Displays explore the history of area shipbuilding and also honor submariners and submarines built in Manitowoc. One of the engines of the Straits of Mackinac trainferry *Chief Wawatam* is on display. The World War II sub *Cobia* is adjacent to the museum and open for tours. Open all year. *(wisconsinmaritime.org)*

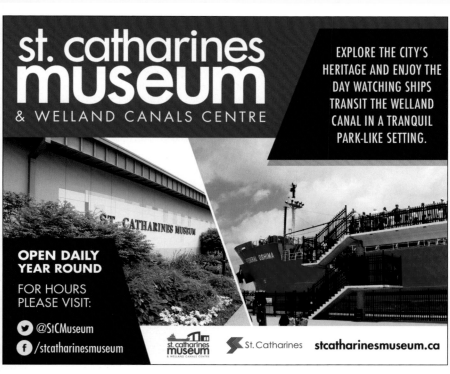

Stacks *and* Flags

Close-up view of the Polish Steamship Co. stack. *(Alain Gindroz)*

COLORS OF THE GREAT LAKES

Abaco Marine Towing
Clayton, NY

Algoma Central Corp.
St. Catharines, ON

American Steamship Co.
Williamsville, NY

Andrie Inc.
Muskegon, MI

Andrie Specialized
Norton Shores, MI

ArcelorMittal Mines Canada
Port Cartier, QC

Ashton Marine Co.
North Muskegon, MI

Basic Marine Inc.
Escanaba, MI

Bay City Boat Lines
Bay City, MI

**Bay Shipbuilding Co.
Fincanteri Marine Group**
Sturgeon, Bay, WI

Beaver Island Boat Co.
Charlevoix, MI

Blue Heron Co.
Tobermory, ON

Buffalo Dept. of Public Works
Buffalo, N.Y.

Busch Marine Inc.
Carrollton, MI

Calumet River Fleeting
Chicago, IL

Canada Steamship Lines
Montreal, QC

Canada Steamship Lines
Montreal, QC

Canadian Coast Guard
Ottawa, ON

**Carmeuse North America
(Erie Sand & Gravel)**
Erie, PA

Causley Marine Contracting LLC
Bay City, MI

**Central Marine Logistics Inc.
Operator for ArcelorMittal**
Griffith, IN

Chicago Fire Dept.
Chicago, IL

Cleveland Fire Dept.
Cleveland, OH

Cooper Marine Ltd.
Selkirk, OH

Croisières AML Inc.
Québec, QC

Dann Marine Towing
Chesapeake City, MD

Dean Construction Co.
Belle River, ON

Detroit City Fire Dept.
Detroit, MI

Diamond Jack's River Tours
Detroit, MI

Duc D'Orleans Cruise Boat
Corunna, ON

Durocher Marine
Cheboygan, MI

Eastern Upper Peninsula Transportation Authority
Sault Ste. Marie, MI

**Essroc Canada Inc.
Algoma Central – Mgr**
North York, ON

Fraser Shipyards Inc.
Superior, WI

**G3 Canada Ltd.
Algoma Central – Mgr**
Winnipeg, MB

Gaelic Tugboat Co.
Detroit, MI

Gananoque Boat Line
Gananoque, ON

Genesis Energy
Houston, TX

Geo. Gradel Co.
Toledo, OH

Goodtime Cruise Line
Cleveland, OH

**Grand Portage /
Isle Royale Trans. Line**
Superior, WI

Gravel & Lake Services
Thunder Bay, ON

Great Lakes Dock & Materials
Muskegon, MI

**Great Lakes Fleet Inc.
Key Lakes Inc.– Mgr.**
Duluth, MN

Great Lakes & International Towing & Salvage
Burlington, ON

Great Lakes Maritime Academy
Traverse City, MI

Great Lakes Science Center
Ann Arbor, MI

Great Lakes Towing Co.
Cleveland, OH

Groupe C.T.M.A.
Cap-aux-Meules, QC

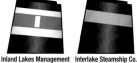

Groupe Desgagnés Inc.
Québec City, QC

Groupe Desgagnés Inc.
Québec City, QC

Groupe Desgagnés Inc.
Québec City, QC

Hamilton Port Authority
Hamilton, ON

Heritage Marine
Two Harbors, MN

Inland Lakes Management
Alpena, MI

Interlake Steamship Co.
Richfield, OH

J.W. Westcott Co.
Detroit, MI

Kindra Lake Towing
Chicago, IL

The King Company
Holland, MI

Lafarge Canada Inc.
Montreal, QC

Lafarge North America Inc.
Southfield, MI

Lake Erie Island Cruises
Sandusky, OH

Lakehead Tugboats Inc.
Thunder Bay, ON

Lake Michigan Carferry Service Inc.
Ludington, MI

Le Groupe Océan Inc.
Québec, QC

Lower Lakes Towing Lower Lakes Transportation
Port Dover, ON / Williamsville, NY

Luedtke Engineering
Frankfort, MI

MCM Marine Inc.
Sault Ste. Marie, MI

MacDonald Marine Ltd.
Goderich, ON

Madeline Island Ferry Line Inc.
LaPointe, WI

Malcolm Marine
St. Clair, MI

Manitou Island Transit
Leland, MI

Marine Tech LLC
Duluth, MN

Mariposa Cruise Line
Toronto, ON

McAsphalt Marine Transportation
Scarborough, ON

McKeil Marine Ltd.
Hamilton, ON

McKeil Marine Ltd.
Burlington, ON

McNally International
Hamilton, ON

Midwest Maritime Corp.
Milwaukee, WI

Miller Boat Line
Put-in-Bay, OH

Ministry of Transportation
Downsview, ON

Montreal Port Authority
Montreal, QC

Muskoka Steamship & Historical Society
Gravenhurst, ON

Nadro Marine Services
Port Dover, ON

New York State Marine Highway Transportation
Troy, NY

Owen Sound Transportation Co. Ltd.
Owen Sound, ON

Pere Marquette Shipping
Ludington, MI

Port City Steamship Port City Tug Inc.
Muskegon, MI

Purvis Marine Ltd.
Sault Ste. Marie, ON

Roen Salvage Co.
Sturgeon Bay, WI

Ryba Marine Construction
Cheboygan, MI

Sea Service LLC
Superior, WI

Selvick Marine Towing Corp.
Sturgeon Bay, WI

Shoreline Sightseeing Co.
Chicago, IL

Société des Traversiers Du Québec
Québec, QC

Soo Locks Boat Tours
Sault Ste. Marie, MI

St. James Marine Co.
Beaver Island, MI

St. Lawrence Cruise Lines Inc.
Kingston, ON

St. Lawrence Seaway Development Corp.
Massena,NY

St. Lawrence Seaway Management Corp.
Cornwall, ON

St. Marys Cement Group
Toronto, ON

Sterling Fuels Ltd.
Hamilton, ON

Svitzer Canada Ltd.
Halifax, NS

Thousand Islands & Seaway Cruises
Brockville, ON

Thunder Bay Tug Services Ltd.
Thunder Bay, ON

Toronto Drydock Ltd.
Toronto, ON

Toronto Fire Services
Toronto, ON

Toronto Port Authority
Toronto, ON

United States Army Corps of Engineers
Chicago, IL

United States Coast Guard 9th Coast Guard District
Cleveland, OH

United States Fish & Wildlife Service
Elmira, MI

United States National Park Service
Houghton, MI

U.S. Oil Div. U.S. Venture Inc.
Appleton, WI

VanEnkevort Tug & Barge
Escanaba, MI

SALTWATER FLEETS ON THE SEAWAY

ABC Maritime
Nyon, Switzerland

Ace Tankers CV
Amsterdam, Netherlands

Alliance Tankers
Hamilton, Bermuda

Ardmore Shipping Ltd.
Cork, Ireland

Armador Gemi Isletmeciligi Ticaret Ltd.
Istanbul, Turkey

ARA Group
Werkendam, Netherlands

Atlantska Plovidba
Dubrovnik, Croatia

Bernhard Schulte Group
Hamburg, Germany

BigLift Shipping
Amsterdam, Netherlands

Blystad Group
Oslo, Norway

Briese Schiffahrts GMBH & Co. KG
Leer, Germany

Canadian Forest Navigation Co. Ltd.
Montreal, QC, Canada

Carisbrooke Shipping LTD
Cowes, United Kingdom

Chemfleet Shipping
Istanbul, Turkey

Chemikalien Seetransport
Hamburg, Germany

Chemnav Inc.
Athens, Greece

Clipper Cruises Ltd.
Nassau, Bahamas

Clipper Group AS
Copenhagen, Denmark

Coastal Shipping Ltd. (Div. Woodward Group)
Goose Bay, NL, Canada

C.O.E. Shipping GMBH & Co.
Buxtehude, Germany

Columbia Shipmanagement
Hamburg, Germany

Cosco Southern Asphalt Shipping Co.
Guangzhou, China

Danser Van Gent
Delfzijl, Netherlands

Duzgit Gemi Insa Sanayi
Istanbul, Turkey

Eastern Pacific Shipping — Singapore

 Empire Chemical Tankers — Piraeus, Greece

 Elbe Shipping GMBH — Drochtersen, Germany

 Enzian Ship Management — Zürich, Switzerland

 Fednav International Ltd. — Montreal, QC, Canada

 Fednav International Ltd. — Montreal, QC, Canada

 Finbeta — Savona, Italy

 Fairfield Chemical Carriers — Wilton, CT, USA

 Freese Reederei Group — Stade, Germany

 Greenfleet Shipping Ltd. — Nassau, Bahamas

 Hansa Heavy Lift GMBH — Bremen, Germany

 Harren & Partner Schiffahrts GMBH — Bremen, Germany

 Hermann Buss GMBH — Leer, Germany

 Herning Shipping AS — Herning, Denmark

 Intersee Schiffahrts-Gesellschaft MbH & Co. — Haren-Ems, Germany

 Intership Navigation Co. — Limassol, Cyprus

 Jo Tankers — Spijkenisse, Netherlands

 Johann M.K. Blumenthal GMBH & Co. — Hamburg, Germany

 Jumbo Shipping Co. SA — Rotterdam, Netherlands

 Kallianis Bros Shipping — Athens, Greece

 Knutsen O.A.S. Shipping — Haugesund, Norway

 Lauranne Shipping BV — Ghent, Netherlands

 Marconsult Schiffahrt GMBH & Co. KG — Hamburg, Germany

 Mastermind Shipmanagement Ltd. — Limassol, Cyprus

 Mega Chemical Tankers Ltd. — Singapore, Singapore

 Mineralien Schiffahrt Spedition — Schnaittenbach, Germany

 Navigation Maritime Bulgare Ltd. — Varna, Bulgaria

 Neste Shipping OY — Espoo, Finland

 Nordana Shipping Co. — Copenhagen, Denmark

 Nordic Tankers A/S — Copenhagen, Denmark

 Oceanex Inc. — Montreal, QC, Canada

 OSM Group AS — Kristiansand, Norway

 Parakou Shipping Ltd. — Hong Kong, China

 Pearl Seas Cruises LLC. — Guilford, CT

 Peter Dohle Schiffahrts — Hamburg, Germany

 Phoenix Shipping and Trading SA — Piraeus, Greece

 Polish Steamship Co. — Szczecin, Poland

 Pot Scheepvaart BV — Delfzijl, Netherlands

 Principal Maritime Management LLC — Southport, CT

 Rederiet Stenersen AS — Bergen, Norway

 Reederei Karl Schlüter GMBH & Co. KG — Rendsburg, Germany

 Reederei Nord GMBH — Hamburg, Germany

 Rigel Schiffahrts GMBH — Bremen, Germany

 Sloman Neotun Shiffahrts — Bremen, Germany

 Spliethoff's — Amsterdam, Netherlands

 Sunship Schiffahrtskontor KG — Emden, Germany

 Tarbit Tankers B.V. — Dordrecht, Netherlands

 TB Marine Shipmanagement GMBH & Co. — Hamburg, Germany

Team Tankers Management AS
Hellerup, Denmark

Thorco Projects
Hamburg, Germany

Transal Denizcilik Tickaret
Istanbul, Turkey

Tradewind Tankers
Barcelona, Spain

Uni-Tankers A/S
Middelfart, Denmark

Unicorn Tankers International Ltd.
London, United Kingdom

VBG Denizcilik Sanaya VE Ticaret AS
Istanbul, Turkey

W. Bockstiegel Reederei KG
Emden, Germany

Wagenborg Shipping
Delfzijl, Netherlands

Yardimci Shipping Group
Istanbul, Turkey

Yilmar Shipping & Trading Ltd.
Istanbul, Turkey

Zealand Shipping BV
Almere, Netherlands

FLAGS OF REGISTRY

Bahamas

Barbados

Belgium

Bermuda

Bulgaria

Canada

China

Croatia

Cyprus

Denmark

Finland

France

Germany

Greece

Hong Kong

India

Ireland

Israel

Italy

Japan

Liberia

Lithuania

Malta

Monaco

Netherlands

Norway

Panama

Philippines

Poland

Russia

Singapore

Spain

St.Vincent and The Grenadines

Sweden

Switzerland

Taiwan

Turkey

Ukraine

United Kingdom

United States

Vanuatu

Yugoslavia

FLEET HOUSEFLAGS

Algoma Central Corp.
St. Catherines, ON

American Steamship Co.
Williamsville, NY

Andrie Inc.
Muskegon, MI

**ArcelorMittal
Central Marine Logistics**
Griffith, IN

**Canada Steamship
Lines Inc. (CSL)**
Montreal, QC

**Canadian Coast
Guard**
Ottawa, ON

**Canadian Forest
Navigation Co. Ltd.**
Montreal, QC

Fednav Ltd.
Montreal, QC

Gaelic Tugboat Co.
Detroit, MI

**Great Lakes Fleet Inc.
Key Lakes Inc. - Mgr.**
Duluth, MN

**Great Lakes
Maritime Academy**
Traverse City, MI

Great Lakes Towing Co.
Cleveland, OH

Groupe Desgagnés Inc.
Québec, QC

**Inland Lakes
Management Inc.**
Alpena, MI

Interlake Steamship Co
Richfield, OH

J.W. Westcott Co.
Detroit, MI

LaFarge Canada Inc.
Montreal, QC

**Lake Michigan
Carferry Service Inc.**
Ludington, MI

Le Groupe Océan Inc.
Québec, QC

**Lower Lakes Towing Ltd.
Lower Lakes Transportation Co.**
Port Dover, ON / Williamsville, NY

**McAsphalt Marine
Transportation Ltd.**
Scarborough, ON

McKeil Marine Ltd.
Burlington, ON

**Owen Sound
Transportation Co. Ltd.**
Owen Sound, ON

**Pere Marquette
Shipping Co.**
Ludington, MI

Polish Steamship Co.
Szczecin, Poland

Purvis Marine Ltd.
Sault Ste. Marie, ON

**St.Lawrence Seaway
Development Corp.**
Massena, NY

**St.Lawrence Seaway
Management Corp.**
Cornwall, ON

Spliethoff's
Amsterdam, Netherlands

**U.S. Army Corps
of Engineers**
Cincinnati, OH

**U.S. Coast
Guard**
Cleveland, OH

Wagenborg Shipping
Delfzijl, Netherlands

Other Flags of Note

**Dangerous Cargo
On Board**

Pilot On Board

Diver Down

Commodore Perry War of 1812
flag, often flown by lake vessels

Extra Tonnage

Ports · Cargoes
Locks · Canals

U.S. Coast Guard cutter Hollyhock working aids to navigation. *(Steve Jowett)*

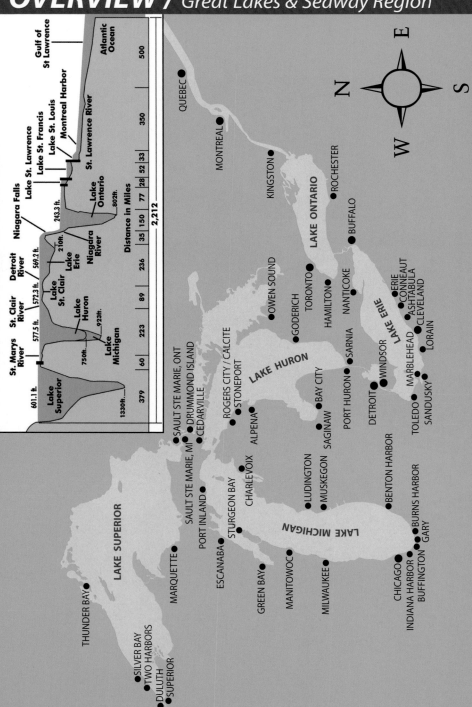

PORTS / *Loading & Unloading*

CSL Laurentien at South Chicago, assisted by the tug Massachusetts.
(Christine Douglas)

Taconite ore is loaded for delivery to lower lakes steel mills at Duluth, Two Harbors, Taconite Harbor and Silver Bay, Minn., as well as Superior, Wis., and Escanaba and Marquette, Mich. Limestone-loading ports are Port Inland, Cedarville, Drummond Island, Calcite, Rogers City and Stoneport, Mich., and Marblehead, Ohio. Coal ports are Superior, Wis., S. Chicago, Ill., and the Ohio ports of Toledo, Sandusky, Ashtabula and Conneaut. Petroleum is loaded aboard vessels at Sarnia, Ont., and E. Chicago, Ind. Grain export ports include Duluth, Minn.; Milwaukee and Superior, Wis.; and the Ontario ports of Thunder Bay, Sarnia and Owen Sound.

The primary U.S. iron ore and limestone receiving ports are Cleveland and Chicago, along with Gary, Burns Harbor and Indiana Harbor, Ind.; Detroit, Mich; and Toledo, as well as Lorain, Ashtabula and Conneaut, Ohio. Nanticoke, Hamilton, and Sault Ste. Marie, Ont., are major ore-receiving ports in Canada. Coal is carried by self-unloaders to power plants in the U.S. and Canada. Most grain loaded on the lakes is destined for export via the St. Lawrence Seaway, although some is carried to Toledo and Buffalo, N.Y. Cement from Alpena and Charlevoix, Mich., is delivered to terminals from Lake Superior to Lake Ontario. Tankers bring petroleum products to cities as diverse in size as Cleveland, Ohio, and Cheboygan, Detroit, Escanaba and Muskegon, Mich. Self-unloaders carry limestone, coal, road salt and sand to cities throughout the region.

AVERAGE RUNNING TIMES

Times listed are for downbound passages. Reverse for upbound times. Times vary with speed / weather / traffic.

LAKE SUPERIOR
Duluth/Superior – Soo Locks .... 24 hrs
Marquette or Thunder Bay – Soo Locks .... 12 hrs

ST. MARYS RIVER
Soo Locks – DeTour, Mich. .... 6 hrs
DeTour – Port Huron .... 19 hrs

LAKE HURON
DeTour – Mackinac Bridge .... 2 hrs
DeTour – Port Huron .... 19 hrs
Harbor Beach – Port Huron .... 4 hrs

LAKE MICHIGAN
Gray's Reef Light – Gary, Ind. .... 22 hrs

LAKE ERIE
Detroit River Light – Toledo .... 1.75 hrs
Detroit River Light – Southeast Shoal .... 3 hrs
Southeast Shoal – Long Point .... 9 hrs
Long Point – CIP 15 (Welland Canal) .... 7 hrs
Detroit River Light – Port Colborne piers
(Welland Canal) .... 19 hrs

LAKE ONTARIO
Welland Canal (Port Weller) – Hamilton .... 2 hrs
Welland Canal (Port Weller) – Cape Vincent, N.Y.
(call-in points at Newcastle, mid-lake and
Sodus Point) .... 12 hrs

CARGOES / *Some of What Lakers Carry*

Algoma Transport unloads salt at Marinette, Wis. (Scott Best)

IRON FINES – Fines (ore less than 6mm in diameter) are created as a result of mining, crushing and processing the larger pieces of ore. See **SINTER**.

LIMESTONE – Common sedimentary rock consisting mostly of calcium carbonate used as a building stone and in the manufacture of lime, carbon dioxide and cement.

AGRICULTURAL PRODUCTS – Wheat, grain, soybeans, canola, flax and oats are shipped on the Great Lakes. Some is used domestically, but most is shipped to international markets overseas.

BUNKER C – A special grade of heavy fuel oil, also known as No. 6 fuel.

CEMENT CLINKER – A material, made by heating ground limestone and clay, that is ground up to a fine powder to produce cement.

CLINKER – The incombustible residue that remains after the combustion of coal.

COAL – Both eastern (high sulfur, used in industry) and western (low sulfur, burned at power plants) coal are shipped aboard Great Lakes vessels.

COKE – A byproduct of blended coals baked in ovens until mostly pure carbon is left. Coke is used to generate the high heat necessary to make steel in blast furnaces.

COKE BREEZE – Byproduct of coke production.

DOLOMITE – Rock similar to limestone but somewhat harder and heavier.

FLUXSTONE – Taconite pellets premixed with limestone, so no limestone needs to be added in a blast furnace.

SCALE – Byproduct of the shaping of iron and steel.

PETROLEUM COKE – Petroleum coke (petcoke) is the bottom end of oil refining – the parts of crude oil that will not vaporize in the refining process. It is mostly used as fuel (often blended with coal) in power plants.

PIG IRON – Crude iron that is the direct product of the blast furnace and is refined to produce steel, wrought iron or ingot iron.

POTASH – A compound used for fertilizer.

SALT – Most salt shipped on the Great Lakes is used on roads and highways during the winter to melt ice.

SINTER – Broken taconite pellets, a.k.a. taconite pellet chips and fines. Small, but still useful in the blast furnace.

SLAG – Byproduct of the steelmaking process is used in the production of concrete and as seal coat cover, a base for paving, septic drain fields and railroad ballast.

TACONITE – A low-grade iron ore, containing about 27 percent iron and 51 percent silica, found as a hard rock formation in the Lake Superior region. It is pelletized for shipment to steel mills (see below).

TRAP ROCK – Rock, usually ground fairly fine, for use as foundations and roads or walkways. It is mined near Bruce Mines, Ont., and loaded there.

Why taconite pellets?

The high-grade iron ore (around 60 percent pure) that was mined on the ranges around Lake Superior was mostly exhausted in the tremendous mining efforts of World War II and in the early 1950s. There was still plenty of iron ore in the ground, but it was only about 20-30 percent iron. To mine and ship all that ore in its natural form would have been expensive, so engineers developed the taconite pelletization process to increase the iron content of the product coming off the ranges headed for the steel mills. Pellets have a number of positive attributes. Their iron content (and the content of other elements) can be precisely controlled so the steel mills know exactly what they are getting. Pellets are relatively moisture free compared with raw iron ore, so they are less prone to freeze in rail cars, storage piles or dock pockets. This means the pellets can be shipped for a much longer season than natural iron ore, so companies need fewer rail cars and ships to carry the same amount of pellets, thus saving money on labor and infrasructure. Pellets are also uniform in size, shape and mass, making them very easy to handle on conveyor belt systems, which makes for speedy, precise ship loading and unloading using a shipboard self-unloading system, again cutting down on costs.

A self-unloader's system of belts carries the cargo from the hold, across the boom and onto the dock.

Vessels transiting the St. Clair River, Lake St. Clair and the Detroit River are under the jurisdiction of Sarnia Traffic and must radio their positions at predetermined locations. Call-in points (bold type on map) are not the same for upbound and downbound traffic. Average running times between call-in points are below. *

UPBOUND	Buoys 1&2	Black River	Stag Isl.	Salt Dock	X-32	Crib Light	Grassy Isl.
Detroit River Lt.	8:10	7:50	7:20	6:00	4:20	4:00	1:35
Grassy Island	6:45	6:25	5:55	4:35	2:55	2:35	
St. Clair Crib	4:10	3:50	3:20	2:00	0:25		
Light X-32	3:50	3:30	3:00	1:35			
Salt Dock	2:10	1:50	1:20				
Stag Isl. Upper	0:50	0:35					
Black River	0:20						

DOWNBOUND	Det. River	Grassy Isl.	Belle Isl.	Crib Light	Light 23	Salt Dock	Black River	7&8
30 min. above buoys 11 & 12	9:05	7:35	6:25	5:10	3:55	3:10	1:20	0:40
Buoys 7 & 8	8:15	6:55	5:45	4:30	3:15	2:30	0:40	
Black River	7:45	6:15	5:05	3:50	2:35	1:50		
Salt Dock	5:55	4:25	3:15	2:00	0:45			
Light 23	5:10	3:40	2:30	1:10				
St. Clair Crib	3:55	2:25	1:10					
USCG Belle Isle	2:40	1:10						
Grassy Isl.	1:30							

* Times can change if vessels stop for fuel or are delayed by other traffic.

Map labels:

BUOYS 11 & 12 DOWNBOUND ONLY

BUOYS 7 & 8 DOWNBOUND ONLY

BUOYS 1 & 2 UPBOUND ONLY

LAKE HURON

SARNIA

PORT HURON

IMPERIAL FUEL DOCK

BLACK RIVER

STAG ISLAND UPPER UPBOUND ONLY

SHELL FUEL DOCK

ST. CLAIR

ST. CLAIR EDISON POWER PLANT RECOR POINT

MARINE CITY

SALT DOCK

ALGONAC

HARSENS ISLAND

LIGHT 23 DOWNBOUND ONLY

X(RAY) 32 UPBOUND ONLY

ST. CLAIR CRIB LIGHT

LAKE ST. CLAIR

USCG BELLE ISLE DOWNBOUND ONLY

J.W. WESTCOTT MAILBOAT

DETROIT

MISTERSKY FUEL

WINDSOR

ROUGE RIVER

STERLING FUEL

GRASSY ISLAND

FIGHTING ISLAND

GROSSE ILE

LIVINGSTONE CHANNEL

AMHERSTBURG CHANNEL

DETROIT RIVER LIGHT

N W E S

MONROE

LAKE ERIE

PELEE PASSAGE

POINT PELEE

PELEE ISLAND

SOUTHEAST SHOAL

TOLEDO

The St. Marys River flows out of the southeast corner of Lake Superior in a southeasterly direction to Lake Huron. Vessels transiting the St. Marys River system are under the jurisdiction of Soo Traffic, part of the U.S. Coast Guard at Sault Ste. Marie, Mich., and must radio their positions on VHF Ch. 12 (156.600 MHz) at predetermined locations. Vessels in the vicinity of the Soo Locks fall under the jurisdiction of the lockmaster, who must be contacted on VHF Ch. 14 (156.700 MHz) for lock assignments.

Call-in points (bold type on map) are not the same for upbound and downbound traffic. Approximate running times between call-in points are at left; times may vary due to other traffic and weather. Because of their size, 1,000-footers take more time to transit than smaller vessels.

Arrival times at the Soo Locks are available at the Information Center located in the locks park. Upbound vessels must make a pre-call to Soo Traffic one hour before entering the river at DeTour, and downbound traffic is required to make a one-hour pre-call above Ile Parisienne.

** Upbound traffic passes Neebish Island on the east side. Downbound traffic passes the island to the west, through the Rock Cut, a channel dynamited out of solid rock in the early 1900s.

Map labels

ILE PARISIENNE
DOWNBOUND ONLY

WHITEFISH BAY

CANADA

GROS CAP
UPBOUND ONLY

WEST PIER
EAST PIER
SAULT STE MARIE, ON
MISSION POINT
SOO LOCKS
BIG POINT
SUGAR ISLAND
LAKE GEORGE
SAULT STE MARIE, MI

U.S.A.

NINE MILE POINT
LAKE NICOLET
BARBEAU
ROCK CUT
NEEBISH ISLAND**
STRIBLING POINT
JOHNSON POINT
WINTER POINT
ST. JOSEPH ISLAND
MUNUSCONG LAKE
MUD LAKE JUNCTION BUOY

RABER
LIME ISLAND
DRUMMOND ISLAND
DETOUR VILLAGE
DETOUR REEF LIGHT

LAKE HURON

N E S W (compass)

UPBOUND

UPBOUND	J'ct. Buoy	Nine Mile	Miss. Point	Clear Locks	Gros Cap
DeTour	1:35	3:35	4:20	5:50	7:25
Junction Buoy		1:50	2:45	4:15	5:50
Nine Mile Point			0:55	2:25	4:00
Mission Point*				1:30	3:05
Clear of Locks					1:35

DOWNBOUND

DOWNBOUND	Gros Cap	Big Point	Clear Locks	Nine Mile	J'ct Buoy	DeTour
Ile Parisienne	0:45	1:55	3:25	4:20	6:20	8:00
Gros Cap		1:10	2:40	3:35	5:35	7:15
Big Point*			1:30	2:25	4:25	6:05
Clear of Locks				0:55	2:55	4:35
Nine Mile Point					2:00	3:40
Junction Buoy						1:40

* Lockmaster only

The Soo Locks at Sault Ste. Marie, Mich., on the St. Marys River, overcome a 21-foot difference in water levels between Lake Superior and lakes Huron, Michigan and Erie.

Under the jurisdiction of the U.S. Army Corps of Engineers, the locks operate on gravity, as do all locks in the St. Lawrence Seaway system. No pumps are used to empty or fill the lock chambers; valves are opened, and water is allowed to seek its own level. All traffic passes through the locks toll-free.

Traffic is dispatched by radio to the appropriate lock according to size, other vessels in the locks area and the time the captain first calls in to the lockmaster. All vessels longer than 730 feet and / or wider than 76 feet are restricted by size to the Poe, or second, lock. A vessel is under engine and thruster control at all times, with crews ready to drop mooring lines over bollards on the lock wall to stop its movement.

As soon as the vessel is in position, engines are stopped and mooring lines made fast. If the vessel is being lowered, valves at the lower end of the lock chamber are opened to allow the water inside to flow out. If the vessel is being raised, valves at the upper end of the chamber are opened to allow water to enter. When the water reaches the desired level, the valves are closed, the protective boom is raised, the gates are opened, and the vessel leaves the lock.

The first canal on the American side was built from 1853-55. That canal was destroyed in 1888 by workers making way for newer, bigger locks.

MacArthur Lock

Named after World War II Gen. Douglas MacArthur, the MacArthur Lock is 800 feet long (243.8 meters) between inner gates, 80 feet wide (24.4 meters) and 31 feet deep (9.4 meters) over the sills. The lock was built in 1942-43 and opened to traffic on July 11, 1943. Vessel size is limited to 730 feet long (222.5 meters) by 76 feet wide (23 meters).

Poe Lock

The Poe Lock is 1,200 feet long (365.8 meters) and 110 feet wide (33.5 meters), and has a depth over the sills of 32 feet (9.8 meters). Named after Col. Orlando M. Poe, it was built in the years 1961-68. The lock's vessel size limit is 1,100 feet long (335.3 meters) by 105 feet wide (32 meters).

Davis and Sabin locks

Dating from the first two decades of the 20th century, these two locks are no longer used. Work began in 2009 to replace them with one new Poe-sized lock, at an estimated cost of more than $500 million. However, the project remains stalled due to lack of funding.

Canadian Lock

The Canadian Lock at Sault Ste. Marie, Ont., has its origin in a canal constructed from 1887-95. The present lock, operated by Parks Canada, is used by pleasure craft, tugs and tour boats.

About the Soo Locks ...

The Empire State Building is 1,250 feet tall. The largest vessel using the Soo Locks is 1,014 feet long. This vessel, the American-flagged *Paul R. Tregurtha*, carried 3,219,646 net tons of cargo through the locks during the 1998 season.

There are about 140 major freighters, barges and tankers engaged almost exclusively in the Great Lakes and Seaway trade. That number is augmented by a variety of saltwater vessels, or "salties," that enter the system during the season.

The Great Lakes shipping season runs from late March to late December. In the spring and fall, a small fleet of icebreakers operated by the U.S. and Canadian coast guards and commercial tugs helps keep navigation channels open.

A vessel traveling from the Atlantic Ocean to Lake Superior through the St. Lawrence Seaway and the Soo Locks rises nearly 600 feet. The first lift, a total of 224 feet, is provided by the seven St. Lawrence Seaway locks that begin at Montreal. The Welland Canal, connecting Lake Erie and Lake Ontario and bypassing Niagara Falls, raises vessels an additional 326 feet. The Soo Locks complete the process.

One short blast of a vessel's whistle while in the lock means "cast off lines."

A red-and-white flag flying from a vessel's mast indicates a pilot is on board. Saltwater vessels pick up pilots at various points in their voyage.

During 1953, 128 million tons of freight moved through the locks. This amazing record stands.

The St. Marys River, running 80 miles (128.7 km) from Isle Parisienne at its north end to DeTour Reef Light at its south end, connects Lake Superior with Lake Huron. It includes two engineering marvels – the Soo Locks at Sault Ste. Marie and the West Neebish Cut at Barbeau, Mich., a channel dynamited out of solid rock that allows traffic to pass to the west side of Neebish Island.

LOCKS & CANALS / *Welland Canal*

The **28-mile (44 km) Welland Canal** is the fourth version of a waterway link between Lake Ontario and Lake Erie, first built in 1829. The present canal was completed in 1932, deepened in the 1950s as part of the Seaway project and further straightened in 1973. Today its eight locks, all Canadian, lift ships 326 feet (100 meters) over the Niagara Escarpment.

Each of the seven Welland Canal locks has an average lift of 46.5 feet (14.2 meters). All locks (except Lock 8) are 859 feet (261.8 meters) long, 80 feet (24.4 meters) wide and 30 feet (9.1 meters) deep. Lock 8 measures 1,380 feet (420.6 m) long.

The largest vessel that may transit the canal is 740 feet (225.5 meters) long, 78 feet (23.8 meters) wide and 26.5 feet (8.08 meters) in draft. **Locks 1, 2** and **3** are at Port Weller and St. Catharines, Ont., on the Lake Ontario end of the waterway. At Lock 3, the Welland Canal Viewing Center and Museum also houses an information desk (which posts a list of vessels expected at the lock), a gift shop and restaurant.

At Thorold, **Locks 4, 5** and **6**, twinned to help speed passage of vessels, are controlled with an elaborate interlocking system for safety. These locks (positioned end to end, they resemble a short flight of stairs) have an aggregate lift of 139.5 feet (42.5 meters). Just south of locks **4, 5** and **6** is Lock **7. Lock 8**, seven miles (11.2 km) upstream at Port Colborne, completes the process, making the final adjustment to Lake Erie's level.

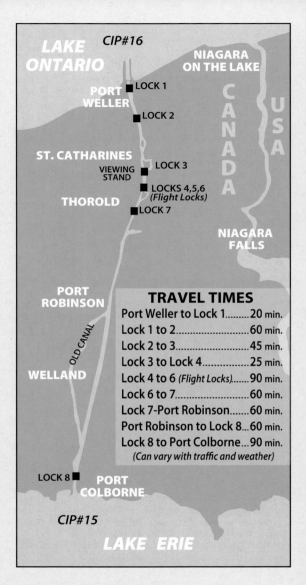

TRAVEL TIMES

Port Weller to Lock 1	20 min.
Lock 1 to 2	60 min.
Lock 2 to 3	45 min.
Lock 3 to Lock 4	25 min.
Lock 4 to 6 *(Flight Locks)*	90 min.
Lock 6 to 7	60 min.
Lock 7-Port Robinson	60 min.
Port Robinson to Lock 8	60 min.
Lock 8 to Port Colborne	90 min.

(Can vary with traffic and weather)

In 1973, a new channel was constructed to replace the section of the old canal that bisected the city of Welland. The Welland Bypass eliminated long delays for canal navigation and for road and rail traffic. Two tunnels allow auto and train traffic to pass beneath the canal.

The average passage time for the canal is 8-11 hours, with the majority of the time spent transiting Locks 4-7. All vessel traffic though the Welland Canal is regulated by a control center, Seaway Welland, which also remotely operates the locks and the traffic bridges over the canal. Vessels passing through the Welland Canal and St. Lawrence Seaway must carry a qualified pilot at all times.

CSL St-Laurent being lowered in Lock 1 of the Welland Canal. (Bill Bird)

Walter J. McCarthy Jr. at the Soo Locks on Engineer's Day, always the last Friday in June, when access to normally off-limits areas is allowed. (Roger LeLievre)

Tanker Sten Baltic entering the Seaway westbound at Montreal. *(René Beauchamp)*

The St. Lawrence Seaway is a waterway extending some 2,038 miles (3,701.4 km) from the Atlantic Ocean to the head of the Great Lakes at Duluth, Minn., including Montreal harbor and the Welland Canal. More specifically, it is a system of locks and canals (U.S. and Canadian), built between 1954 and 1958 at a cost of $474 million and opened in 1959, that allows vessels to pass from Montreal to the Welland Canal at the western end of Lake Ontario. For the Montreal-Lake Ontario section, the average transit time is 24 hours upbound and 22 hours downbound. The difference is mainly due to the current in the St. Lawrence River. The vessel size limit within this system is 740 feet (225.6 meters) long, 78 feet (23.8 meters) wide and 26 feet (7.9 meters) draft. It takes 8-10 days for a ship to go from Lake Superior to the Atlantic Ocean.

LOCK DIMENSIONS

Length.....................766 feet (233.5 meters)
Width...............................80 feet (24 meters
Depth.............................30 feet (9.1 meters)

Closest to the ocean is the **St. Lambert Lock**, which lifts ships some 15 feet (4.6 meters) from Montreal harbor to the level of the Laprairie Basin, through which the channel sweeps in a great arc 8.5 miles (13.7 km) long to the second lock. The **Côte Ste. Catherine Lock**, like the other six St. Lawrence Seaway locks, is built to the dimensions shown in the table above. The Côte Ste. Catherine lifts ships from the level of the Laprairie Basin 30 feet (9.1 meters) to the level of Lake Saint-Louis, bypassing the Lachine Rapids. Beyond it, the channel runs 7.5 miles (12.1 km) before reaching Lake Saint-Louis.

The **Lower Beauharnois Lock**, bypassing the Beauharnois Power House, lifts ships 41 feet (12.5 meters) and sends them through a short canal to the **Upper Beauharnois Lock**, where they are lifted 41 feet (12.5 meters) to reach the Beauharnois Canal. After a 13-mile (20.9 km) trip in the canal and a 30-mile (48.3 km) passage through Lake Saint Francis, vessels reach the U.S. border and the **Snell Lock**, which has a lift of 45 feet (13.7 meters) and empties into the 10-mile (16.1 km) Wiley-Dondero Canal.

After passing through the Wiley-Dondero, ships are raised another 38 feet (11.6 meters) by the **Dwight D. Eisenhower Lock**, after which they enter Lake St. Lawrence, the pool upon which nearby power-generating stations draw for their turbines located a mile to the north.

At the western end of Lake St. Lawrence, the **Iroquois Lock** allows ships to bypass the Iroquois Control Dam. The lift here is only about 1 foot (0.3 meters). Once in the waters west of Iroquois, the channel meanders through the Thousand Islands to Lake Ontario, the Welland Canal and beyond.

Norge, the Royal Yacht of the King of Norway, was a Seaway visitor in 2016. *(Murray Blancher)*

SEAWAY – LOCK LIFTS

St. Lambert Lock	15 ft.
Côte Ste. Catherine Lock	30 ft.
Lower Beauharnois Lock	41 ft.
Upper Beauharnois Lock	41 ft.
Snell Lock	45 ft
Eisenhower Lock	38 ft.
Iroquois Lock	1 ft.

MONTREAL
ST LAMBERT
ST LAMBERT LOCK
COTE STE CATHERINE LOCK
LAKE ST LOUIS
BEAUHARNOIS LOCKS
BEAUHARNOIS CANAL
LAKE ST FRANCOIS
CORNWALL
SNELL LOCK
LONG SAULT
EISENHOWER LOCK
INGLESIDE
MASSENA
MORRISBURG
IROQUOIS
IROQUOIS LOCK
OGDENSBURG
OTTAWA
CANADA
U.S.A.
PRESCOTT
BROCKVILLE
ALEXANDRIA BAY
CAPE VINCENT
KINGSTON
LAKE ONTARIO

N
E
S
W

FOLLOWING THE FLEET

With an inexpensive VHF scanner, boatwatchers can tune to ship-to-ship and ship-to-shore traffic using the following frequency guide.

Calling/distress only	**Ch. 16 – 156.800 MHz**	Calling/distress only
Commercial vessels only	**Ch. 06 – 156.300 MHz**	Working channel
Commercial vessels only	**Ch. 08 – 156.400 MHz**	Working channel
DeTour Reef – Lake St. Clair Light	**Ch. 11 – 156.550 MHz**	Sarnia Traffic - Sect. 1
Long Point Light – Lake St. Clair Light	**Ch. 12 – 156.600 MHz**	Sarnia Traffic - Sect. 2
Montreal – Mid-Lake St. Francis	**Ch. 14 – 156.700 MHz**	Seaway Beauharnois – Sect. 1
Mid-Lake St. Francis – Bradford Island	**Ch. 12 – 156.600 MHz**	Seaway Eisenhower – Sect. 2
Bradford Island – Crossover Island	**Ch. 11 – 156.550 MHz**	Seaway Iroquois – Sect. 3
Crossover Island-Cape Vincent	**Ch. 13 – 156.650 MHz**	Seaway Clayton – Sect. 4
		St. Lawrence River portion
Cape Vincent – Mid-Lake Ontario	**Ch. 12 – 156.600 MHz**	Seaway Sodus – Sect. 4
		Lake Ontario portion
Seaway Pilot Office – Cape Vincent	**Ch. 14 – 156.700 MHz**	Pilotage traffic
Mid-Lake Ontario – Welland Canal	**Ch. 11 – 156.550 MHz**	Seaway Newcastle – Sect. 5
Welland Canal	**Ch. 14 – 156.700 MHz**	Seaway Welland – Sect. 6
Welland Canal to Long Point Light	**Ch. 11 – 156.550 MHz**	Seaway Long Point – Sect. 7
Montreal Traffic	**Ch. 10 – 156.500 MHz**	Vessel traffic
Soo Traffic	**Ch. 12 – 156.600 MHz**	Vessel control, Sault Ste. Marie,
Lockmaster, Soo Locks	**Ch. 14 – 156.700 MHz**	Soo Lockmaster (WUE-21)
Coast Guard traffic	**Ch. 21 – 157.050 MHz**	United States Coast Guard
Coast Guard traffic	**Ch. 22 – 157.100 MHz**	United States Coast Guard
U.S. mailboat, Detroit, MI	**Ch. 10 – 156.500 MHz**	Mailboat *J. W. Westcott II*

Hear vessel traffic online at broadcastify.com – click on the 'Listen' button

The following prerecorded messages help track vessel arrivals and departures

Boatwatcher's Hotline	**(218) 722-6489**	Superior, Duluth, Two Harbors,
		Taconite Harbor and Silver Bay
CSX coal docks/Torco dock	**(419) 697-2304**	Toledo, Ohio, vessel information
Eisenhower Lock	**(315) 769-2422**	Eisenhower Lock vessel traffic
Michigan Limestone dock	**(989) 734-2117**	Calcite, Mich., vessel information
Michigan Limestone dock	**(906) 484-2201**	Press 1 – Cedarville, Mich., passages
Presque Isle Corp.	**(989) 595-6611**	Stoneport vessel information ext. 7
Seaway Vessel Locator	**(450) 672-4115**	
Soo Traffic	**(906) 635-3224**	Previous day – St. Marys River
Soo Traffic – hotline	**(906) 253-9290**	Soo Locks traffic information
Superior Midwest Energy	**(715) 395-3559**	Superior, Wis., vessel information
Thunder Bay Port Authority	**(807) 345-1256**	Thunder Bay, Ont., vessel information
Welland Canal Traffic	**(905) 688-6462**	Welland Canal traffic

MEANINGS OF BOAT WHISTLES

1 SHORT: I intend to leave you on my port side (answered by same if agreed upon).

2 SHORT: I intend to leave you on my starboard side (answered by same if agreed upon). (Passing arrangements may be agreed upon by radio. If so, no whistle signal is required.)

1 PROLONGED: Vessel leaving dock.

3 SHORT: Operating astern propulsion.

1 PROLONGED, SOUNDED AT INTERVALS OF NOT MORE THAN 2 MINUTES: Vessel moving in restricted visibility.

1 SHORT, 1 PROLONGED, 1 SHORT: Vessel at anchor in restricted visibility (optional). May be accompanied by the ringing of a bell on the forward part of the ship and a gong on the aft end.

3 PROLONGED & 2 SHORT: Salute (formal)

1 PROLONGED & 2 SHORT: Salute (commonly used)

3 PROLONGED & 1 SHORT: International Shipmasters' Association member salute

5 OR MORE SHORT BLASTS SOUNDED RAPIDLY: Danger

Spotlight

Ships · Sailors
Adventures

**Crewman lowered to
the dock via bosun's
chair at Marquette,
Mich.** *(Lee Rowe)*

147

Kaye E. Barker
upbound with a
bone in her teeth.
(Marc Dease)

Sky's the limit
Drones mean new views for photographers

There's no question drones have opened a whole new world for boat photographers.

By now, most of us have seen the stunning images a drone's platform can provide. But until a few years ago, such great angles were only available to those with the cash to rent an airplane or helicopter. A decent drone package can now be had for just under $1,000, although professional setups can cost much more.

Federal Hudson
(Marc Dease)

The appeal is obvious. First, there's the flexibility to get a shot from almost any vantage point. Trees and power lines are not in the way. Then there's the time factor. Land-bound photographers have only a few seconds to snap the perfect shot, but a drone's battery life and range are its only limitations. And a drone can go out to meet a boat over water in areas that were previously inaccessible to most photographers.

Marc Dease, of Point Edward, Ont., and Dan Vaught of DeTour Village, Mich., are two of the best-known drone users, thanks to their eye-catching posts on social media.

Before pedestrian traffic was prohibited on the Blue Water Bridge between Port Huron and Sarnia in about 1996, Dease used to love shooting still photos from the roadway. His drone gives him a similar perspective, with a few improvements.

"It's one step better than the bridge. I go to the boats instead of waiting for the boats to come to me," he says. Another advantage: He doesn't have to worry about what side the sun is on. "The drone gives me access all day."

The drones are controlled by an app loaded on an iPad or other smart device. A signal transmits the image the drone's camera is seeing back to the device so the operator can view it. A joystick allows the user to control height, speed and angle. If the signal is lost, the drone is programmed to return to the point from which it was launched.

Dease upgraded from his first drone recently to a Phantom 4 PRO to improve quality. Vaught operates as a hobbyist, but he is working on his Unmanned Aircraft Systems certification. He is registered with the FAA as required by law, since his drone weighs between 0.55 pounds and 55 pounds.

Dease credits Vaught, whom he has never met, for his interest in drone photography. "I saw his videos, I thought they were cool, and I had to get one," he recalls. When Vaught bought a cheap drone for his young son a few years ago, he became hooked himself.

Vaught's drone has a range of about three miles, but he usually only flies it to about a mile out. It can fly a few feet above the ground or water or up to several thousand feet, but legally it has to remain below 400 feet above ground level. The wind limit for a drone is 20-25 mph, much better than earlier models.

Vaught and Dease say they have had few issues from freighter captains regarding their drones, and they have

Continued on Page 150

Dan and his drone.
(Yvonne Bosley)

American Century dwarfs Vaught's small boat / launch pad.
(Dan Vaught)

Buffalo on the St. Marys River.
(Sam Hankinson)

even developed relationships with some of the skippers as a result of their photography. Dease notifies the ones he knows on Facebook when he will be flying. "I think they find it pretty cool," he says.

Common sense is key. "I've been welcomed by some crews and warned not to be around others," Vaught explains, "but the rule of thumb is don't interfere with their operation or put the drone in any position to cause damage or injury. You always keep in mind the possibility of the drone shutting down or failing. The self-imposed rules I stick to are do not fly in front of the pilothouse without approval from the captain or crew, no low-level flights over the boat itself if it's underway, and no flying over crew members. I do have contact with a few of the captains and crews. Some will even update me on when they'll be in the area."

Another drone user, Sam Hankinson of Grand Haven, Mich., says he began his interest in drones differently than the others – he built his own.

"In my sophomore year of high school I designed and built one in my engineering class. I was an inexperienced pilot, and the maximum amount of time I had it in the air was less than a minute. I crashed it multiple times, fixing it each time until I damaged it beyond repair. That experience allowed me to learn how drones work and what electronics are inside that contribute to a functional aerial photography tool."

Continued on Page 152)

Mississagi arrives as Calumet departs Port Dolomite near Cedarville, Mich. (Dan Vaught)

Rt. Hon. Paul J. Martin passing Sarnia. (Marc Dease)

Arthur M. Anderson at Mission Point. *(Dan Vaught)*

When Hankinson stepped up to a DJI Phantom 3 model, he had enough prior knowledge to get it off the ground quickly. "I was reluctant to fly at first, given my history of crashes," Hankinson recalls, "but I soon learned the Phantom 3 is much different than a self-built drone and has many advantages. The most helpful tool is the 'return to home' feature. If the drone loses connection with the receiver, it comes back to the location from where it took off. This comes in handy when you're chasing a ship a half a mile down the St. Marys River and can't make visual contact with your machine."

Hankinson said drones have changed how he boatwatches. "Living in a less active port, the easiest photo opportunities I have are when a ship is coming in or departing. The places where they tie up are accessible but don't provide good angles. In the past, I would pass up an opportunity to see a ship if it was at the dock and not going anywhere because I knew I wouldn't get good pictures. With drone, I can get great photos of a ship whether it is inbound off the lake or tied up at a dock."

As one would expect, losing an expensive drone in the water is an issue for drone photographers. "Besides damaging property or injuring someone, that's my biggest concern," Vaught admits. "Usually, over water, if you have a crash or shut down, that's it. It's lost and you're out $1,300 to $1,500.

Alpena passes Pine Island in the lower St. Marys River. (Dan Vaught)

Capt. Henry Jackman above Point Edward, Ont. (Marc Dease)

The manufacturer of the drones I use considers flying over water a violation of the warranty. Eighty or ninety percent of the time, my drone is over the water, but that's the risk I'm willing to take to get the shots I want.

"I've taken thousands of pictures and have been out over the water hundreds of times, and I still get a small knot in my stomach whenever I do it. There's always that nag in the back of your mind that it won't be coming back," he adds.

To guard against loss, Vaught straps a GetterBack, a product familiar to fishermen, to the drone's framework. If the drone does go in the water, a bobber on a 100-foot Kevlar line will float to the surface so the drone can be retrieved.

Dease still remembers the time he almost tanked his drone. "I was watching the boat and not paying attention. It got lower and lower to about two feet from the water. If it goes in the water, it's gone. If I crash it on land, it's gone. It's gone either way," he says. – **Roger LeLievre**

Cruise ship Victory 1 near Sault Ste. Marie. (Sam Hankinson)

Algoma Discovery passes the tip of Sugar Island. (Sam Hankinson)

Stewart J. Cort downbound in the lower St. Marys River. (Dan Vaught)

Their ship came in

Couple's 'LRO' goes from lake boat to longtime retirement project

From the air. (Matt Miner)

More than 10 years ago, when a Michigan couple purchased most of the front end of a retired Great Lakes vessel and installed it on property overlooking the lower St. Marys River in Michigan's Upper Peninsula, they knew they had their work cut out for them.

Time has proved Marc and Jill VanderMeulen are up to the challenge presented by restoring a big steel chunk of the retired laker *John W. Boardman*. Time itself has also proved to be a challenge. The work just doesn't seem to progress as quickly as they – and others – would like.

"It keeps," Marc says of the project, which they have dubbed the LRO, for Large Rusty Object. "I just wish things could go faster," Jill adds.

The couple, who commute 325 miles north from their home base at Holland, Mich., can only work seasonally, during vacations and weekends. A lot of progress has been behind the scenes and involves foundation work (moving stone and rock is serious business) and, most recently, rehabbing and installing decorative antique fencing for security. Chipping old paint, cleaning old woodwork, running utilities and repainting the exterior in its original Huron Cement Co. green so that it wasn't an eyesore for the neighbors, also took time.

Four decks tall, the section weighs more than 120 tons and perhaps as much as 300 tons, according to the house movers who installed it on shore. It is positioned on a bow-shaped concrete platform so that it overlooks DeTour Passage and Potaganissing Bay. Before the couple bought the forward end of the vessel, it sailed the Great Lakes from 1923 until 1980 as a powdered-cement carrier. Originally named *John W. Boardman*, it was rechristened *Lewis G. Harriman* in 1965. When she was laid up in 1980, she was used for cement storage at Milwaukee and Green Bay, Wis. The couple has restored the boat's original *John W. Boardman* name.

In 2003, her usefulness at an end, the *Harriman* was sold to Purvis Marine Limited of Sault Ste. Marie,

Continued on Page 158

John W. Boardman in her sailing days. (VanderMeulen Collection)

Steamboat Gothic: Marc and Jill VanderMeulen in front of the John W. Boardman. (Chris Winters)

The Large Rusty Object arrives at DeTour in 2005. *(Jill VanderMeulen)*

At the Purvis scrapyard in 2004. *(Roger LeLievre)*

Ont., for scrap. Enter the VanderMeulens. They looked first at the Canadian lakers *Quedoc* and *Vandoc,* also being scrapped, but they were much newer, had too much metal and lacked the charm – and the beautiful interiors – of the *Harriman.* They struck a deal with Jack Purvis in the fall of 2005, and soon the section – complete with crew and captain's quarters, windlass and dunnage rooms and pilothouse – was loaded on a barge and floated down the St. Marys River to its new home, where it was brought ashore on six, 50-ton rollers by a team of house movers. Although it sounds simple, the engineering required was daunting, and delays due to weather stretched the project out for months. The project also required a zoning variance from DeTour Village.

By comparison, a newer laker would have been much larger, heavier and therefore more expensive to move and maintain. The couple estimates that same cut from a boat like the *Edward L. Ryerson* would yield 18 full bathrooms and require reuse as a hotel.

"We didn't get the concrete work done till 2012. It was only supposed to take 90 days," Jill recalls. "The house movers thought that they would be finished 30 days after the barge arrived in DeTour. They did all that had been agreed to, but it took seven years, working part-time.

"Everything takes much longer than you think. We just keep plodding on, little by little."

Most of the collectible items had been removed by the time the VanderMeulens came on the scene. However they have slowly been acquiring replacements for pilothouse equipment. The original steering pole was missing, but they were able to purchase a surplus pole that was once used on the *J. Burton Ayers.* The bronze tip on the end is from the recently scrapped steamer *Courtney Burton.*

"We know that it's not the place to spend the winter," he explains. "I think that Michigan law requires that a B&B be your residence, so if that happens, we will be living in the boat during the summer and are looking forward to that," Marc explains. Otherwise, they maintain a more traditional cottage next door.

"A seasonal B&B is our hope," adds Jill, "but we'll see what transpires. We have a lot of people lined up to be guests. They are waiting for us to hurry up."

Still, the project was never intended to be a money-making enterprise and never will be. "We wanted to preserve part of a pilothouse-forward laker – initially only a pilothouse – but are very pleased with the way things have worked out," says Marc "If we can share it with others through tours or as a B&B then that will provide us with some entertainment and perhaps the funds for continued painting."

Now that more than 10 years have elapsed since they embarked upon their challenge, do the couple have any regrets? "We would have had regrets had we not done it," Marc says.

"The LRO was a retirement project that came early, but the entire boat would be rebar in China had we not purchased the forward structure when it was available," he adds. The couple also wants to say thanks to passing vessels for the salutes that have made chipping and painting much more fun over the past decade.

"We plan to live in DeTour full-time in a few years, and our commute to work on the boat will then be about 100 feet," he concludes. – *Roger LeLievre*

Hoisting a vintage desk aboard (upper right); old boat meets new foundation (right); woodwork (far right); desk in place (below)

The VanderMeulens wave to a passing freighter, hoping for a salute. (Roger LeLievre)

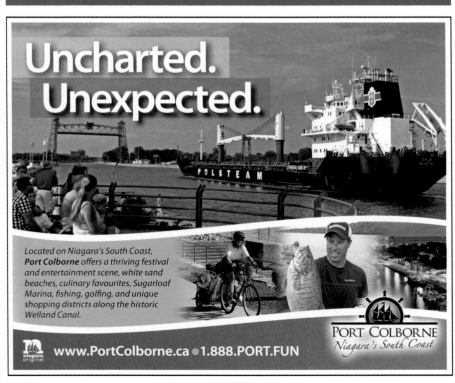

Historic Gallery

Tanker Britamlube in the 1950s. *(Edward O. Clark, courtesy of Skip Meier)*

In this 1953 image, Ernest T. Weir has just been towed from the graving dock at the American Shipbuilding Co. in Lorain, Ohio. The vessel was scrapped in 2016 as American Fortitude. Tug New Mexico is the smoker. (Mark Cowles Collection)

Beechglen loading grain at Thunder Bay, Ont., c. the1980s. (Tom Manse Collection)

BEECHGLEN

Ruth Hindman of 1910 downbound in the1960s. (Emory A. Massman, Michelson Collection)

Richard M. Marshall (later John Dykstra) and Harry W. Croft meet in the Detroit River in the mid-1950s. (Elmer Treloar)

U.S. Steel's William B. Schiller showing her age in 1973. She was retired in 1978. (Roger LeLievre)

Otto M. Reiss in American Steamship Co. colors in 1969. (Roger LeLievre)

N.M. Paterson & Sons' Quedoc on Lake St. Clair in 1973. (Roger LeLievre)

Ryerson royalty: Capt. George Fisher (left) greets Edward L Ryerson, Mrs. Nora Ryerson, Philip D. Block and Joseph L. Block on August 6, 1960. (Steve Haverty Collection)

United States Gypsum loading at the B&O Coal Dock, Lorain, Ohio. (Tom Manse Collection)

George H. VanVleck of the Petrol Traffic Co. towing a barge, circa 1875. (Peter B. Worden Collection Marine Historical Society of Detroit)

Steamer Westdale in 1975. She was scrapped in 1981 as H.C. Heimbecker. (Roger LeLievre)

WESTDALE

Wooden steamer Gettysburg with two schooner-barges in tow, Sault Ste. Marie, 1897. *(Peter B. Worden Collection, Marine Historical Society of Detroit)*

GEORGE M. STEINBRENNER

Golden Hind in 1983. (Eric Treece)

George M. Steinbrenner of the once-large Kinsman fleet in 1972. (Roger LeLievre)

A Lake Superior sunset astern of the Oakglen in 1984. (Bob Campbell)

Elbert H. Gary arrives to unload U.S. Steel's Gary Works' first cargo in1908. The vessel lasted until 1973, when it was scrapped as R.E. Webster. (Tom Manse Collection)

Simcoe eastbound in the Welland Canal at Port Colborne in 1982. (Eric Treece)

Walter A. Sterling's christening at Lorain, Ohio, in 1961. We know her today as Lee A. Tregurtha. (Tom Manse Collection)

WALTER A. STERLING
THE CLEVELAND-CLIFFS STEAMSHIP CO

USCG Acacia and helicopter assist S.T. Crapo in ice. *(Peter B. Worden Collection)*

Judith M. Pierson from the Blue Water Bridge in 1977. (Bob Campbell)

Fred A. Manske inbound at Muskegon, Mich., in 1974. (Matt Miner Collection)

Deluxe service for a passenger boarding the Milwaukee Clipper. (Tom Manse Collection)

An iced-up Cecelia Desgagnés on the Detroit River. (Mike Nicholls)

Deck view of the whaleback steamer Frank Rockefeller meeting the whaleback Thomas Wilson towing barges 117 and 118. The image was taken between1896 and 1900. (Michelson Collection)

U.S. Steel fleet's Eugene W. Pargny lining up for the Soo Locks. The Pargny was scrapped in 1984. (Tom Manse)

EUGENE W. PARGNY

Smoky grain boat Brookdale. (Emory A. Massman, Michelson Collection)

Roger Blough transfers pellets into the A.H. Ferbert as part of a test in 1973. (Tom Manse Collection)

Quebecois stuck in St. Marys River ice during the 1970s. (Roger LeLievre)

B. W. DRUCKENMILLER

Theodore Roosevelt and tug Lou-Ellla early in the 20th century. (Tom Manse Collection)

B.W. Druckenmiller loading new cars in this early 1960s image at the Nicholson Dock in Detroit. (Emory A. Massman, Michelson Collection)

GREAT LAKES GLOSSARY

AAA CLASS – Vessel design popular on the Great Lakes in the early 1950s. *Arthur M. Anderson* is one example.

AFT – Toward the back, or stern, of a ship.

AHEAD – Forward.

AMIDSHIPS – The middle point of a vessel, referring to either length or width.

ARTICULATED TUG/BARGE (ATB) – Tug-barge combination. The two vessels are mechanically linked in one axis but with the tug free to move, or articulate, on another axis.

BACKHAUL – The practice of carrying a revenue-producing cargo (rather than ballast) on a return trip from hauling a primary cargo.

BARGE – Vessel with no engine, either pushed or pulled by a tug.

BEAM – The width of a vessel measured at the widest point.

BILGE – Lowest part of a hold or compartment, generally where the rounded side of a ship curves from the keel to the vertical sides.

BOW – Front of a vessel.

BOW THRUSTER – Propeller mounted transversely in a vessel's bow under the waterline to assist in moving sideways. A stern thruster may also be installed.

BRIDGE – The platform above the main deck from which a ship is steered/navigated. Also: PILOTHOUSE or WHEELHOUSE.

BULK CARGO – Goods, loose or in mass, that generally must be shoveled, pumped, blown or scooped out of a vessel.

BULKHEAD – Wall or partition that separates rooms, holds or tanks within a ship's hull.

BULWARK – The part of the ship that extends fore and aft above the main deck to form a rail.

DATUM – Level of water in a given area, determined by an average over time.

DEADWEIGHT TONNAGE – The actual carrying capacity of a vessel, equal to the difference between the light displacement tonnage and the heavy displacement tonnage, expressed in long tons (2,240 pounds or 1,016.1 kilograms).

DECK SPRINKLERS: The reason for water spraying on a vessel's deck is to help cool the upper part of a boat and prevent hogging (bending due to temperature differences above and below the waterline). With decks exposed to the sun all day, the surface can get very hot. The hull of the boat underwater stays cooler. Hogging can affect cargo capacity and the depth to which a boat can load.

DISPLACEMENT TONNAGE – The actual weight of the vessel and everything aboard her, measured in long tons. The displacement is equal to the weight of the water displaced by the vessel. Displacement tonnage may be qualified as light – indicating the weight of the vessel without cargo, fuel and stores – or heavy, indicating the weight of the vessel loaded with cargo, fuel and stores.

DRAFT – The depth of water a ship needs to float. Also, the distance from keel to waterline.

FIT OUT – The process of preparing a vessel for service after a period of inactivity.

FIVE-YEAR INSPECTION – U.S. Coast Guard survey, conducted in a drydock every five years, of a vessel's hull, machinery and other components.

FLATBACK – Lakes slang for a non-self-unloader.

FOOTER – Lakes slang for 1,000-foot vessel.

FOREPEAK – The space below the forecastle.

FORWARD – Toward the front, or bow, of a ship.

FREEBOARD – The distance from the waterline to the main deck.

GEARLESS VESSEL – One that is not a self-unloader.

GROSS TONNAGE – The internal space of a vessel, measured in units of 100 cubic feet (2.83 cubic meters) = a gross ton.

HATCH – An opening in the deck through which cargo is lowered or raised. A hatch is closed by securing a hatch cover over it.

IMO # – Unique number issued by International Maritime Organization, or IMO, to ships for identification. Not all vessels have an IMO number.

INTEGRATED TUG/BARGE (ITB) – Tug-barge combination in which the tug is rigidly mated to the barge. *Presque Isle* is one example.

IRON DECKHAND – Mechanical device that runs on rails on a vessel's main deck and is used to remove and replace hatch covers.

JONES ACT – A U.S. law that mandates that cargoes moved between American ports be carried by U.S.-flagged, U.S.-built and U.S.-crewed vessels.

KEEL – A ship's steel backbone. It runs along the lowest part of the hull.

LAID UP or **LAY-UP** – Out of service.

MARITIME CLASS – Style of lake vessel built during World War II as part of the nation's war effort. *Mississagi* is one example.

NET REGISTERED TONNAGE – The internal capacity of a vessel available for carrying cargo. It does not include the space occupied by boilers, engines, shaft alleys, chain lockers or officers' and crew's quarters. Net registered tonnage is usually referred to as registered tonnage or net tonnage and is used to calculate taxes, tolls and port charges.

RIVER CLASS – Group of vessels built in the 1970s to service smaller ports and negotiate narrow rivers.

SELF-UNLOADER – Vessel able to discharge its own cargo using a system of conveyor belts and a movable boom.

STEM – The extreme forward end of the bow

STEMWINDER – Vessel with all cabins aft.

STERN – The back of the ship.

STRAIGHT-DECKER – Non-self-unloading vessel.

STEM – The extreme forward end of the bow.

TACONITE – Processed, pelletized iron ore. Easy to load and unload, this is the primary type of ore shipped on the Great Lakes and St. Lawrence Seaway. Also known as pellets.

TOLL – Fee charged against a ship, cargo and passengers for a complete or partial transit of a waterway covering a single trip in one direction.

TURKEY TRAIL – Route from North Channel (above Manitoulin Island) into the St. Marys River, named for the many courses which zigzag through the area's islands, shoals and ports.

VESSEL LOG / *Record your own ship spottings*

Date	Vessel Name	Location

Radcliffe R. Latimer backing in at Goderich, Ont., to load salt. (Shane Ruther)

ADVERTISER INDEX   *Thank you!*

The information in this book, current as of March 1, 2017, was obtained from the U.S. Army Corps of Engineers, the U.S. Coast Guard, the Lake Carriers' Association, Lloyd's Register of Shipping, NOAA, Transport Canada, The St. Lawrence Seaway Authority, Internet Ships Register, Shipfax, Tugfax, BoatNerd.com and individual vessel owners / operators.

MORE KYS PHOTOS ONLINE

Every year, *Know Your Ships* gets nearly 1,000 great photo submissions. Unfortunately, there isn't room in the book for them all, so we've created a gallery of some of these images at **knowyourships.com**. Please stop by and take a look.

Carferry Badger outbound at Manitowoc, Wis. (Connor Siemers)

Michigan's Maritime College

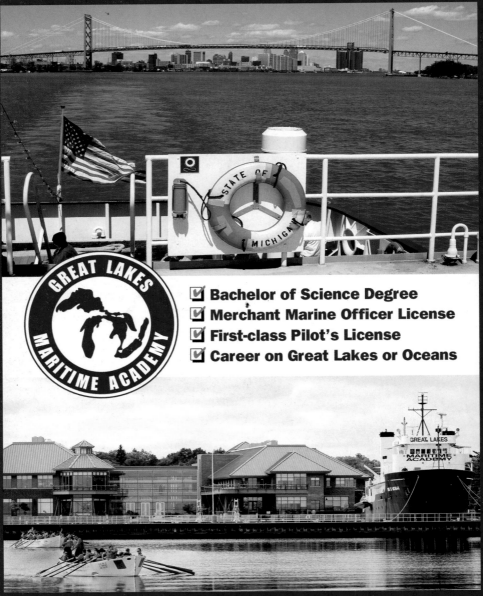

- ☑ Bachelor of Science Degree
- ☑ Merchant Marine Officer License
- ☑ First-class Pilot's License
- ☑ Career on Great Lakes or Oceans

GREAT LAKES MARITIME ACADEMY

nmc.edu/maritime • 877-824-7447